The ESL Miscellany

A Treasury of Cultural and Linguistic Information

Fourth "Silver Anniversary" Edition

Raymond C. Clark • Patrick R. Moran • Arthur A. Burrows

PRO LINGUA ⬤ ASSOCIATES

Pro Lingua Associates, Publishers

P.O. Box 1348
Brattleboro, Vermont 05302-1348 USA

Office: 802 257 7779
Orders: 800 366 4775
Fax: 802 257 5117
Webstore: www.ProLinguaAssociates.com
Email: info@ProLinguaAssociates.com
SAN: 216-0579

At Pro Lingua
our objective is to foster
an approach to learning and teaching
that we call **interplay**, the **inter**action
of language learners and teachers with their materials,
with the language and culture,
and with each other in active,
creative and productive
play.

This book was designed and set in Century Schoolbook type by Arthur A. Burrows; the cover uses the Monotype Corsiva and Palatino faces. It was printed and bound by United Graphics in Mattoon, Illinois. The photographs of American gestures are by Michael Jerald. The maps are from MapArt by Cartesia. Original drawings are by Patrick Moran. The road signs are copyright 2005 Richard C. Moeur, rendered by (http://www.trafficsign.us/). The folk art and other illustrations are selected from two collections of clip art: *Art Explosion®: 750,000 Images,* Copyright 1995-2000 © by Nova Development Corporation and its licensors, and *The Big Book of Art™.* Copyright 1997-2002 by Hermera Technologies Inc. and its licensors. The front cover art, "Earth in Light," is Copyright © by photographer Arthur Matkovsiy, agency Dreamstime.com.

Printed in the United States of America

Fourth edition, first printing 2007.
32,000 copies in print.

Acknowledgements

As we became involved in the revision of our ESL Miscellany, we inevitably were reminded of the many people who contributed in one way or another since the very first edition in 1981. Our acknowledgement for all this help must be made in a very general way. However, we do want to express our thanks to a few people who have made a special contribution.

First and foremost of these has been the late **Richard Yorkey** of St. Michael's College in Vermont. Dick sent us many useful ideas and resources as we developed the first few editions. In constructing many of our word lists, we borrowed heavily from Dick's collection of lists.

At the very beginning of the first edition, we had considerable help from **Eleanor Boone, Rick Gildea, Mike Jerald,** and **Mary Clark.** We also had help from **Marilyn Funk** and **John Croes.** In the first edition, **Peg Clement** contributed her collection of American gestures, on which the selection in this book is based; for this most recent edition, we again thank **Mike Jerald** for his photography and **Adrienne Major, Liza Aldana, Veronica McKay,** and **Cole Madden** for their modeling.

Susannah Clark was our chief editorial assistant for the first edition, and **Mary Clark** suggested the title for the book. **Diane Larsen-Freeman** looked over the first rendition of the Linguistic Aspect. **Bonnie Mennell** and **Karen Kale** reviewed our list of communicative topics. **Anders Burrows** helped develop the topics on photography, cinema, and video and the media. **Thor Carlson** added to the topic on automobiles and compiled the list of computer acronyms.

Now that our fourth edition is a reality, we invite you to contact us with your suggestions for the next edition.

RCC, AAB, PRM

Pronouncement on Pronouns

In this book, we at Pro Lingua Associates are offering a solution to the vexing "he/she" pronoun problem. We have come to the conclusion that when a reference is made to third person singular, and that person is indefinite (and hence gender is unknown or unimportant), we will use the third person plural forms, they, them, their(s). We are fully aware that historically these forms represent grammatical plurality. However, there are clear instances in the English language where the third person plural form is used to refer to a preceding indefinite, grammatically singular pronoun. Examples:

Everyone says this, don't **they**?
Nobody agrees with us, but we will ignore **them**.

If you will accept the examples above, it is not a major step to find the following acceptable:

The user of this book should find this easier because **they** can avoid the confusion of *he* or *she*, the awkwardness of *he or she*, and the implicit sexism of using *he* for everybody.

So in this book, you will find statements such as, . . . *the teacher who is using this book to prepare **their** own lessons.* The reader of our text may disagree with our solution, but we ask them to consider that it is time to change the usage of gender-marked pronouns when they are clearly inappropriate. This is our solution, and we encourage you to try it out. And we invite your comments.

Contents

THE LINGUISTIC ASPECT

Grammar

THE COMMUNICATIVE ASPECT

THE CULTURAL ASPECT

THE METALINGUSITIC ASPECT
AND MISCELLANEOUS MATERIALS

THE PARALINGUISTIC ASPECT

The ESL Miscellany

Introduction

The Purpose and Contents
of the Miscellany

This book is a compendium of useful and interesting information for teachers and learners of English as a Second Language. Although the book focuses on North American English, it will also be useful to teachers and students of other varieties of English. Teachers will find this book useful as a resource for developing material as they supplement, expand, replace, adapt, or develop from scratch a complete curriculum. This one book does not contain everything that the teacher/materials developer needs to know, but we believe it is the most comprehensive one-volume reference available to the lesson writer.

In addition to its usefulness in developing materials, this book offers another function as a guideline/checklist for teachers who teach "a little of this and a little of that." The problem with this kind of eclecticism, of course, is that it is not always easy to know if everything is being covered. This book will not be able to tell teachers everything they need to know about North American English, but it can serve as a comprehensive outline. By consulting the list of Situations, for example, the teacher can rather quickly review which conversational situations have been covered and what remains to be covered.

A third use for this book is that many of the lists can be copied and used as hand-outs. For example, the summary of religions in the U.S. and Canada could be copied and given to the students as the point of reference for a question-answer practice or discussion of religion. For that reason we encourage copying of these lists for classroom use.

We suggested earlier that students of North American English will also find this book useful, but it is likely that it will be especially valuable to advanced students of North American English who are in need of a one-volume guide that will help them determine what they already know and what they should focus their study on. We think this book will be of particular interest to advanced students who are preparing to be teachers of English as a Second Language.

The **Miscellany** is divided into five parts. Parts I and II contain information about the language itself. This information is classified as two major aspects: Linguistic and Communicative. The linguistic aspect contains information that in some way deals with what is commonly called the phonology, lexicon, and grammar of the language. However, this linguistic aspect is not a grammar, but rather a series of lists of words and forms that exemplify some grammar point. For example, under Phrasal Verbs, there will be no rules for the use of these verbs.

Instead, there will be a list of separable and inseparable phrasal verbs. In other words, it is assumed that the user will have some understanding of how phrasal verbs function in English.

The communicative aspect does not deal with linguistic forms such as "go, went, gone" but outlines ways in which the language is used to send and receive messages. We have included lists of *functions* such as asking, introducing, telling, etc. Also in the communicative aspect section, we have included vocabulary lists that outline potential *topics* of conversations and *situations,* the contexts in which communicative functions and topics of conversation are carried out.

In Part III we have compiled several lists that form an outline of North American culture. Each list can be used as the basic data upon which can be based a discussion or controlled conversation about some facet of North American culture. Part III can be used as the basis for an orientation to immigration and resettlement in the United States and Canada.

Part IV is a pot-pourri of information that is, in general, metalinguistic. In other words, the information in this part will help the teacher and the learner facilitate the teaching/learning process. But there is also information that does not fit neatly into any of the other categories and is best labeled as miscellaneous.

Part V needs little explanation. It contains some examples of communicative systems that parallel the language itself. Hence, we have called it the paralinguistic aspect. Of greatest interest is a photographic catalog of 61 gestures that are commonly recognized and understood in North America. We have provided titles and minimal explanations for the gestures, but otherwise we leave it up to you, the user of this book, to discuss, compare, practice, and even add to this listing.

We will be the first to admit that this volume is far from complete. The information is such that it changes almost as fast as it is updated. As we prepare for the next edition, we welcome your comments and suggestions.

In preparing this fourth edition, some of the material from previous editions no longer seemed as relevant and appropriate as it once did. Since we have added new material, it seemed reasonable to drop some, too. However, we know that each topic we have dropped will be missed by some teachers who have found the material, for example, on nursery rhymes, contraception, human and animal body parts, curses, and vulgarities, useful in working with specific students. So that we don't disappoint these teachers, we are making this information available for free at our webstore, ProLinguaAssociates.com, linked to the *ESL Miscellany* announcement.

PRO LINGUA ASSOCIATES
Brattleboro, 2007

The Interplay Lesson Plan

On the next page we offer a lesson plan that may be helpful to the teacher who is using material from this book to prepare their own lessons. For that matter, this lesson plan can be used for most teaching activities.

The plan is based on Pro Lingua's concept of **Interplay**: The **inter**action of the teacher and learner with the material, with the language and the culture, and with each other in active, creative, and productive **play**.

The basic format comprises three stages in the implementation of most lessons: **Before**, **During** and **After**. *Before* teaching, the typical lesson is based on the students (who), the context of the teaching (when and where), the objective of the lesson (why), and the lesson content (what). *During* is the time in which the teacher and the students are actively involved face-to-face in teaching and learning. *After* focuses on assessing the lesson and looking forward to review and future lessons.

A few brief definitions may be useful.

Students: Although it is usually unnecessary to state explicitly who the students are, it is, nevertheless, always useful to consider, as the lesson is planned, the age, proficiency level, and goals of the students.

Context: For purposes of maintaining a record of the lesson for future reference, it may be helpful to state the time and place of the teaching.

Objective(s): In simple terms, the objective is a statement of *what the students should be able to do* as a result of the lesson. There may be more than one objective, but unless there is at least one objective for the lesson, it may lack focus, and the assessment of the objective may be difficult to carry out.

Linguistic Content: The lesson may or may not have a specific linguistic content, but if it does, it will be in the area of *pronunciation, vocabulary,* or *grammar.*

Functional/Strategic Content: This aspect of the content is concerned with communicative competence. Typically, functional content involves "-ing words," such as *asking, demanding, explaining,* and strategic skills, such as *rejoindering, interrupting, confirming,* and *clarifying.*

Topical Content: This involves the "message," especially the vocabulary associated with topics, such as *clothing, restaurants, business, sports,* and *music.*

3

Cultural Content: There may be a cultural content to the lesson. For example, *a holiday, a folktale, family structure,* and *rites of passage, from birth to death.*

Presentation: Typically, this part of the lesson is teacher-centered as the teacher *introduces the material* to the students. The presentation of the new material is often preceded by review of old material or schema-building in which the teacher sets the stage for the introduction of the new material.

Practice: Once the material is presented, the teacher and students engage in relatively *controlled interaction* with error correction so that the students will gain skill in using the new material.

Production: The final part of the lesson features the students *using* the material with each other to accomplish a communicative task. Typically, the teacher stands aside and observes and encourages the students as they become more fluent at manipulating the material in real or realistic communication.

Assessment: At the end of the lesson, or shortly thereafter, the teacher looks back at the objective *to measure* the success of the lesson. This can be done formally as a quiz or informally as monitoring the students and noting successes and errors.

Assignment: The teacher may ask the students to do *homework* that is based on the content of the lesson.

Follow-up: The teacher notes how and when the lesson content can or should be *reviewed or recycled* in future lessons.

The Lesson Plan

Before

Students:

Teaching/Learning Context:

Objective:

Content

Linguistic:

Functional/Strategic:

Topical:

Cultural:

During

Presentation:

Practice:

Production:

After

Assessment:

Assignment:

Follow-up:

愛

The
Linguistic
Aspect

A Note on Phonetic Symbols:

There are 26 letters in the English alphabet. However, there are (depending on how you classify them) at least 38 distinct sounds in spoken English. Complicating the picture, some of the letters of the English alphabet are really not necessary, for example, C, Q, and X.

> C can be replaced by S or K: city = sity and cake = kake
> Q , which is normally followed by U, can be replaced by KW quit = kwit
> X can be KS: box = boks

In short, some letters have to do double duty. For example, the final consonant sound in the word "much" is a single sound spelled with two letters, CH. In many ESL texts, this sound is represented by ʃ or č. In this book, however, we will use CH simply because we do not want to use special phonetic symbols. We think our students have enough of a problem learning the 26 letters that they will see in their everyday lives. Therefore, on page 10, "Basic Sounds of English," we offer our phonetic spelling of English using the ordinary symbols of the alphabet. For your information, on page 252 in the Metalinguistic Aspect, we have included three different phonetic alphabets.

A note on "A Grammar Sequence":

There are 33 steps in the grammar sequence. There is much more to the grammar of English than the series of steps presented here. However, the learner who has encountered the grammatical features in these 33 steps will be well along toward a basic mastery of the grammar of English. The particular sequence presented here is, of course, only one possible sequence to be used as the basis for a grammatical syllabus. Nevertheless, it is our hope that our sequence will be a useful guide for what grammatical features are usually taught before others.

The Alphabet

A B C D E F G

H I J K L M N O P

Q R S T U V

W X Y Z

a b c d e f g

h i j k l m n o p

q r s t u v w x y z

A B C D E F G

H I J K L M N O P

Q R S T U V

W X Y Z

a b c d e f g

h i j k l m n o p

q r s t u v w x y z

2: Common Consonant Clusters

Initial Consonant Clusters (two or more sounds)

BL   BR   CL   CR   DR   DW   FL   FR   GL   GR   PL   PR

QU   SC   SCH   SCR   SK   SL   SM   SN   SP   SPL   SPR   ST

STR   SW   TR   TW

Final Consonant Clusters (two sounds)

BL able	CT act	FT left	LD old	LF shelf	LK bulk
LP help	LT halt	MP lamp	NC since	NCH lunch	ND hand
NG orange	NK ink	NT hunt	RD hard	RG large	RK park
RL girl	RM arm	RN corn	RP tarp	RT art	SK ask
SP clasp	ST must				

Consonant Digraphs (two oe three letters representing one sound)

CH much	CK luck	DG edge	GU guard	GH ghost, laugh, ø
GN sign	KN knife	LK walk	MB thumb	NG sing	PH phone
SH shut	TCH watch	TH thigh, thy	TI action	WH where, whose
WR write				

1: Basic Sounds of English (phonemes)

Symbol	Example		Symbol	Example
		Vowels		
iy	beet		ou	bout
i	bit		er	Burt
ey	bait		uw	boot
e	bet		yuw	beaut
a	bat		u	bull
uh	but		ow	boat
ay	bite		oy	boy
ah	bot		aw	ball
		Consonants		
p	pin		b	bill
t	tin		d	dill
k	kin		g	gill
f	fat		v	vat
th	thigh		*th*	thy
s	sip		z	zip
sh	ash		zh	azure
ch	chip		j	jip
m	mop		n	not
h	hum		ng	hung
l	lot		r	rot
w	wet		y	yet

2: Major Phoneme-Grapheme (sound-letter) Correspondences in English

Phoneme Graphemes   *Phoneme   Graphemes*

Vowels

iy	beet, beat, he, here, please either, brief, city, key	**ou**	out, now
i	bit	**er**	her, fur, word, bird
ey	cake, bait, day, great, eight	**uw**	boot, blue, new, rule
e	bet	**yuw**	unit, cute, view, beauty
a	bat	**u**	book, bull, would
uh	but, son, above, double	**ow**	no, boat, slow, hope
ay	by, bite, high, lie	**oy**	boy, oil
ah	not, father	**aw**	ball, haul

Consonants

p	pepper	**b**	bubble
t	tattle, walked	**d**	dill, middle, lived
k	can, black, kin	**g**	gill, luggage
f	fat, phone	**v**	vat
th	thigh	***th***	thy
s	sip, city, glass	**z**	zip, has, jazz
sh	ash, action, sugar	**zh**	azure
ch	chip, catch	**j**	jet, edge, gem
m	mop, bummer, comb	**n**	not, banner
h	hum, who	**ng**	hung, think
l	lot, wall	**r**	rot, arrive, write
w	wet, quit	**y**	yet, _unit

11

3: Pronunciation of English Consonants

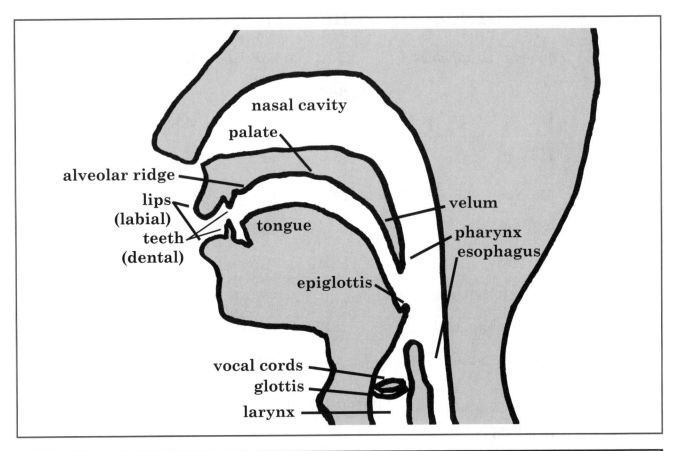

Point of Articulation	labial	labial-dental	dental	alveolar	palatal	velar	glottal
stops vl	p			t		k	
vd	b			d		g	
fricatives vl		f	th	s	sh		h
vd		v	*th*	z	zh		
affricatives vl					ch		
vd					j		
nasals vd	m			n		ng	
liquids vd				l, r			
glides vd	w				y		

4: Common Spellings of Vowels

iy

beat	meet	fill	skill	race	stain	left
cheap	queen	film	spit	rage	tail	leg
clean	see	fish	split	rake		lend
cream	seed	fit	stick	safe	bay	less
deal	seem	fix	still	sale	clay	let
dream	sheep	gift	strip	same	day	melt
each	sheet	give	swim	scale	gray	mend
east	sleep	hill	thick	shade	hay	neck
heal	speed	him	thin	shake	lay	net
heat	steel	his	this	shame	may	next
lead	steep	hit	trick	shape	pay	pen
leaf	street	if	trip	snake	pray	pet
lean	sweet	ill	win	space	ray	press
least	tree	in	wind	stage	say	red
leave	weed	inch	wish	state	stay	rent
meal	week	inn	with	strange	tray	rest
mean		it	wrist	take	way	self
meat	be	kick		tame		sell
neat	he	kill		taste	they	send
reach	me	kiss	**ey**	trade	weigh	sense
read	she	lid		wage		set
real	we	lift	age	wake	**e**	shelf
sea		lip	base	wave		smell
seat	chief	list	cage		bed	spell
speak	field	live	cake		beg	spend
steam	piece	milk	cape	aid	bell	swell
stream	thief	mill	case	claim	belt	tell
tea	yield	miss	date	fail	bend	tent
teach		mix	face	faint	best	test
weak	seize	pick	fade	faith	cent	them
	cheese	pig	flame	gain	check	then
deed	these	pin	grave	mail	chest	well
deep		print	hate	nail	debt	west
feed	**i**	quick	lake	paid	desk	wet
feel		rich	late	pain	dress	when
free	big	ship	make	paint	egg	yes
green	bill	silk	male	plain	end	yet
greet	bit	since	name	rail	fresh	
keep	dig	sit	pale	rain	get	bread
knee	dip		paste	raise	help	breath
	dish		plate	sail		
	ditch					

dead
deaf
death
head
health
sweat
wealth

edge
else
friend

a

act
add
am
as
ask
at
bck
bad
bag
band
bank
bath
black
camp
cat
catch
chance
class
crack
crash
damp
dance
drag
fact
fan
fast
fat
flag
flat
gap

gas
glad
glass
grand
grass
half
hang
hat
have
lack
lamp
land
last
mad
map
mass
mat
pack
pad
pan
pass
past
path
sad
sand
staff
stamp
stand
tap
tax
thank
that
trap
wrap

uh

brush
bunch
bus
but
club
cup
cut

drum
duck
dull
dust
fun
gun
hunt
hut
judge
jump
just
luck
lump
lunch
lung
much
mud
must
nut
pump
rub
rug
run
rush
rust
shut
such
suck
sun
thumb
thus
trunk
trust
up

from
front
love
month
none
of
once
some
son
ton

rough
touch
tough
young

blood
flood

u

book
brook
cook
crook
foot
good
hook
look
shook
took
wood
wool

bush
full
pull
push
put

could
should
would

uw

boot
broom
cool
food
fool
hoop
loop
mood
moon

noon
pool
roof
room
shoot
smooth
soon
spoon
too
tool
tooth

choose
loose
lose
move
prove
shoe

blew
crew
few
new
screw
stew
threw

rude
rule
tube
tune
use

group
soup
through
wound
youth

fruit
juice
suit

due
true
truth

do
to
who

view

ow

bone
close
hole
home
hope
joke
lose
nose
note
owe
rope
stone
stove
vote
whole

bold
both
clothes
cold
comb
fold
gold
hold
host
most
old
post
roll

boat
coal
coast
coat
float
goat
load
loan

road
roast
soap
throat

blow
bow
bowl
flow
grow
know
own
row
show
slow
snow
throw

go
no
so

though
toe

oy

boil
boy
coin
join
joint
joy
noise
oil
point
soil
spoil
toy
voice

14

Open aw

all
ball
call
chalk
fall
false
hall
salt
small
talk
tall

cloth
cost
cross
dog
long
loss
off
soft
strong
wrong

draw
law
paw
raw
saw
straw

cause
fault
pause
sauce

cough
ought
thought

broad

ou

cloud
count
doubt
ground
hour
house
loud
mouse
mouth
noun
ounce
our
out
proud
round
shout
sound
sour
south

bow
brown
cow
crowd
down
drown
how
now
town

ah

block
box
clock
dot
drop
lock
lot
not
on
pot
rock

shop
spot
top

ay

bite
crime
die
dine
dive
drive
fine
fire
hide
ice
knife
life
like
line
live
mine
nice
pile
pipe
price
pride
rice
ride
ripe
shine
side
size
slide
smile
strike
tide
time
tribe
while
white
wide
wife
wine

wipe
wise
write

bind
blind
bright
child
fight
find
high
kind
light
mild
mind
night
right
sight
sign
tight
wild

by
cry
dry
fly
fry
my
sky
try
type
why

buy
die
lie
tie
eye
I

ar

arm
art
bar

car
card
charge
dark
far
farm
hard
harm
march
mark
park
part
sharp
star
start
yard

heart
guard

eyr

air
chair
fair
hair
pair
stairs

bare
care
dare
rare
share

bear
swear
tear
wear

their
there
where

iyr

beard
clear
dear
ear
fear
hear
near
tear
year

cheer
steer
fierce
here

er

bird
birth
dirt
firm
first
girl
shirt
sir
skirt
stir
thirst

burn
church
curve
fur
hurt
nurse
turn
urge

word
work
world
worm
worse
worth

earn
earth
learn
search

her
serve
term
verb

or

born
cork
corn
for
fork
form
lord
nor
north
or
sort
storm

force
horse
more
shore
sore
store

course
court
pour

board
oar
roar

war
warm
warn

door
floor

5: Basic Lexical Stress Patterns

/ —

able	double	heavy	morning	pretty	stranger
agent	early	honest	mountain	prison	subject
always	effort	hurry	music	profit	summer
answer	either	keyboard	nation	promise	supper
beauty	empty	lady	neighbor	question	system
better	enter	landlord	never	rapid	table
brother	equal	language	noisy	rather	teacher
busy	ever	lawyer	nothing	ready	ticket
careful	father	leader	number	river	travel
carry	favor	lesson	office	rubber	under
center	fellow	listen	often	ruler	useful
circle	finger	market	owner	safety	valley
college	flower	matter	paper	science	village
corner	follow	measure	parent	second	visit
danger	foreign	member	pencil	sister	window
daughter	freedom	middle	person	sleepy	woman
distance	garden	mixer	poison	speaker	yellow
dollar	happy	monster	practice	stomach	zero

— /

about	arrive	contain	hotel	prepare	review
above	attend	control	improve	pretend	succeed
accept	because	decide	include	produce	success
account	become	degree	inform	pronounce	suggest
across	before	delay	instead	protect	supply
admit	begin	depend	intend	receive	surround
adopt	behind	describe	machine	refer	today
afraid	believe	destroy	mistake	refuse	tonight
again	belong	direct	observe	regret	unite
ago	below	discuss	omit	remain	unless
agree	beside	disease	oppose	remind	until
allow	between	employ	perform	reply	without
alone	beyond	event	perhaps	report	
along	collect	exact	police	respect	
among	complete	except	polite	result	
around	connect	explain	prefer	return	

16

—/—

acceptance	apartment	companion	description	imagine	religion
admission	appearance	condition	destruction	important	remember
advantage	appointment	consider	develop	invention	reporter
adventure	approval	container	dictation	mechanic	solution
advisor	arrival	December	diploma	musician	successful
agreement	attendance	decision	effective	opinion	suggestion
already	attractive	delighted	election	perfection	together
ambition	banana	deliver	exactly	performance	tomorrow
amusement	collection	department	familiar	possession	umbrella
another	commuter	departure	idea	relation	whoever

/ — —

animal	curious	generous	mystery	possible	satisfy
article	difficult	gentleman	nowadays	prejudice	substitute
beautiful	document	government	numeral	president	sympathy
capital	embassy	grandfather/	opposite	probable	tendency
century	enemy	mother	origin	property	valuable
certainly	energy	industry	passenger	quality	various
character	excellent	institute	personal	quantity	visitor
citizen	exercise	interview	politics	radio	wonderful
company	frequently	liberty	poverty	recently	yesterday
criminal	funeral	medicine	powerful	relative	

6: Noun-Verb Stress Patterns

Noun	*Verb*
/—	—/
address	address
annex	annex
conduct	conduct
conflict	conflict
contract	contract
contrast	contrast
convert	convert
decrease	decrease
defect	defect
extract	extract
object	object
increase	increase
insult	insult
intrigue	intrigue
permit	permit
produce	produce
progress	progress
project	project
protest	protest
rebel	rebel
record	record
reject	reject
subject	subject
suspect	suspect
estimate	estimate

7: Pronunciation of -s Suffix

Voiceless /s/	_Voiced /z/_	_Voiced /iz/_

Nouns

banks	brothers	bridges
books	cars	buses
cents	days	classes
clocks	dollars	colleges
exits	doors	garages
minutes	friends	glasses
mistakes	girls	houses
months	homes	inches
nights	hotels	languages
parents	lessons	lunches
pints	mornings	offices
quarts	planes	ounces
seats	problems	packages
shops	roads	pages
stamps	rooms	pieces
streets	schools	places
tickets	taxis	prices
weeks	words	sentences

Verbs

asks	buys	catches
drinks	gives	changes
gets	goes	closes
helps	knows	finishes
likes	leaves	fixes
makes	listens	freezes
puts	lives	guesses
sits	needs	kisses
sleeps	opens	loses
speaks	pulls	notices
stops	reads	practices
takes	returns	pronounces
talks	says	pushes
thanks	sees	reaches
thinks	spells	realizes
waits	studies	uses
walks	turns	watches
wants	understands	wishes

8: Pronunciation of -ed Suffix

Voiceless /t/	*Voiced /d/*	*Voiced /id/*
asked	answered	accepted
checked	believed	assisted
discussed	called	corrected
dropped	changed	counted
finished	cleaned	decided
helped	closed	departed
hoped	enjoyed	divided
introduced	explained	doubted
jumped	filled	ended
liked	learned	expected
looked	listened	folded
missed	lived	handed
picked	loved	hated
placed	moved	included
practiced	played	invited
pushed	pulled	needed
shopped	returned	noticed
stopped	showed	pointed
talked	spelled	repeated
thanked	studied	started
walked	tried	visited
washed	turned	waited
watched	used	wanted

All words have been selected from Pro Lingua's *Learner's Lexicon*, 1200-word level.

9: Basic Intonation Patterns

1. I bought a new com|pu|ter.   Statement (final word is multisyllabic)

2. Did you get it at |Office Shop?| Yes/No question

3. I bought it at |Brown's.| Statement (final word is one syllable)

4. When did you |buy| it?   WH question

5. You like to shop there, |don't| you?   Tag question expecting agreement

6. So, you got another H|T,| |didn't| you?   Tag question for information or clarification

7. Don't you like the new |Bells?| Negative question expressing surprise

8. I looked at a |Bell,| an H|T,| and a |Trac.| Series

9. So, did you get an H|T| or a |Trac?| Alternative

10. I bought a |used| |HT.| Focused information

11. If I have enough |money,| I'll get a |print|er.   Continuation of a phrase or clause. (Here, in the 'result' clause.)

21

10: Minimal Pairs

Vowels

/iy/	/i /
sheep	ship
leave	live
seat	sit
green	grin

/iy/	/ey/
eat	ate
see	say
week	wake
creep	crepe

/iy/	/e/
meet	met
mean	men
seeks	sex
beast	best

/i/	/ey /
it	ate
kick	cake
chin	chain
give	gave

/i/	/e/
pick	peck
did	dead
sit	set
knit	net

/i/	/a/
big	bag
it	at
sit	sat
zig	zag

/i /	/uh/
big	bug
live	love
sick	suck
rib	rub

/ey/	/e/
wait	wet
date	debt
pain	pen
raid	red

/ey/	/a/
snake	snack
ate	at
made	mad
hate	hat

/ey /	/uh /
ape	up
lake	luck
rain	run
came	come

/ey/	/ow/
taste	toast
say	so
break	broke
wake	woke

/e/	/a/
dead	dad
said	sad
men	man
bed	bad

/e /	/uh /
beg	bug
ten	ton
many	money
net	nut

/e/	/ah/
get	got
step	stop
red	rod
net	not

/a/	/uh/
grab	grub
swam	swum
mad	mud
cap	cup

Vowels (Continued)

/a/	/ah/
an	on
map	mop
cat	cot
lack	lock

/a/	/ay/
am	I'm
sad	side
dad	died
back	bike

/uh/	/ah/
hug	hog
cup	cop
luck	lock
nut	not

/uh/	/u/
luck	look
buck	book
stud	stood
tuck	took

/uh/	/ow/
cut	coat
must	most
come	comb
but	boat

/uh/	/aw/
gun	gone
cut	caught
bus	boss
dug	dog

/ah/	/u/
lock	look
pot	put
cod	could
shock	shook

/ah/	/ow/
hop	hope
got	goat
want	won't
rod	road

/ah/	/aw/
cot	caught
sod	sawed
are	or
tock	talk

/ah/	/ou/
are	hour
shot	shout
dot	doubt
got	gout

/aw/	/oy/
all	oil
jaw	joy
ball	boil
bald	boiled

/u/	/uw/
full	fool
pull	pool
soot	suit
could	cooed

/u/	/ow/
bull	bowl
cook	coke
should	showed
brook	broke

/ow/	/oy/
toe	toy
old	oiled
bold	boiled
cone	coin

/ou/	/ay/
mouse	mice
tower	tire
proud	pride
found	find

/ou/	/oy/
owl	oil
vowed	void
sow	soy
bough	boy

/oy/	/ay/
toy	tie
boy	buy
voice	vice
alloy	ally

23

Consonants

/p/	/b/
pig	big
cap	cab
pie	buy
rapid	rabid

/b/	/v/
boat	vote
best	vest
curb	curve
cupboard	covered

/l/	/r/
light	right
bowl	boar
collect	correct
lead	read

/ch/	/sh/
cheap	sheep
catch	cash
watch	wash
cheese	she's

/j/	/sh/
jeep	sheep
jade	shade
jack	shack
gyp	ship

/j/	/ch/
gin	chin
joke	choke
jeer	cheer
junk	chunk

/j/	/y/
juice	use
jet	yet
jam	yam
wage	weigh

/g/	/k/
bag	back
grape	crepe
glass	class
gap	cap

/th/	/t/
death	debt
thigh	tie
thin	tin
three	tree

/th/	/s/
think	sink
thing	sing
mouth	mouse
thin	sin

/th/	/d/
they	day
lather	ladder
their	dare
breathe	breed

/f/	/v/
fine	vine
fail	veil
life	live
safe	save

/v/	/w/
vine	wine
veered	weird
veal	we'll
over	ower

11: Pronunciation Problem Areas for Selected Learners

VOWELS. Virtually all learners will have difficulty distinguishing the /i/iy/ and the /e/ey/ vowel contrasts. Many will also have difficulty with the lower vowels: /a/ah/uh/aw/, and the back vowels /u/uw/. Other vowel problem areas are noted in the list below.

CONSONANTS. Very few languages use /th ~ *th*/, therefore these sounds are troublesome for all. Otherwise, language-specific consonant problems are listed below.

Arabic:	e/i	p/b	f/v			
Chinese:	a/e	l/n	l/w	r/w/l	w/v	
Czech:	e/a	w/v	th/t	d/*th*	w/v	
Farsi:	w/v	r				
French:	ch/j	r	h			
German:	ow	w/v	r			
Greek:	s/sh	s/z	r	h		
Hindi:	e/a	f/p	v/b	w/v		
Italian:	h	r				
Japanese:	s/sh	t/ch	b/v	l/r		
Korean:	p/f	b/v	s/sh	l/r		
Polish:	w/v	l/w	r	ng		
Portuguese:	sh/ch	j/zh	s/sh	l/w		
Russian:	a/e	er	w	ng		
Serbo-Croation:		a/e	w/v			
Spanish:	b/v	ch/sh	j/y	s/z	r	
Thai:	i/e	ey/e	p/f	w/v	sh/ch	l/r
Turkish:	e/a	v/w				
Vietnamese:	e/a	p/f/b				

25

1: Affix Chart

Prefixes		Function/ Meaning
un- non- in- anti- mal- a- mis- dis-		Negative
uni- multi- mono- semi- bi- poly- tri- equi- pan-		Quantity
en- be-		Verb
pre- intra- post- extra- inter-		Position
super- sub- sur- epi- hypo- hyper- para-		Relationship
ex- ab- in- trans- ad- pro- de- se- re-		Movement
syn- contra- co-		With or Against

Suffixes		Function/ Meaning
-er -ist -ant -ian -ary		"Doer" Noun
-en -ate -ify -ize		Verb
-ance -ship -ity -ness -hood -ion -age -ment -dom -ism		Noun
-able -al -less -en -ful -ous -y -ary -ish -ive -ic		Adjective
-ly -wise -ward		Adverb

2: Common Affixes

PREFIXES

Prefix	Meaning	Example
a-, an-	not	amoral, atypical, amorphous
ab-	away from	abnormal, abrupt, abstain
ad-	toward, to	administer, adhere, adapt
ante-	before, in front of	anteroom, antecedent, antedate
anti-	against, opposite	antidote, antipathy, antiseptic
arch-	chief, prime	archbishop, archangel, archenemy
auto-	self	automatic, automobile
be-	to cause, intensely	belittle, befriend, beware, bedecked, befuddled
bene-	well	benefactor, benefit, benevolent
bi-	two	bisect, bifocal, bigamy
circum-	around, on all sides	circumscribe, circumnavigate, circumvent
con-	with	conversation, confound, convoy
col-	with	collage, collateral, collapse
cor-	with	correlate, correspond, correct
co-	with	co-worker, co-exist, co-author
contra-	against, opposite	contradict, contraband, contravene
counter-	against, opposite	counteract, counterbalance, countermand
de-	not, away from, down from	descend, deflate, deviate
di-	apart, away, not	diverge, diminish, dilute, divorce
di-	twice, two-fold, double	dichotomy, digraph, dilemma
dia-	through, completely	diameter, diaper, diaphanous, diaspora
dif-	apart, away, not	diffuse, differ, difficult
dis-	apart, away, not	distrust, disinterested, disorder
en-	make, create	engage, enact, entrust
epi-	above, around, additional	epicenter, epidemic, epidermis
equi-	equal	equivalent, equinox, equilibrium
ex-, e-	out from, former	exit, excavate, ex-governor, egress, exhale
extra-	outside, beyond	extraordinary, extrasensory, extravagant
hetero-	different	heterogeneous, heterosexual
homo-	same	homogeneous, homosexual
hyper-	extremely	hyperactive, hyperventilate, hyperbole
hypo-	below, beneath	hypodermic, hypocrisy, hypotenuse
in-	into, not	inhale, inept, innocent
im-	into, not	impel, imbalance, immoral
il-	into, not	illuminate, illiterate, illegal, illegible
ir-	into, not	irradiate, irregular, irresponsible, irresolute
inter-	between, at intervals	intersperse, intermittent, intervene
intra-	within	intracellular, intramural
intro-	motion inward	introduce, introspective, introvert
macro	large	macrocosm, macrobiotics, macro-organism
mal-	ill, badly, bad, wrong	malfunction, malnutrition, malevolent
mega-	big	megaphone, megaton, megalopolis, megabyte
micro-	small	microscope, microphone, micro-organism
mini-	small, little	minivan, miniskirt, minimal
mis-	wrong, wrongly, not	misunderstanding, misuse, mistrust

27

Prefix	Meaning	Example
mono-	single, one	monophonic, monologue, monomania
multi-	many	multisided, multiplex, multivitamin
neo-	new	neophyte, neoclassical, neonatal
non-	not	nonexistent, nonpayment, nonconformist
ob-	against	obstinate, obscure, object
pan-	all, whole, completely	Pan African, panorama, pandemic
para-	beyond, outside, near	parabola, paramilitary, paradox, paramedic
pen-	almost	peninsula, penultimate
per-	motion through, thoroughly	percolate, perfect, perceive
peri-	around, about, enclosing	perimeter, periscope, periphery
poly-	many	polygamy, polyglot, polychrome
post-	behind, after	posterity, posthumous, postscript
pre-	before, earlier, in front of	preconceived, premonition, predict
pro-	forward, before, in favor of	propulsion, prologue, project
proto-	earliest, first, original	prototype, proto-American, protocol
re-	back, again	reappear, recapture, reclaim, return
retro-	backwards	retrospect, retroactive, retroflex
se-	aside, apart	seclusion, secede, seduce
semi-	half, partly	semiannual, semicircle, semiprecious
sub-	under, below	subway, submarine, subnormal, submerge
super-	over, above, extra	superimpose, supernatural, superfluous
sur-	above, additional	survey, surtax, surface
syn-,sym-	together	synchronize, synthesis, sympathy
tele-	distant	telegraph, telepathy, television
trans-	across, over, through, beyond	transition, transcend, transgress
tri-	three	trimester, trilateral, trillion
ultra-	beyond, excessively	ultraliberal, ultramodern, ultraviolet
un-	not	unimportant, unflattering, unattractive
uni-	one	uniform, unicameral, unique
vice-	one who takes the place of another	vice-president, viceroy, vice-consul

NOUN SUFFIXES

Suffix	Meaning	Example
-ance,-ence	act of	attendance, precedence, reliance
-ancy, -ency	state of	hesitancy, presidency, consistency
-age	action, condition, collection	message, bondage, marriage, postage, baggage
-ant, -ent	one who, that which	stimulant, participant, student, president
-ar	one who	bursar, liar, beggar
-ary, -ory, -ery, -ry	one who, place where, study of	secretary, library, history, conservatory, winery, bakery, chemistry
-dom	domain, condition of	freedom, wisdom, kingdom
-ee	one who is	employee, refugee, absentee
-eer	one who	profiteer, racketeer, pamphleteer
-er	one who	painter, receiver, baker
-ess	one who (female)	actress, poetess, lioness
-hood	state of	boyhood, falsehood, manhood
-ian	one who	beautician, musician, librarian

Suffix	Meaning	Example
-ics	science, art, or practice of	graphics, mathematics, athletics, dramatics
-ion, -ation, -sion, -tion	state, action, institution	fixation, exploration, starvation, foundation, organization, preservation, suspension, competition
-ism	doctrine, point of view	mannerism, idealism, realism
-ist	one who, believer	segregationist, realist, cyclist
-ity	state, quality	sanity, rapidity, elasticity
-ment	state, quality, act of	amazement, payment, embodiment
-ness	state of	fullness, shyness, sickness
-ocracy	system, style of government	democracy, autocracy, plutocracy
-or	one who	actor, governor, inspector
-ship	state, condition	friendship, dictatorship, membership

ADJECTIVE SUFFIXES

Suffix	Meaning	Example
-able, -ible	capable of	capable, edible, visible
-al	like, pertaining to	criminal, practical, musical
-ary, -ory	connected with, engaged in	ordinary, budgetary, compensatory
-ed	covered with, affected by	wooded, clothed, blessed
-en	made of, resembling	wooden, ashen, silken
-ful	full of, having	useful, hopeful, successful
-ic	like, pertaining to	democratic, heroic, specific
-ish	like, pertaining to	foolish, childish, selfish
-ive	like, pertaining to	active, explosive, sensitive
-less	without	speechless, childless, harmless
-like	having the qualities of	childlike, cowlike, statesmanlike
-ly	having the qualities of	beastly, manly, worldly
-oid	like, resembling	spheroid, humanoid, paranoid
-ous	like, pertaining to	courageous, ambitious, grievous
-ward	manner, position	awkward, backward, forward

ADVERB SUFFIXES

Suffix	Meaning	Example
-ly	in a _ manner	happily, strangely, comically
-ward(s)	direction of movement	backward(s), earthward, homeward
-wise	in the manner of, as far as _ is concerned	crabwise, clockwise, corkscrew-wise, education-wise, weather-wise

VERB SUFFIXES

Suffix	Meaning	Example
-ate	to cause, to make	placate, indicate, irritate
-en	to become, to make	deafen, ripen, widen
-ify	to cause, to make	beautify, diversify, simplify
-ize	to cause, to make	symbolize, hospitalize, publicize

29

3: Common Roots

Root	Meaning	Example
agr	field, farm	agriculture, agronomy
anthro	man	anthropoid, misanthrope
aqua	water	aquatic, aqueduct
astro	star	astrology, astronaut
aud	hear	auditorium, audience
biblio	book	bibliography, bibliophile
bio	life	biology, biography
celer	speed, hasten	accelerate, celerity
chronos	time	chronicle, chronology
cap, capt, cip	take	capture, reciprocate
cep, cept, ceive	take	reception, conceive
ced, cess, cede	go, move along	success, proceed
cid	kill	suicide, genocide
clud, clus	close, shut	seclusion, include
cosmo	world	cosmopolitan, cosmonaut
crat	power	democrat, autocrat
cred	believe, trust	credit, incredulous
cur, curr	run	incur, current
demo	people	democrat, demography
dict	say	diction, contradict
duc, duct	lead	induce, abduct, educate
fac, fact	make, do	manufacture, factory
fec, fect	make, do	infect, effect
fer	carry, bear	infer, conference
fic, fict	make, do	efficacious, fiction
flect	bend	inflection, deflect
frater	brother	fraternal, fratricide
fund, fus	pour	refund, effusive
gen, gener	birth, race	generation, regenerate
geo	earth	geology, geography
glot	tongue	polyglot, glottal
gram	written	telegram, grammar
graph	write	autograph, biography
gress, grad	go, step	progress, gradual
hydr	water	dehydrate, hydrant
ject, jact	throw	project, rejection
jud	judgement	judicial, judicious
lect, leg	read, choose	collect, legend, elect
logo, log, logy	study, word	anthropology, chronology, analog
loq, loc	speak	eloquent, locution

Root	Meaning	Example
manu, mani	hand	manuscript, manicure
mar	sea	maritime, submarine
mater	mother	maternal, matriarch
med	middle	intermediary, medium
min	smaller, less	diminish, minute
mit, mis	send, let go	transmit, missile, missionary
mort	death	mortician, mortal
mot, mob, mo	move, start	motion, motivate
naut	sailor	astronaut, nautical
necro	death	necromancer, necropolis
neuro	nerve	neurology, neurotic
nom	name	nomenclature, nominal
nom	knowledge, law	autonomy, astronomy
pater	father	paternal, patriotic
path	suffering, ill	pathetic, pathology
ped, pod	foot	pedal, tripod
pend	hang, weigh	depend, ponderous, pending
phil	love	philosophy, philanthropist
phob	fear	hydrophobia, phobia
phon	sound, voice	phonology, telephone
photo	light	photography, photosynthesis
plex, pli, ply	fold	complexity, pliant, plywood
plic	fold	complicate, duplicate, implicate
poli	city	cosmopolitan, politician
port	carry	portable, import
pos, pon	place, put	postpone, position
psych	of the mind	psychic, psychology
reg, rect	rule, manage	direct, regulate
rupt	break	rupture, disrupt
scop	watch/look at	microscopic, telescope
scrib, scrip	write	inscribe, conscription
soph	wise	sophisticated, philosophy
spec, spic	see, watch	inspect, despicable
sta, stat	stand	stable, station
stit, sist	to set up, establish	constitution, insist
tact, tang	touch	tactile, tangible
ten, tain, tin	hold, keep	contain, tenacious
tend, tens, tent	stretch, weaken	extend, tenuous
typ	image	typical, typewriter
vacu	empty	vacuum, evacuate
ven	love	venerate, venereal
ven	come	prevent, convene, intervene
voca	call	vocal, invocation
vor	eat, devour	voracious, carnivorous

31

4: Common Suffixed Words

Noun

action
completion
condition
connection
decision
definition
description
direction
discussion
division
introduction
permission
prediction
preposition
production
question
station
television
translation

conversation
demonstration
examination
explanation
identification
invitation
location
occupation
preparation
pronounciation
reservation
taxation

brother
computer
container
doctor
employer
eraser
father
mother
lawyer
leader
marker
neighbor
owner
refrigerator
robber
ruler
sister
stranger
sweater
teacher
typewriter
waiter
worker

musician
patient
president
artist
dentist
dictionary
vocabulary
discovery
laundry

absence
acceptance
assistance
difference
distance
entrance
license
patience
preference

agency
emergency

departure
failure
furniture
measure
mixture
picture
signature
temperature

advertisement
agreement
apartment
argument
assignment
employment
government
requirement

baggage
college
garage
marriage
package

approval
arrival
criminal
decimal
terminal

ability
activity
electricity
reality
relationship
freedom
business

Verb

advertise
memorize
realize
identify
frighten
demonstrate
translate

Adjective

busy
chilly
cloudy
dirty
easy
empty
foggy
healthy
heavy
hungry
icy
muddy
noisy
oily
rainy
shiny
stormy
tasty
thirsty
windy

awful
beautiful
careful
successful
wonderful

nervous
various
careless
considerable
enjoyable
possible
probable
artistic
electric
public
expensive
conditional
national
natural

Adverb

actually
awfully
certainly
closely
fairly
finally
partly
probably
quickly
quietly
really
simply
slowly
specially
successfully
suddenly
usually

Words are taken from Pro Lingua's *Learner's Lexicon,* 1200-word level.

5: Irregular Noun Plurals

A. Vowel change

man > men
woman > women

foot > feet
tooth > teeth

goose > geese
mouse > mice

B. *-en* Suffix

child > children

ox > oxen

C. f > v

thief > thieves
wife > wives
life > lives
knife > knives
calf > calves

half > halves
hoof > hooves
leaf > leaves
loaf > loaves
self > selves

sheaf > sheaves
shelf > shelves
wolf > wolves

D. Same

sheep > sheep
deer > deer
moose > moose
fish > fish
trout > trout

salmon > salmon
bass > bass
series > series
means > means
species > species

Chinese > Chinese
Japanese > Japanese
Swiss > Swiss

E. No singular

scissors
tweezers
tongs
trousers
slacks

shorts
pants
pajamas
(eye) glasses
spectacles

binoculars
clothes
people

F. Borrowed Greek and Latin words

analysis > analyses
basis > bases
hypothesis > hypotheses
parenthesis > parentheses
synopsis > synopses
thesis > theses
crisis > crises

stimulus > stimuli
nucleus > nuclei
alumnus > alumni
radius > radii
syllabus > syllabi
medium > media
memorandum > memoranda

curriculum > curricula
phenomenon > phenomena
criterion > criteria
vortex > vortices
matrix > matrices
index > indices

6: Compound Word Chart

N = N+N fireplace raincoat keyboard	N = N + V-ing bookkeeping sightseeing shoplifting	ADJ = ADV/ADJ + V-en new born quick frozen absent minded
N = ADJ+N blackbird software short circuit	N = V + N push button pickpocket cookbook	ADJ = ADJ + ADJ audio-visual deaf mute African-American
N = N +V-er baby sitter stockholder bus driver	ADJ = N + ADJ age-old jet black duty-free	ADJ = NUM + N ten-foot seven-member two-dollar
N = V + part breakdown grownup drop-off	ADJ = N + V-ing man eating fact-finding breathtaking	V = PART + V overcome outdo input
N = N + V handshake lifeguard headache	ADJ = N + V-en typewritten bow-legged heart broken	V = N + V window shop brainwash sleepwalk
N = V-ing + N dining room firing squad chewing gum	ADJ = ADV/ADJ + V-ing far reaching good looking well-meaning	V = ADV/ADJ + V download dry clean fast forward

The boxes have been half-filled to allow you to insert other compound words

7: A Collection of Common Collocations

Food Pairs with *AND*

bacon and eggs
bacon, lettuce,
   and tomato
bread and butter
fish and chips

half and half
meat and potatoes
milk and honey
pork and beans
salt and pepper

soup and sandwich
spaghetti and
   meatballs
sugar and spice
surf and turf

Noun Pairs with *AND*

aches and pains
brothers and sisters
cats and dogs
cops and robbers
cowboys and Indians

dos and don'ts
fame and fortune
husband and wife
ladies and gentlemen
life and death

peace and prosperity
odds and ends
sticks and stones
supply and demand
thunder and lightning

Other Pairs with *AND*

back and forth
betwixt and between
down and out
each and every
far and away
fast and furious
few and far between
first and foremost
forever and ever
forgive and forget
front and center
fun and games
hard and fast

high and mighty
hit and run
hot and bothered
lost and found
more and more
nice and easy
now and forever
off and on
out and out
over and done with
over and over
pure and simple
rise and shine

rough and tumble
safe and sound
sick and tired
spick and span
stop and go
straight and narrow
thick and thin
time and again
tried and true
up and coming
up and down
war and peace
wear and tear

Pairs with *OR*

dead or alive
do or die
double or nothing
feast or famine
friend or foe
give or take

hit or miss
life or death
more or less
no ifs, ands, or buts
on or about
plus or minus

rain or shine
ready or not
right or wrong
sink or swim
trick or treat
win or lose

Adjective + Noun

confirmed bachelor
happy ending
inveterate smoker

moldy bread
rancid butter

rotten apple
sonic boom

35

Adjective Pairs

bare naked	hard hit	slap happy
bone dry	high powered	sound asleep
dirt cheap	picture perfect	stark naked
freezing cold	razor sharp	tough minded
hard headed	red hot	wide awake

Containers, etc.

a bag of potatoes	a dozen eggs	a pound of meat
a bottle of wine	an ear of corn	a quart of milk
a bouquet of flowers	a head of lettuce	a roll of toilet paper
a box of cereal	a jar of honey	a six-pack of beer
a bunch of bananas	a jug of cider	a stick of butter
a bushel of apples	a loaf of bread	a tub of butter
a can of soup	a pack of gum	a tube of toothpaste
a clove of garlic		

Animal Sounds

a bird chirps	a duck quacks	a mouse squeaks
a cat meows	a frog croaks	an owl hoots
a chick peeps	a hen clucks	a pig grunts
a cow moos	a horse neighs	a rooster crows
a dog barks	a lion roars	a snake hisses

Animal Similes

blind as a bat	happy as a clam	sly as a fox
busy as a bee	proud as a peacock	strong as an ox
crazy as a loon	silly as a goose	stubborn as a mule
free as a bird	slippery as an eel	wise as an owl

Similes with *LIKE*

cry like a baby	purr like a kitten	shake like a leaf
drink like a fish	roar like a lion	sleep like a log
drive like a maniac	run like a deer	smell like a rose
eat like a pig	sell like hotcakes	work like a dog
hop like a bunny		

More Similes with *AS*

American as apple pie	easy as pie	naked as a jaybird
bright as a button	flat as a pancake	nutty as a fruitcake
cool as a cucumber	high as a kite	pretty as a picture
dead as a doornail	old as the hills	sober as a judge

Verb + Noun

catch a cold
commit suicide
do a favor
   an assignment
   homework
   housework
   the dishes
drive a car
fly a flag
   a kite
   a plane
get busy
   dressed
   even
   going
   involved
   lost
   mad
   pregnant
   sick
   tired
   to sleep
   some/nowhere
   well
   with it
give directions
   a gift
   a hand
   permission

have an advantage
   a baby
   children
   a drink
   a good/bad time
   an excuse
   a headache
   an idea
   a job
   a seat
   the time
   time
make an appointment
   a bed
   a bet
   a copy
   a date
   a decision
   do
   friends
   love
   money
   a phone call
   progress
   a request
   sense
   waves
operate an elevator
paddle a canoe
play ball
   cards
   dead
   a game
   possum

sail a boat
take advantage of
   a bath
   the blame
   a break
   a bus
   care
   dictation
   a drink
   effect
   one's medicine
   a nap
   notes
   offense
   a picture
   place
   a plane
   responsibility
   a seat
   a shower
   a swim
   a train
   someone's word
say one's prayers
   grace
   hello/goodbye (for me)
tell one's fortune
   a joke
   a lie
   a secret
   a story
   the truth

8: Nationality and Place Words
Members of the United Nations

Place	Person	Adjective
Afghanistan	Afghan(s), Afghanistani	Afghan, Afghani
Albania	Albanian(s)	Albanian
Algeria	Algerian(s)	Algerian
Andorra	Andorran(s)	Andorran
Angola	Angolan(s)	Angolan
Antigua and Barbuda	Antiguan(s), Barbudan(s)	Antiguan, Barbudan
Argentina	Argentine(s), Argentinean(s)	Argentine, Argentinean
Armenia	Armenian(s)	Armenian
Australia	Australian(s), Aussie(s) (colloq.)	Australian
Austria	Austrian(s)	Austrian
Azerbaijan	Azerbaijani(s)	Azerbaijan, Azerbaijani
Bahamas, The	Bahamian(s)	Bahamian
Bahrain	Bahraini(s)	Bahraini
Bangladesh	Bangladeshi(s)	Bangladeshi
Barbados	Barbadian(s)	Barbadian
Belarus	Belarussian(s)	Belarus
Belgium	Belgian(s)	Belgian
Belize	Belizean(s)	Belizean
Benin	Beninese	Beninese
Bhutan	Bhutanese, Bhutani(s)	Bhutanese, Bhutani
Bolivia	Bolivian(s)	Bolivian
Bosnia and Herzegovina	Bosnian(s)	Bosnian
Botswana	Motswana (sing.), Batswana (pl.)	Motswana (sing.), Batswana (pl.)
Brazil	Brazilian(s)	Brazilian
Brunei	Bruneian(s)	Bruneian
Bulgaria	Bulgarian(s)	Bulgarian
Burkina Faso (Upper Volta)	Burkinabe (Voltan(s)	Burkinabe (Voltan)
Burundi	Murundi (sing.) Burundi (pl.)	Burundi, Kirundi (lang.)
Cambodia (Kampuchea)	Cambodian(s)	Cambodian
Cameroon/Cameroun	Cameroonian(s)	Cameroonian
Canada	Canadian(s)	Canadian
Cape Verde	Cape Verdean(s)	Cape Verdean
Central African Republic	Central African(s), Centrafrican(s)	Central African, Centrafrican
Chad	Chadian(s)	Chadian
Chile	Chilean(s)	Chilean
China, Peoples Republic of	Chinese	Chinese
Colombia	Colombian(s)	Colombian
Comoros	Comorian(s)	Comorian
Congo, Dem. Republic (Zaire)	Congolese	Congolese
Congo, Republic of	Congolese	Congolese (Zairean)
Costa Rica	Costa Rican(s)	Costa Rican
Côte d'Ivoire (Ivory Coast)	Ivorian(s)	Ivorian
Croatia	Croatian(s)	Croatians
Cuba	Cuban(s)	Cuban
Cyprus	Cypriot(s)	Cypriot
Czech Republic	Czech(s)	Czech

Place	Person	Adjective
Denmark	Dane(s)	Danish
Djibouti	Djibouti(s)	Djibouti
Dominica	Dominican(s)	Dominican
Dominican Republic	Dominican(s)	Dominican
East Timor	Timorese	East Timorese
Ecuador	Ecuadorian(s)	Ecuadorian
Egypt	Egyptian(s)	Egyptian
El Salvador	Salvadoran(s)	Salvadoran
Equatorial Guinea	Equatorial Guinean(s)	Equatorial Guinean
Eritrea	Eritrean	Eritrean
Estonia	Estonian(s)	Estonian
Ethiopia	Ethiopian(s)	Ethiopian
Fiji	Fijian(s), Fiji Islander(s)	Fijian
Finland	Finn(s)	Finnish
France	Frenchman/woman (men/women)	French
Gabon	Gabonese	Gabonese
Gambia, The	Gambian	Gambian
Georgia	Georgian	Georgian
Germany	German	German
Ghana	Ghanaian	Ghanaian
Greece	Greek	Greek
Grenada	Grenadian	Grenadian
Guatemala	Guatemalan	Guatemalan
Guinea	Guinean	Guinean
Guinea-Bissau	Guinean	Guinean
Guyana	Guyanese	Guyanese
Haiti	Haitian(s)	Haitian
Honduras	Honduran(s)	Honduran
Hungary	Hungarian(s)	Hungarian
Iceland	Icelander(s)	Icelandic
India	Indian(s)	Indian
Indonesia	Indonesian(s)	Indonesian
Iran	Iranian(s)	Iranian
Iraq	Iraqi(s)	Iraqi
Ireland	Irishman (-men, -women)	Irish
Israel	Israeli(s)	Israeli
Italy	Italian(s)	Italian
Jamaica	Jamaican(s)	Jamaican
Japan	Japanese	Japanese
Jordan	Jordanian(s)	Jordanian
Kazakhstan	Kazakh(s)	Kazakh
Kenya	Kenyan(s)	Kenyan(s)
Kiribati (Gilbert Islands)	Kiribati(s)	Kiribati (Gilbertese)
Korea, North	North Korean(s)	North Korean
Korea, South	South Korean(s)	South Korean
Kuwait	Kuwaiti(s)	Kuwaiti
Kyrgyzstan	Kirgiz(es)	Kirgiz
Laos	Lao(s), Laotian(s)	Lao, Laotian
Latvia	Latvian(s)	Latvian

Place	Person	Adjective
Lebanon	Lebanese	Lebanese
Lesotho	Mosotho (sing.), Basotho (pl.)	Basotho, Sesotho (lang.)
Liberia	Liberian(s)	Liberian
Libya	Libyan(s)	Libyan
Liechtenstein	Liechtensteiner(s)	Liechtenstein
Lithuania	Lithuanian(s)	Lithuanian
Luxembourg	Luxembourger(s), Luxembourgian(s)	Luxembourgish, Luxembourgian
Macedonia	Macedonian(s)	Macedonian
Madagascar	Malagasy(ies)	Malagasy
Malawi	Malawian(s)	Malawian
Malaysia	Malaysian(s)	Malaysian
Maldives	Maldivian(s)	Maldivian
Mali	Malian(s)	Malian
Malta	Maltese	Maltese
Marshall Islands	Marshall Islanders	Marshallese
Mauritania	Mauritanian(s)	Mauritanian
Mauritius	Mauritian(s)	Mauritian
Mexico	Mexican(s)	Mexican
Micronesia	Micronesian(s)	Micronesian
Moldova	Moldovan(s)	Moldovan
Monaco	Monegasque(s)	Monegasque
Mongolia	Mongolian(s)	Mongolian
Montenegro	Montenegran(s)	Montenegran
Morocco	Moroccan(s)	Moroccan
Mozambique	Mozambican(s)	Mozambican
Myanmar (Burma)	Burmese	Burmese
Namibia	Namibian(s)	Namibian
Nauru	Nauruan(s)	Nauruan
Nepal	Nepalese	Nepalese, Nepali
Netherlands, The (Holland)	Dutchman (men, women)	Dutch
New Zealand	New Zealander(s)	New Zealand
Nicaragua	Nicaraguan(s)	Nicaraguan
Niger	Nigerien(s)	Nigerien
Nigeria	Nigerian(s)	Nigerian
Norway	Norwegian(s)	Norwegian
Oman	Omani(s)	Omani
Pakistan	Pakistani(s)	Pakistani
Palau	Palauan(s)	Palauan
Panama	Panamanian(s)	Panamanian
Papua New Guinea	Papua New Guinean(s)	Papua New Guinean
Paraguay	Paraguayan(s)	Paraguayan
Peru	Peruvian(s)	Peruvian
Philippines	Filipino(s) (-a(s))	Filipino
Poland	Pole(s)	Polish
Portugal	Portuguese	Portuguese
Qatar	Qatari(s)	Qatari
Romania, Rumania	Romanian(s)	Romanian
Russia	Russian(s)	Russian
Rwanda	Rwandan(s)	Rwandan

Place	Person	Adjective
St. Kitts and Nevis	St. Kittitian(s), Nevisian(s)	St. Kittitian, Nevisian
St. Lucia	St. Lucian(s)	St. Lucian
St. Vincent and the Grenadines	Vincentian(s)	Vincentian
Samoa	Samoan(s)	Samoan
San Marino	Sammarinese (sing.) (-inesi (pl.))	Sammarinese (sing.) (-inesi (pl.))
Sao Tome and Principe	Sao Tomean(s)	Sao Tomean
Saudi Arabia	Saudi(s)	Saudi (Saudi Arabian)
Senegal	Senegalese	Senegalese
Serbia	Serb(s)	Serbian
Seychelles	Seychellois	Seychellois
Sierra Leone	Sierra Leonean(s)	Sierra Leonean
Singapore	Singaporean(s)	Singaporean
Slovakia	Slovakian(s)	Slovakian
Slovenia	Slovenian(s)	Slovenian
Solomon Islands	Solomon Islander(s)	Solomon Islander
Somalia	Somali(s)	Somali
South Africa	South African(s)	South African
Spain	Spaniard(s)	Spanish
Sri Lanka (Ceylon)	Sri Lankan(s) (Ceylonese)	Sri Lankan (Ceylonese)
Sudan	Sudanese	Sudanese
Surinam	Surinamer(s)	Surinamer
Swaziland	Swazi(s)	Swazi
Sweden	Swede(s)	Swedish
Switzerland	Swiss	Swiss
Syria	Syrian(s)	Syrian
Tajikistan	Tajik(s)	Tajik
Tanzania	Tanzanian(s)	Tanzanian
Thailand	Thai(s)	Thai
Togo	Togolese	Togolese
Tonga	Tongan(s)	Tongan
Trinidad and Tobago	Trinidadian(s), Tobagonian(s)	Trinidadian, Tobagonian
Tunisia	Tunisian(s)	Tunisian
Turkey	Turk(s)	Turkish
Turkmenistan	Turkoman (-men)	Turkoman
Tuvalu (Ellice Islands)	Tuvaluan(s)	Tuvaluan
Uganda	Ugandan(s)	Ugandan
Ukraine	Ukrainian(s),	Ukrainian
United Arab Emirates	Emirati(s)	Emirati(s)
United Kingdom of Great Britain	Briton(s), Brits	British
United States of America	American(s)	American
Uruguay	Uruguayan(s)	Uruguayan
Uzbekistan	Uzbeki(s), Uzbek(s)	Uzbeki, Uzbek
Vanuatu	ni-Vanuatu	ni-Vanuatu
Venezuela	Venezuelan(s)	Venezuelan(s)
Vietnam	Vietnamese	Vietnamese
Yemen	Yemeni(s)	Yemeni
Zambia	Zambian(s)	Zambian
Zimbabwe	Zimbabwean(s)	Zimbabwean

This list includes all the members of the United Nations as of the publication of this edition. The names of other geographical regions and major cities of the United States and the world are available as ESL Miscellany supplements on our website www.ProLinguaAssociates.com.

1: A Grammar Sequence

This grammar sequence is only a handy guide to what can and should be covered in a basic English course. The list represents a series of steps from very basic phrase structures and transformations to increasingly complex or unusual structures. Some of the steps are large, and some small, and some will be easier than others. It is by no means a complete outline of the grammar of English. However, mastery of this list, along with commensurate progress in pronunciation, vocabulary development, and communicative skills would enable a student to function reasonably independently in an English-speaking world.

1. **Affirmative Statement Word Order**   *I am reading this sentence now.*
      Subject noun phrase + verb phrase + object noun phrase + adverbial
      Subject Pronouns   *I, you, he, she , we, they*
      Present forms of *BE*   *am, are , is*
      Subject - verb agreement with *BE*   *I am,* etc.
      Present progressive aspect   *am reading*
          BE + **V** *-ing*
      Determiner + Object noun   *this sentence*

2. **Negative Statement Word Order**   *I am not reading a French sentence.*
      Placement of *not* after 1ˢᵗ auxiliary
      Determiner + adjective + noun   *a French sentence*

3. **Yes/No Question**   *Are you learning English?*
      Inversion of subject and 1ˢᵗ auxiliary
      Short answer   *Yes, I am.*

4. **Simple Present Tense Aspect**
   with Stative Verbs
      Affirmative statement   *I need English.*
      3ʳᵈ person singular –*S*   *She needs English.*
      Negative statement   *I do not know that word.*
          Do insertion; placement of *not* **after** *do*
      3ʳᵈ person singular with *do*   *She does not know that word.*
      Yes/No question with *do*   *Do you like English?*
      Do **insertion and inversion of**
          subject and *do*
      Short answer   *Yes, I do. /Yes, she does.*
                                                                No, I do not. /No he does not.
      Common Stative Verbs   *cost, feel, have, hear, know, like,*
                                                                need, want, understand

5. **Simple Present with Copula _BE_**   *He is a student.*
    Affirmative statement   *She is a teacher.*
    _BE_ **+ noun phrase**   *is a teacher.*
    Indefinite article   *a teacher*
    Definite article   *The teacher is in the classroom.*
    _BE_ **+ prepositional phrase**   *is in the classroom*
    _BE_ **+ adjective**   *The students are busy.*
    Regular plural _–S_   *students*

6. **Yes/No Question and Negation**   *Are you an English teacher?*
   with Copula _BE_   *I am not a teacher.*
    Inversion of Subject and _BE_   *Are you*
    Placement of _not_ **after** _BE_   *am not*
    Indefinite article _an_   *an English teacher*

7A. **Contraction of** _Not_   *She isn't a math teacher.*
                        He isn't taking this course.
                        They don't speak Spanish.
                        She doesn't know the answer.
    _AM_ **exception**   *I'm not happy.*

7B. **Contraction of** _BE_   *She's a very good teacher.*
    Intensifier   *very*

8. **Simple Past Tense**   *I learned a new word.*
    regular _–ed_ **suffix**
    Did in questions and negatives   *Did you like the class?*
                        We didn't know the answer.
    Common irregular past forms   *I knew the answer.*
                        begin, bring, buy, cost, drink, eat, forget,
                        go, have, make, read, say, see, sleep,
                        speak, take, teach, tell, think
    Common adverbs of time   *yesterday, last X, ago*

9A. _WH_ **subject Question Words with**   *Who is she?*
    copula _BE_   *What is he?*
                        Where is he?

9B. _WH_ **subject Question Words with**
    Other Verbs   *Who speaks Russian?*
                        What happened?

9C. _WH_ **Predicate Question Words**   *What do you want?*
                        Where are you going?
                        Who did you see?
                        When did you return?

9D. *HOW:* formulaic

How are you?
How do you do?

10. **Locative and Temporal Prepositions in Prepositional Phrases**

at school, in the park, on the street,
to the bank, from the store, near the
post office, under the desk,
at three o'clock, on Monday, in 2008

11. **Coordination with** *and, but, or*

the bank and the post office
I went home and read the paper.
She knows the answer, and he does too.
She speaks well, but he doesn't.

    adverbs: *also, too, either*

I also need a pen or a pencil.
I need a pen, too.
She doesn't need a pen, and I don't either.

    Indefinite pronoun: *one(s)*

She likes the red one, but
I like the blue ones.

12. **Modal Verbs:**
    Can **(ability)**
    Requests and permission
    with *can, may*
    Polite requests with *would, could*
      and *please.*

I can do that.
Can you help me?
May I go now?
Could you give me a hand, please?
Would you please do me a favor?

13. **Imperative (affirmative),**
    Demonstratives and invitations
      Negative imperative
      Hortative
      Negative hortative
      Invitation with *shall* **and**
        would you like (to)
      Demonstratives as Pronouns:
      this, that, these, those

Give me this blue one.
Don't take that red one.
Let's buy these pens.
Let's not buy those pens.
Shall we go now?
Would you like this or that?
I want these.
She wants those.

14. **Object Pronouns:** *me, you, him,*
    her, it, us, them
    Direct and indirect object
    position

Please give me this one.

Please give it to me.
Please give me the book.

15. **Nonreferential** *there, here*

There is a bus station on the corner.
Here comes the bus.

    How + **adj and** **nonreferential** *it*

How far is it to the station?
How long does it take?

    Adverbial *there, here*

Is it raining there?
It's a nice day here.

16A. **Phrasal Modal:** *have to, have got to*   *I have to go.*
    Contraction of *have*   *I've got to go home.*

16B. **Phrasal Modal:** *be going to*   *I'm going to take the bus.*

16C. **Future Predictive** *Will*   *I'll arrive at three o'clock.*
    Contraction of *will*   *I won't be late.*

17. **Present Habitual Tense-Aspect**   *I go to work at 8 o'clock.*
    With frequency adverbs: *I usually eat lunch at noon.*
    always, usually, sometimes, never
    Position with copula BE and   *I am always on time.*
      auxiliaries   *I can usually finish by four.*
    Time expressions: *I do it every day.*
      all (day, month year, etc.)   *I don't do it all day, but*
      every (other)   *I do it every other day.*
    Frequency questions: *How often,*   *How often do you do that?*
      ever   *Do you ever do that?*
    Fronting of *usually* **and**   *Usually I leave at three.*
      sometimes   *Sometimes I go at two.*

18. **Why with adverbial clause and**   *Why do you do that?*
    subordinator *because*   *I do it because I have to.*
    How come **and** *what ..for*   *How come you're late?*
      What did you do that for?

19A. **Tag questions:** Agreement   *It's a nice day, isn't it?*
    intonation
    Affirmative tag   *It isn't easy, is it?*

19B. **Tag questions:** Information   *You're leaving soon, aren't you?*
    intonation   *You aren't leaving now, are you?*

20A. **Possession:** *Whose*   *Whose book is this?*
    Possessive adjectives: *my, your,*   *That's my book.*
      his, her, its, our, their
    –S **suffix**   *That one is Maria's.*
    of **possessive phrase**   *in the middle of the book*

20B. **Possessive Pronouns:** *mine, yours,*   *That book is hers.*
    his, hers, its, ours, theirs
    Which/what **+ Noun**   *Which book is his?*
      What book are you reading?
    Whose, which **as pronouns**   *Whose is that?*
    Idiomatic *belongs to*   *That book belongs to me.*

21. **Comparison of Adjectives:** *–er, –est*
    more, most

    I need a __bigger__ car.
    I don't want a __more expensive__ car.
    Yoshi has __the fastest__ car.
    Margot has __the most economical__ car.

    Comparative constructions:
    –er than, more X than
    Equative constructions: *as .. as*
    the same as, different from

    His computer is __slower than__ mine.
    My laptop is __more portable than__ his.
    My cell phone is __as nice as__ yours.
    Your mouse is __the same as__ mine, but
    *   his is __different from__ ours.*

    the same X as

    My computer has __the same memory as__ his.

22. **Present Perfect Tense Aspect**
    Have + –en
    With adverbs: *just, recently,*
    since, already, yet, never,
    for (ten years, etc.), up to now

    I have __seen__ that film.
    She has __just__ returned from Boston.
    I've __already__ done that, but she hasn't
    done __it yet__.
    I have __never__ been to Australia.
    I have __practiced__ yoga __for several years__.
    __Up to now__ I have __always__ had a Ford.

23. **Noun Phrase: Count and**
    noncount nouns
    With determiners: indefinite
    specific: *a, some, ø*
    Definite: *the*

    I'll have a vegetable and rice.

    I'd like __a__ hot dog and __some__
    mustard, but I don't want __ø__ relish.
    __The__ hot dog was good, but __the__ mustard
    wasn't.

    Generic

    I like __ø__ apples. __The__ apple is very
    nutritious.

24. **Noun Phrase:**
    Quantifiers *much, many*

    I don't have __much__ money, and
    *   I have __many__ debts.*

    Statements, questions,
    and negatives
    with *some, any*
    with count nouns: *few, a few,*
    several
    with noncounts: *little, much, a lot of*

    I don't have __any__ twenties. Do you have
    *   __any__ tens? No, but I have __some__ fives.*
    There were __few__ people there, and __a few__
    left early. However, __several__ people stayed.
    She has __little__ money, __a lot of__ courage,
    *   but not __much__ luck.*

    with count or noncount: *all, most,*
    almost, no

    Almost __all__ the customers bought something.
    __Most__ of them spent a lot of money. There
    *   were __no__ complaints.*

25A. Modals: Prediction with *will, might, may*

The rain will be heavy, but it may end by evening. There might be more rain tomorrow.

25B. Modals: Probability with *may, might, could, ought to, should, must*

RRRRRRing! That may be Alfredo.
Yeah, but it might be Anna. And it could be Yukiko. No, it ought to be Franz. It's two o'clock; it should be Jon. You're all wrong. It must be Antonio. He promised to call at two.

26. Phrasal Verbs:
    Intransitive:
    Transitive Inseparable:
    with adverb/preposition:
    Transitive Separable:
    Pronoun object placement

My car broke down in the desert.
They broke into a store.
He broke up with her.
He broke the engine down into five sections.
He broke it down.

27A. Past Progressive Tense-Aspect

Yesterday at two o'clock I was driving home.

    Time expressions: *at/on/in* with *o'clock, Monday, 2005*

In 2003 I was studying for the TOEFL.

27B. Past Progressive with adverbial Time Clause with *when*

I was taking a shower *when the phone rang*.

28. Modals: Advice with *should, ought to, had better*
    Contraction of *had*
    Use of *or else*
    Ability with *be able to*
    Prohibition with *cannot*
    Obligation with *have to, must*

You should see a doctor.
You ought to take this medicine.
You'd better get some rest
    or (else) you won't
    be able to go with us.
I'm sorry, you cannot drive.
You have to use a seat belt.
You must yield to pedestrian.

    No Obligation with *don't have to*

You don't have to wear a helmet.

29. More Questions
    Embedded WH questions
    WH + infinitive
    Negative Questions
    Short answer

I know where he is.
Do you know where to go?
Don't you know the answer?
No, I don't.

30. **Future Time**
    with present progressive *I am leaving tomorrow.*
    with simple present   *I leave a two o' clock.*
    with *be about to*   *We are about to leave.*
    Future Progressive   *I will be taking the train.*
    Time expressions: *tomorrow,* *She's going tomorrow.*
     soon, at/on/in   *We're leaving soon.*
              Tomorrow at two o'clock I'll be
              flying to Europe.

31. **Infinitives and Gerunds**
    Verbs followed by infinitives: *I want to go.*
     want, learn, wait, teach, tell,
     ask, need, prefer
    Verbs followed by Gerunds: *I enjoy singing.*
     dislike, keep, miss, practice
    Verbs followed by either: *I like singing.*
     begin, have, love, prefer, stop *I stopped to look. I stopped looking.*
    Verbs followed by object and
    simple verb: *hear, notice, see, watch* *We watched them leave.*

32. **Causative Verbs**   *We made him go.*
    Verbs followed by simple form *We had him go by taxi.*
     make, have, let   *I didn't let her go.*
    followed by infinitive *get* *She got us to change our minds.*

33. **Noun Phrase word order** *both my two big brothers*
    Pre-determiners: *both, all, half* *both brothers*
    core determiners: *a, the, some* *a brother*
     my, your, his, her, its, our, their *my brother*
     this, that, these, those *that brother*
     each, every, some   *every brother*
    Post determiners: *two, first, next,* *two brothers*
     many, much, a lot of, several
    Intensifiers: *very, quite, rather,* *very big*
     somewhat, too, enough, repetition *too big, big enough, my big big brothers*
    Adjective ordering: *opinion, size,* *beautiful, big, long, rusty, old,*
     shape, condition, age, color, origin *black, German Mercedes*

34. Adverbials

Prepositional phrases	*to the city*
Adverb phrases	*very slowly*
Adverbial clauses:	
time	*after I go*
cause	*because I have to go*
concession	*although I cannot go*
condition	*if I go*
Word order: Manner/direction, place/position, time/frequency, purpose, reason	*rapidly • to the mall • on Elm Street • at two o' clock • every Friday • to shop • because he gets paid on Friday*

35. Conditional Verb Clauses

Future Predictive	*If it rains, I won't go, but she will.*
	If it should (happen to) stop, I'll go.
Factual	*If I get up too early, I am grumpy.*
	Whenever it rains our roof leaks.
Imaginative	*If I had enough money I'd take a vacation.*
	If I were you, I'd go to Hawaii.
	If I had gone to Hawaii, I would have gotten a nice tan.

36. Modal Verbs in Past Time

He had to do it, but you didn't have to.
Andy should have done it.
I couldn't have done it.
Cindy might have done it.
Bill must have done it.

37. Phrasal Modals

We had better go.
We are supposed to go now.
I would rather go later.
She is willing to go later.
I am not able to go now.

38. Passive Voice

Simple past	*The flowers were planted yesterday.*
With *by* phrase	*They were planted by the Garden Club.*
Simple future	*More flowers will be planted tomorrow.*
Simple present	*They are planted every spring.*

39. Participles as Modifiers

–ing vs *–ed*	*The movie was boring. I was bored.*

40. Other Past Time Verb Phrases
Iterative *used to /would*   *We used to/would swim every day.*
Noniterative *used to*   *I used to like swimming.*

Interrupted future past   *I was going to go to the beach, but it rained.*

41. Reflexive/Emphatic Pronouns
Reflexive   *I hurt myself.*
Emphatic   *I myself was not hurt.*
Unaided   *I did it all by myself.*

42. Past and Future Perfect tense/aspects
Past perfect   *I had never done that before.*
Future perfect   *By next year I will have done that several times.*

43. Perfect Progressive tense/aspects
Present perfect progressive   *She has been studying Spanish since 1999.*
Future perfect progressive   *By next year she will have been studying Spanish for several years.*
Past perfect progressive   *She had been studying Spanish for one year when she first went to Mexico.*

44. Complementation
Embedded *that* noun clause   *I know that he is here.*
Embedded Yes/No question   *Do you know if/whether she is here?*
Embedded negative clause   *I don't know if/whether he is here.*
Embedded WH question   *I don't know where they are.*

45. Generalized *–ever*   *Wherever he went he planted apple trees.*
                                        Whoever saw him was amused.
                                        He wore whatever he pleased.
                                        He ate whenever he wanted to.

46. Impersonal Pronouns
you   *You can't drive fast when it's slippery.*
we   *We should slow down in bad weather.*
they   *They usually salt the roads in the winter.*
one   *One should be careful driving when it snows.*

47. **Other Subjunctive**
    with "control" verbs　　　　*He advised that she take only four courses.*
    with certain adjectives　　　*It is important she pass them.*
    with wish　　　　　　　　　*I wish that she would listen to him.*
    hope vs. wish　　　　　　　*I hope that she will.*

48. **Conjunctive Adverbs**
    addition　　　　　　　　　*I know that. Moreover, she does too.*
    result　　　　　　　　　　*I know that. Therefore, I won't go.*
    concession/contrast　　　　*I know that. However, I'll go anyway.*

49. **Relative Clauses**
    with *who/that*　　　　　　*She is the person who/that knows you.*
    　　　　　　　　　　　　　She is the person who(m)/that you know.
    with *when*　　　　　　　　*I'll never forget the day when we met.*
    with *where*　　　　　　　*This is the place where she lives.*
    restrictive vs. nonrestrictive　*My friend who is from New York is here.*
    　　　　　　　　　　　　　My friend, who is from New York, is here.

50. **Reported Speech**
    Statements　　　　　　　*He said (that) he was OK.*
    Questions　　　　　　　*He asked if I was OK.*
    Commands　　　　　　　*He told me to tell you he was OK.*

51

2: Tense/Aspect Chart

	Simple	Perfect	Progressive	Perfect Progressive
	Active • Passive	Active • Passive	Active • Passive	Active
Future	I will teach English English will be taught	I will have taught English English will have been taught	I will be teaching English	I will have been teaching English
Present	I teach English English is taught	I have taught English English has been taught	I am teaching English English is being taught	I have been teaching English
Past	I taught English English was taught	I had taught English English had been taught	I was teaching English English was being taught	I had been teaching English

3: Stative Verbs

agree	desire	hear	own	taste
appear	dislike	imagine	prefer	tend
appreciate	doubt	know	realize	think
be	dread	like	regret	trust
believe	equal	look like	remember	understand
belong	fear	love	require	want
care	feel	mean	resemble	weigh
consider	forget	need	see	wish
contain	guess	note	seem	
cost	hate	notice	smell	
depend	have	owe	suppose	

4: Linking Verbs

act	My cat is acting very strange nowadays.
appear	She appeared confused by his answer.
be	She is a teacher. She is very skillful. She is in her office now.
become	He became dissatisfied with his progress. Eventually, he became a wonderful teacher.
feel	She feels quite pleased with the results.
get	She got angry when the company fired her.
go	This bottle of milk is going bad.
grow	It's growing darker with every minute.
look	You look terrible.
remain	This strange mystery remains unsolved.
seem	Our last assignment seemed quite easy.
smell	Your new perfume smells wonderful.
sound	Her explanation sounds very strange to me.
taste	Your oyster stew tastes great.
turn	The leaves in my yard have turned red.

Less common: lie, rest, stand, come, fall, run

5: Irregular Verbs
Past participle ends with *n:*

arise	arose	arisen	mow	mowed	mown/mowed
awake	awoke	awoken/awaked	prove	proved	proven
be	was/were	been	ride	rode	ridden
bear	bore	born	rise	rose	risen
beat	beat	beaten	run	ran	ran
begin	began	begun	see	saw	seen
bite	bit	bitten	sew	sewed	sewn/sewed
blow	blew	blown	shake	shook	shaken
break	broke	broken	shine	shone/shined	shone/shined
choose	chose	chosen	show	showed	shown
do	did	done	slay	slew	slain
draw	drew	drawn	sow	sowed	sown/sowed
drive	drove	driven	speak	spoke	spoken
eat	ate	eaten	spin	spun	spun
fall	fell	fallen	steal	stole	stolen
fly	flew	flown	stride	strode	stridden
forbid	forbid/forbade	forbidden	strike	struck	stricken/struck
forget	forgot	forgotten	strive	strove	striven
forgive	forgave	forgiven	swear	swore	sworn
forsake	forsook	forsaken	swell	swelled	swollen/swelled
freeze	froze	frozen	take	took	taken
get	got	gotten	tear	tore	torn
give	gave	given	throw	threw	thrown
go	went	gone	undertake	undertook	undertaken
grow	grew	grown	wake	woke	woken/waked
hide	hid	hidden	wear	wore	worn
know	knew	known	weave	wove	woven
lie	lay	lain	win	won	won
mistake	mistook	mistaken	write	wrote	written

Past participle ends with d:

bind	bound	bound	lead	led	led
bleed	bled	bled	make	made	made
breed	bred	bred	pay	paid	paid
dive	dove/dived	dove/dived	read	read	read
feed	fed	fed	say	said	said
flee	fled	fled	sell	sold	sold
find	found	found	slide	slid	slid
grind	ground	ground	speed	sped	sped
have	had	had	stand	stood	stood
hear	heard	heard	tell	told	told
hold	held	held	understand	understood	understood
lay	laid	laid	wind	wound	wound

Past participle ends with *t:*

bend	bent	bent	lose	lost	lost
bring	brought	brought	mean	meant	meant
build	built	built	meet	met	met
buy	bought	bought	seek	sought	sought
catch	caught	caught	send	sent	sent
creep	crept	crept	shoot	shot	shot
deal	dealt	dealt	sit	sat	sat
feel	fought	fought	sleep	slept	slept
fight	felt	felt	spend	spent	spent
keep	kept	kept	spit	spat	spat
kneel	knelt	knelt	sweep	swept	swept
leave	left	left	teach	taught	taught
lend	lent	lent	think	thought	thought
light	lit	lit	weep	wept	wept

Past participle ends with *d* or *t,* but the verb does not change:

bet	bet	bet	quit	quit	quit
bid	bid	bid	rid	rid	rid
burst	burst	burst	set	set	set
cast	cast	cast	shed	shed	shed
cost	cost	cost	shut	shut	shut
cut	cut	cut	slit	slit	slit
fit	fit	fit	split	split	split
hit	hit	hit	spread	spread	spread
hurt	hurt	hurt	thrust	thrust	thrust
let	let	let	wet	wet	wet
put	put	put			

Past participle ends with *m, g,* or *k:*

become	became	become	sink	sank	sunk
come	came	come	sling	slung	slung
dig	dug	dug	spring	sprang	sprung
drink	drank	drunk	stink	stank/stunk	stunk
fling	flung	flung	strike	struck	struck
hang	hung/hanged*	hung/ hanged*	swim	swam	swum
ring	rang	rung	swing	swung	swung
shrink	shrank	shrunk	wring	wrung	wrung
sing	sang	sung			

*different meanings

6: Intransitive and Transitive Verbs

Most English verbs can be used in either an intransitive or a transitive way. (Transitive verbs take a direct object.)

> Example: (intransitive) *She writes every day.* (transitive) *She is writing a book.*

The verbs in the following lists are <u>usually</u> only intransitive or transitive.

> Example: (intransitive) *He acted in Hamlet every night, and*
> (transitive) *every night he accepted a standing ovation.*

However, some of them may be used either way.

> Example: (intransitive) *She lived in Manhattan, but* (transitive) *she lived a good life.*

A. Intransitive Verbs

act	dream	live	sit
agree	fall	look	sleep
appear	go	matter	stand
arrive	happen	occur	step
belong	laugh	rain	talk
care	lie	remain	think
come	listen	rise	wait

B. Transitive Verbs

accept	cost	have	pick
admit	cover	hear	put
allow	demand	hold	raise
beat	destroy	include	realize
bring	discover	join	say
build	enjoy	kill	send
buy	expect	know	suppose
carry	express	lay	take
catch	feed	let	tell
cause	find	like	wear
consider	force	make	
contain	give	mean	

7: Phrasal Verbs
A. Separable

Example: (beat up) She beat up Freddy. She beat Freddy up.

Verb	Meaning	Example
beat up	hurt physically	She beat Freddy up.
blow out	extinguish	The children wanted to blow the matches out.
break down	disassemble	Max broke his bike down into sixty parts.
bring up	raise children	Their parents brought the children up to respect the law.
call off	cancel	The umpire called the game off.
call up	telephone	Call me up tomorrow.
do over	do again	The teacher asked me to do the assignment over.
fill out	complete	Fill these forms out and come back tomorrow.
get up	arouse from bed	Jane gets her children up by six every morning.
give back	return	The teacher gave the papers back.
give up	abandon	We had to give the puppy up to its real owner.
hand in	submit	The students handed their exams in late.
hang up	place on hook	He always hangs the phone up when I'm speaking.
keep up	maintain	It costs a lot to keep that car up.
leave out	omit	I've published; don't leave that out on my resume.
let down	lower	Let your hair down.
look over	review, examine	Look the test over before beginning.
look up	search for	I spent hours looking those words up.
make out	distinguish	The envelope was wet. He couldn't make her address out.
make up	compose, invent	They made a list up of people willing to contribute.
make up	use cosmetics	She made her daughter's face up for the party.
pack up	gather in a container	The carpenter packed his tools up at five o'clock sharp.
pass out	distribute	The captain passed aspirin tablets out to all of us.
pick out	choose	He picked a tie out to go with his shirt.
pick up	lift, collect	Someone picks the garbage up on Tuesday.
put away	put in the customary place	Put your toys away, children.
put off	postpone	Another meeting? Let's put it off.
put on	don	It's better to put your socks on before your shoes.
put out	extinguish	The fireman put the blaze out.
take back	return	My new radio doesn't work; I'm taking it back to the store.
take off	remove	They took their coats off when they entered.
take up	raise, discuss	Take that issue up with the manager.
talk over	discuss	The defendant talked his case over with lawyers.
throw away	discard	Don't throw those old magazines away.
try on	test the fit and appearance	She never tries clothes on when she shops.
try out	test	They tried the car out and decided not to buy it.
turn down	reject	The boss turned my request for a raise down.
turn down	lower the volume	Turn that television down! It's giving me a headache!
turn in	deliver, submit	The hub-cap thief turned himself in to the police.
turn off	stop power, shut off	Turn the lights off when you leave.
turn on	start power, put on	I turned the lights on to see better.
use up	finish	We've used all our sugar up.

B. Inseparable

Example: (get on)　She got on the bus as I was getting off.

Verb	Meaning	Example
believe in	have faith in	He says he doesn't believe in God.
break up with	end a relationship	Betsy broke up with her boyfriend.
break into	enter forcibly	Somebody broke into our house yesterday.
call on	ask to respond	The teacher never calls on me.
call on	visit	We called on the Smiths last week.
catch up on	become up to date	It took me a day to catch up on my email.
come down with	get sick	My son came down with chicken pox.
come to	total	The bill came to one hundred dollars.
come up with	find	He always comes up with a good answer.
count on	depend on	You can count on me. I'll be there.
cut down on	reduce	She wants to cut down on her smoking.
dwell on	keep attention on	Please don't dwell on that. I've learned!
feel up to	be able	I'm tired, and I don't feel up to going out.
get along with	be friendly	He gets along with everybody.
get around	avoid	Somehow she gets around all the rules.
get out of	escape	We were lucky to get out of that mess.
get over	recover from	I finally got over my bad cold.
get through	finish	I couldn't get through the test in time.
go into	explain	He went into great detail when I asked him.
go over	review	Let's go over all the questions.
keep on	continue	He never stops – just keeps on talking.
look after	care for	My aunt looks after the kids on Monday.
look into	investigate	Detective Smith is looking into the murder.
look like	resemble	She looks like her grandmother.
look up to	respect	Young boys look up to famous athletes.
pick on	tease	That bully likes to pick on my friend.
put up with	tolerate	I won't put up with that rude behavior.
read up on	study	I read up on the history before I went there.
run into	meet accidentally	Guess who I ran into yesterday.
run across	find accidentally	She ran across the old letter and cried.
see in	find attractive	I don't know what she sees in him.
take after	resemble	He takes after his father.
take over	get control	John took over and calmed everyone down.
take up	begin	He took up the violin at the age of fifty.
talk back to	answer rudely	My children never talk back to me.
turn into	change into	Cinderella's coach turned into a pumpkin.
wait on	attend, serve	He waited on tables for a living.

C. Intransitive

Verb	Meaning	Example
blow up	explode	What a disaster! The building blew up.
break down	stop working	The car broke down on the bridge.
break up	end a relationship	Maria and Ted broke up.
check in	arrive	We checked in at two o'clock.
check out	leave	It's 11 o'clock. It's time to check out.
come back	return	She never comes back from school on time.
come over	visit informally	Come over for lunch some time.
come to	regain consciousness	She fainted, but she soon came to.
come up	occur	I'm sorry I was late. Something came up.
fall apart	disintegrate	Her new toy suddenly fell apart.
foul up	make a mistake	I really fouled up and lost my job.
freak out	become hysterical	When I told her about Jim, she freaked out.
get by	barely succeed	His motto is do enough just to get by.
get in	arrive	My flight finally got in at 11 p.m.
get up	arise	He gets up early.
give in	surrender	We were losing, but we wouldn't give in.
give up	quit	Don't give up. We can still win.
go along	agree	She goes along with all his suggestions.
go away	leave	Please go away; I'm busy now.
go off	sound	I was late because my alarm didn't go off.
go on	happen	What's going on here?
grow up	mature	Grow up and act like an adult.
hang out	be with someone	I'm hanging out with my friends these days.
let up	decrease	The rain wouldn't let up.
log on	go on line	I logged on to your web site this morning.
look out	beware	Look out! There's a car coming.
look up	improve	Things are looking up. I have a new job.
make out	succeed	She made out well on those investments.
pan out	result	His big plan didn't pan out, and he failed.
pass out	faint	It was very hot, and she passed out.
settle down	become quiet	All right, kids, settle down and get to work.
shape up	improve	He shaped up and made a lot of progress.
ship out	leave	Shape up or ship out.
show up	appear	His ex-wife showed up at the ceremony.
sink in	realize	The truth finally sank in and he cried.
space out	forget	I spaced out and missed my appointment.
speak up	vocalize	If you don't speak up, you won't succeed.
take off	leave	I don't like this concert. Let's take off.
throw up	vomit	I don't feel well. I'm going to throw up.

8: Modal Verb Chart

Meaning		Modal	Pre	Fut	Past	Expression	Examples
Obligation	unavoidable	**must**	✓	✓	had to	need to have to	We must pay our taxes by the 15th of April. You must be at school and at your desk before the bell rings.
	necessity	**must**	✓	✓	had to	need to have to	We had to drink brackish water in order to survive. The crops must have water or they will die.
	prohibition	**must not**	✓	✓	it was prohib- ited	be forbidden to	You must not smoke in an arsenal. You must not play in the streets.
	no obligation	**not have to**	✓	✓	didn't have to		She doesn't have to be at home before 10:00 p.m. They don't have to come to class.
	avoidable obligation	**should**	✓	✓	should have	be supposed to	You should do your homework every day. We should return these books to the library today.
		ought to	✓	✓	ought to have		
Advisability		**should**	✓	✓	should have		You look terrible, you should see a doctor. You ought to have knocked before entering.
		ought to	✓	✓	ought to have		
	obligation with implied consequences	**had better**	✓	✓	had better have		You had better pay me back before I leave. She'd better watch her language.
	strong advisability, recom- mendation	**must not**	✓	✓	✗	should not	You mustn't go out alone. It's dangerous. She mustn't drive so fast. She'll have an accident.
Preference		**would rather**	✓	✓	would rather have	would prefer, would sooner	I'd rather do it myself. He'd rather have read the book.

✓ indicates that the modal is used in this time reference with no change in its form.
✗ indicates that the modal is not found in this time reference in any form.
Where the modal changes its form, the new form is indicated.

Ability	ability	**can**	✓	✓	could	be able to, know how to	I can speak Russian. He couldn't understand a word.
	former ability	**could**	✗	✗	could	used to be able to	He could run a 4-minute mile in those days. I couldn't express myself then.
Possibility	theoretical and/or factual	**can**	✓	✓	could have	it is possible, maybe, perhaps	Any citizen can become a senator. Could man have decended from apes? We could go to the movies tonight. The road may be blocked. He may buy a new car next year. He might have taken another road home.
		could	✓	✓	could have		
		may	✓	✓	may have		
		might	✓	✓	might have		
Probability	expectation	**should**	✓	✓	should have	expect	He should be here any minute now. They ought to have finished now.
		ought to	✓	✓	ought to have		
	inference	**must**	✓	✗	must have	have to, have got to	It's very muddy; it must have rained a lot.
		can't	✓	✗	can't have	it is not possible	She can't be hungry; she just ate.
		couldn't	✓	✓	couldn't have		He couldn't have flown a plane; he died in 1512.
Willingness		**will**	✓	✓	✗	not mind	Stay there, I'll do the dishes.
Invitation	you	**could**	✓	✓	✗	would like, can, will	Could you go to the dance with me? Would you come to dinner tonight?
		would	✓	✓	✗		
Request	he, she, we, they, I	**may**	✓	✓	✗	can, might	May I leave the room? Could Johnny stay overnight?
		could	✓	✓	✗		
	you	**would**	✓	✓	✗	can, will	Would you open the window? Could you please lower your voice?
		could	✓	✓	✗		
Permission		**may**	✓	✓	was allowed to, was permitted to	be allowed to, be permitted to	You may leave the room. She may marry whomever she likes. Johnny can't stay over.
		can	✓	✓			

61

9: Direct and Indirect Objects

A. Verbs that require the direct object before the indirect object

Verbs that usually require *to**

Example: *He admitted his mistake to his father*

admit	explain	prove	report
announce	introduce	recommend	say
describe	mention	remember	speak
			suggest

Verbs that usually require *for*

Example: *She answered the phone for me.*

answer	correct	keep	pronounce
cash	design	open	repeat
change	fill	prepare	sign
close	fix	prescribe	translate

B. Verbs that can have the indirect object before the direct object**

Verbs that usually require *to* or Ø

Example: *He brought the apple to Eve. He brought Eve the apple.*

bring	offer	sell	teach
deny	owe	send	tell
give	pass	show	throw
hand	pay	sign	write
lend	read	take	

Verbs that normally require *for* or Ø

Example: *She built a cage for her pet snake. She built her pet snake a cage.*

build	cook	get	order
buy	do	hire	save
call	draw	leave	type
catch	find	make	

*Some verbs can be used with either **to** or **for,** but note the difference in meaning.
Example: *He brought the apple to Eve. He brought an apple for Eve.*

**The direct object is usually not a pronoun when it comes after the indirect object.
Example: *He brought her the apple,* but not: *He brought Eve it.*

10: Verbs That Are Followed by an Infinitive

A. No object

Example: *He agrees to meet at noon.*

agree	deserve	learn	swear
appear	desire	manage	volunteer
arrange	fail	mean	offer
care	guarantee	tend	wait
claim	happen	promise	wish
consent	hesitate	refuse	
decide	hope	seem	
demand	know how	struggle	

B. With object

Example: *She advised the man to duck.*

advise	dare	instruct	require
allow	encourage	invite	teach
authorize	forbid	oblige	tell
cause	force	order	train
challenge	get	permit	urge
command	help	persuade	warn
convince	hire	remind	

C. With or without object

Example: *He asks her to leave. He asks to be excused.*

ask	expect	prefer	want
beg	need	prepare	would like

63

11: Verbs Followed by Gerunds

Example: *She admits going to see the movie.*

admit	discuss	mind	risk
anticipate	dislike	miss	suggest
appreciate	enjoy	postpone	tolerate
avoid	finish	practice	understand
can't help	get through	quit	
complete	give up	recall	
consider	imagine	recollect	
delay	keep	recommend	
deny	keep on	resent	
	mention	resist	

12: Verbs Followed by Infinitives or Gerunds

Example: *He can afford to vacation in Italy. He can afford vacationing in Italy.*

(can)afford	forget*	love	remember*
attempt	go	neglect	start
(can) bear	hate	plan	(can) stand
begin	hesitate	prefer	stop*
choose	intend	pretend	threaten
dread	like	regret*	try*

13: Perception Verbs Followed by Simple Verbs**

Example: *She felt him approach.*

feel	observe	see	watch
hear	overhear	sense	witness
notice	perceive	smell	

*The meanings of these verbs are often slightly different when they are followed by an infinitive rather than a gerund.
Example: *He stopped to listen to the speech. He stopped listening to the speech.*

**These verbs may also be followed by a gerund. Example: *She felt him approaching.*

14: Noun and Adjective Phrase Word Order

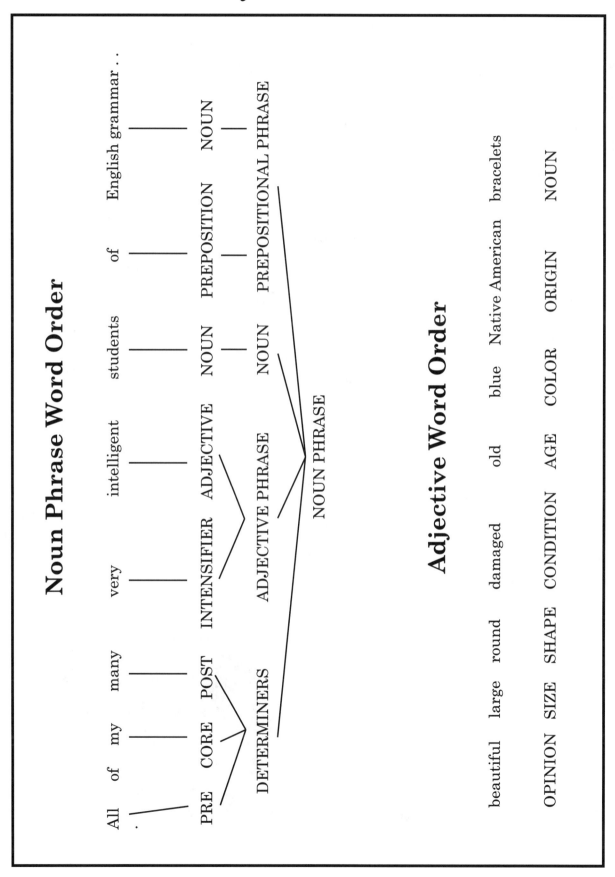

Noun Phrase Word Order

All of my many very intelligent students of English grammar . . .

PRE CORE POST   INTENSIFIER ADJECTIVE   NOUN   PREPOSITION   NOUN

DETERMINERS   ADJECTIVE PHRASE   NOUN   PREPOSITIONAL PHRASE

NOUN PHRASE

Adjective Word Order

beautiful   large round   damaged   old   blue   Native American   bracelets

OPINION   SIZE SHAPE   CONDITION   AGE   COLOR   ORIGIN   NOUN

15: Order of Determiners
in the Noun Phrase

Pre-Determiners

Quantifiers
all
both
many of, a lot of
none of, two of

Multipliers
double
twice
three times

Fractions
(one) half (of)

Core Determiners

Articles
a/an
the
some

Possessive Adjectives
my, your, his, her
our, your, their

Possessive Noun
X's, Joe's

Demonstratives
this, that, these, those

Quantifiers
some/any
each, every
either, neither
no

Post Determiners

Cardinal Numbers
one, two, etc.

Ordinals
first, second
next, last
another

Quantifiers
many, much
few, a few
little, a little
more/less
most/least

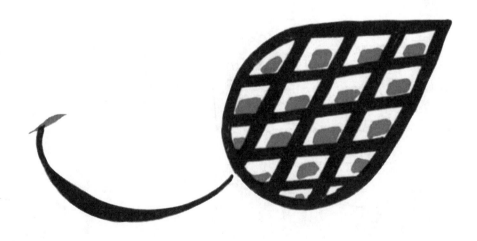

16: Pronouns

Personal Pronouns

Subject	Object	Possessive Adjective	Possessive	Reflexive/ Emphatic
I	me	my	mine	myself
you	you	your	yours	yourself
he	him	his	his	himself
she	her	her	hers	herself
it	it	its	its	itself
we	us	our	ours	ourselves
you	you	your	yours	yourselves
they	them	their	theirs	themselves

Impersonal Pronouns

one	one	one's		oneself

Indefinite Pronouns

	–body	**–one**	**–thing**
some–	somebody	someone	something
any–	anybody	anyone	anything
no–	nobody	no one	nothing
every–	everybody	everyone	everything

Interrogative Pronouns   *As Adjectives*

WHAT	What hit me?	What color do you like?
WHICH	Which do you like?	Which car is yours?
WHOSE	Whose is this?	Whose car is that?

17: Articles

	Specific		*Generic*
	Indefinite	**Definite**	
Count Singular	I ate **an** apple and **a** banana.	**The** apple was green. **The** banana was black.	**An/The** apple is more nutritious than **a/the** banana.
Count Plural	I also ate (**some**) pears.	**The** pears were red.	Ø Pears are also nutritious.
Noncount	I ate (**some**) fruit.	**The** fruit was delicious.	I eat **ø** fruit for lunch.
Proper		Apples are grown in **ø** Vermont.	

18: Noncountable (Mass) Nouns*

A. Abstract	B. Matter, material	C. Generic terms
advice	air	business
age	beer	change
beauty	blood	equipment
capitalism	bread	fruit
communism	butter	furniture
democracy	cake	jewelry
energy	chalk	luggage
fun	cheese	machinery
happiness	coal	mail
help	coffee	money
honesty	electricity	news
information	fog	propaganda
justice	fish	scenery
kindness	gold	slang
knowledge	grass	stationery
laughter	hair	traffic
liberty	ice	vegetation
life	ink	weather
play	iron	
recreation	juice	
strength	lumber	
trouble	meat	
truth	milk	
virtue	oil	
wisdom	oxygen	
work	paper	
youth	rain	
	rice	
	smoke	
	snow	
	soap	
	soup	
	sugar	
	tea	
	water	
	wine	
	wood	

* This list is far from complete; it is intended only to be suggestive. We have tried to include high frequency nouns. Add your own to our lists.

69

D. Subject matter

architecture
art
chemistry
civics
economics
engineering
English
geology
grammar
history
literature
mathematics
music
philosophy
physics
science
technology
vocabulary

———————————
———————————
———————————

E. Sports and recreation/activities

baseball
basketball
bridge
camping
dancing
drinking
football
golf
hiking
hockey
homework
hunting
opera
sailing
singing
softball
swimming
television
traveling
volleyball

F. Countable and noncountable nouns*

age
baseball (and other balls)
beer (and other drinks)
business
change
company
dope
glass
iron
paper
play
room
smoke
tape
tea (party)
work
youth

*This list(F) contains words that can have dual meanings: one countable meaning and a different non-countable meaning. Example: *The game of American **football** is played with an oddly shaped ball called a **football**.*

Many non-count nouns, if used to refer to items or units, can also be used as count nouns. Example: *We work at home and do a lot of business there. I run one business here and my wife runs two others.*

19: Quantifiers with Count and Noncount Nouns

Noncount only	Count or noncount	Count only
much	all	many
not much	almost all	several
a little	most	quite a few
little	a lot of	a few
	quite a lot of	just a few
	not all	not many
	some/any	a couple of
	hardly any	few
	scarcely any	

20: Prepositions

about	away from	from	out of
above	because of	in	outside
according to	before	in back of	over
across (from)	behind	in front of	past
against	below	inside	plus
along	beneath	in spite of	regardless of
alongside	beside	in the middle	since
among	between	like	through
around	but (for)	minus	to
as	by	near	toward(s)
as . . as	close to	next to	under
as far as	despite	of	underneath
as for	during	off	up
at the top/bottom of	down	on	up to
as to	except for	on the left/	until/till
as well as	far from	right/corner of	with
at	for	opposite	within

21: Verb + Preposition Combinations

A. Verb + preposition + object

Example: *They agree on everything.*

agree on	care for	hear about	succeed in
agree with	comment on	hear from	talk about
approve of	complain about	laugh at	talk to
argue with	consent to	listen to	think about
arrive at	consist of	look at	vote for
arrive in	count on	object to	wait for
believe in	decide on	pay for	wish for
belong to	depend on	rely on	work for

B. Verb + object + prepostion + object

Example: *She adds fertilizer to her garden soil.*

add ___ to/with ___	explain ___ to ___	prefer ___ to ___
blame ___ for ___	excuse ___ for ___	remind ___ of ___
compare ___ with/to ___	introduce ___ to ___	thank ___ for ___
congratulate ___ on/for ___	keep ___ for ___	subtract ___ from ___

22: Participles As Modifiers

Example: *He thinks her work is amazing. He is amazed by her work.*

amazing	amazed	fascinating	fascinated
amusing	amused	frightening	frightened
annoying	annoyed	interesting	interested
astonishing	astonished	intriguing	intrigued
boring	bored	irritating	irritated
challenging	challenged	pleasing	pleased
confusing	confused	satisfying	satisfied
convincing	convinced	shocking	shocked
disappointing	disappointed	surprising	surprised
disgusting	disgusted	terrifying	terrified
disturbing	disturbed	thrilling	thrilled
embarrassing	embarrassed	tiring	tired
exciting	excited	touching	touched

23: Time Expressions
for the 12 Tense-Aspect Constructions

1. Present Simple

always	often	usually	sometimes
never	every (day)	once a (week)	at/on/in

2. Past Simple

yesterday	last (night/week/year)	at/on/in	ago

3. Future Simple

tomorrow	next (week)	soon	at/on/in

4. Present Perfect

for (ten years, etc.)		since (1968)	already	just
so far	up to now	until now	all her life	lately
yet	recently	finally	never/ever	

5. Past Perfect

already .. when	just .. when	before	after
until	no sooner ... than	as soon as	when

6. Future Perfect

by	by the time	before	already

7. Present Progressive

now	at the moment	these days	still	at/on/in

8. Past Progressive

already ...when	just ... when	at/on/in

9. Future Progressive

tomorrow ... when	soon	at/on/in

10. Present Perfect Progressive

for	since	lately	recently

11. Past Perfect Progressive

for ... when	before	after

12. Future Perfect Progressive

for ... by

24: Adverbials

Order of Adverbials

Mike walks to town very rapidly on Main Street every morning
Direction   Manner   Position   Frequency

at eight for exercise because he's trying to get in shape.
Time   Purpose   Reason

Adverbial Subordinators

TEMPORAL

after
before
when
while
as
by the time (that)
since
until/till
as soon as
s/so long as
once
whenever
every time
the first time (that)
  " last   "   "
  " next   "   "
(at) the same time (that)
  "   "   moment "
during the time (that)

CONDITIONAL

if
only if
if only
even if
unless
whether or not
providing (that)
provided (that)
in case
in the event that
except that

MANNER

as if
as though
as
however
in any way that

CAUSAL

because
since
now (that)
as
as/so long as
inasmuch as
insofar as

PURPOSE

so (that)
in order (that)
in the hope that
lest
for fear that

PLACE

where(ver)

CONCESSIVE

although
though
even though
in spite of /despite
  the fact that
regardless of
  the fact that
whatever
however
no matter WH
while
whereas
when

25: Preverbal Adverbs of Frequency

0%	10%	50%	75%	100%
never	rarely	sometimes	often	always
don't ever	seldom	occasionally	frequently	
never ever	hardly ever		usually	
	scarcely ever		generally	
	don't often		regularly	
			nearly always	
			almost always	

Initial
sometimes
occasionally
frequently
usually
generally

Final
sometimes
occasionally
frequently
often

26: Adverbial Participles

Present Participle (-ing)

1. **Basic** – Working on his paper, X . . .
2. **Perfective** – Having worked on his paper, . . .
3. **Perfective-progressive** – Having been working on his paper, X . . .

Past Participle (-en/-ed)

1. **Basic** – Worn out from the work, X . . .
2. **Perfective** – Being worn out from his work, X . . .
3. **Perfective-progressive** – Having been worn out from the work, X . . .

27: Adjective + Preposition Combinations

Example: *She is interested in becoming a judge.*

concerned about	slow at	conscious of	sure to
happy about	quick at	confident of	opposed to
angry about	lucky at	ashamed of	
enthusiastic about	surprised at	sure of	bored with
careful about	amazed at	afraid of	impressed with
excited about		certain of	involved with
glad about	interested in	sick of	annoyed with
worried about	involved in		delighted with
sorry about	disappointed in	upset over	satisfied with
disappointed about		disturbed over	pleased with
pleased about	fond of		disappointed with
	in favor of	accustomed to	
good at	tired of	slow to	
clever at	capable of	quick to	
bad at	aware of	resigned to	

28: Verbs and Adjectives Taking Subjunctive

Verbs

Example: *He **advised** that she **watch** the stock market very carefully. He said it is **important** that she **do** this immediately.*

advise	propose	forbid	require
ask	recommend	desire	stipulate
beg	command	insist	suggest
demand	request	prefer	urge

Adjectives

advisable	essential	desirable	important
best	good	mandatory	urgent
better	imperative	necessary	vital
critical	crucial	required	requisite

76

The Communicative Aspect

The communicative aspect does not deal with linguistic forms, such as *go, went, gone*, the **medium** of communication. It outlines ways in which the language is used to send and receive **messages.** We have further analyzed this communicative aspect into three sub-aspects that are usually present when a message is being communicated. First, there is a **situational context** in which the message is exchanged, the *where*. The **topical content** is the subject matter of the message, the *what*, and the **communicative function** is the manner and purpose of the message, the *how* and *why*.

Contents

Situational Context

The situational context, in its simplest sense, is a definite, identifiable place or setting where communication happens (*a bank,* for example). However, some of the situations in the following pages are not specific places. There are events or chains of events that are common and recurrent in everyday life (for example, a *wedding* or *asking for prices*). There are also contexts which are topics for discussion and cultural exploration (such as *planning nutritious meals*).

In order to communicate effectively in these situations, students need appropriate topical vocabulary, cultural information, and functional language. The materials in the following sections will be helpful.

This section amounts to a series of lists of suggested communicative contexts that could be used in presenting and practicing communicative language and cultural insights. In many cases, vocabulary topics relevant to these contexts are given in the next section. When they are, cross-references are given.

A teacher using this section as a planning guide selects a situation appropriate to the interests and needs of their students and then plans a lesson using any of the topics which seem relevant. For example, looking over the list, the teacher settles on *restaurant* from List 1. Basic Daily Needs. The reference is to topics 1–3, 24, and 32. The teacher finds that these lists suggest both vocabulary and cultural information students will need in a restaurant. They will need to know about *reservations, menus, waiters, orders, checks,* and *tips.* After teaching the lesson, the teacher may hand out photocopies of the relevant topic lists for further vocabulary enrichment.

Once the students have been given a handout, it can be used as the basis for pair work, writing assignments, situational role playing, and many other kinds of in-class and out-of-class activities.

The list of situations given in this section is in the form of an outline or checklist. It is intended to be suggestive rather than exhaustive. It is not intended as a situational sequence or syllabus, but it should help teachers develop sequences of their own appropriate for each class.

1: Basic Daily Needs

Food
kitchen
dining room
cooking
restaurant
using a recipe
planning nutritious meals
storing food safely
grocery shopping
weights and measures
planning to save money
serving meals
eating and drinking

See topics 1–3, 24, 32

Clothing
buying clothes, shoes
repairing clothes, sewing
using a washer, dryer
laundry/laundromat
cleaner

See topics 6, 7, 33

Shelter
types of housing
rooms, including:
  living room
  bedroom
  bathroom
  kitchen
housekeeping
maintenance
yard work

See topic 4

2: Transportation

asking directions
using maps
getting lost
walking—when,where
subway station, subway

See topics 19, 29

bus stop, city bus
bus station, intercity bus
railway station, train
airport, plane
taxis

commuting
buying tickets, tokens
travel agent
customs/immigration
hitchhiking

3: Work

The work place
  home
  work shop/factory
  warehouse
  shipping/freight terminal
  store/department store/mall
  office
  studio
  school
  hospital/clinic/nursing home
  daycare/eldercare center
  hotel
  restaurant
  construction site
  outdoors
  farm
  travel/transportation
See topics 34, 46–50

Work procedures
  housekeeping
  cooking/doing dishes
  gardening/groundskeeping
  cleaning and maintenance
  doing repairs
  using the telephone
  taking messages
  making/keeping appointments
  placing/taking orders
  writing receipts
  making change
  packing/shipping
  dictating/taking dictation
  typing
  filing
  using computers
  planning/following plans

scheduling/following schedules
getting paid
cashing pay checks
supervising/being supervised
following instructions
scheduling staff meetings
following safety regulations
asking for help
dealing with mistakes
changing jobs
applying for work
employment office
job training
health insurance/benefits
social security
compensation insurance
labor unions/union dues
health and safety regulations

4: Health and Safety

advice on a healthy diet
advice on getting exercise
gym, athletics
taking vitamins
taking medicine
drug store
doctor's office

dentist's office
emergency services
   police
   fire
   ambulance
medical center
health clinic

hospital
   emergency
   visiting
medical insurance
personal hygiene
sex and contraception
personal safety

See topics 1–3, 27, 41, 42, 43

5: Personal and Family Needs

interpersonal relationships, roles
   work
   school
   sports
   friendship
   romance
family relationships
family planning
family counseling
children
   siblings
   discipline
   child care
   babysitting
   schooling
   afterschool activities
   birthdays/holidays
camp

See topics 8, 9, 26, 56–58, 63

adult education, training
elderly people
relatives
spiritual
wedding
   ceremony
   wedding party
   bridal dinner
   wedding gown, dress
   bachelor party
marriage
   anniversary
   counseling
   separation, divorce
civil union
living together
   as roommates
   out of wedlock
   common law partners

family activities
family trips
record keeping
retirement
elder care
hospice
death, burial
places of worship
community organizations
   ethnic
   religious
   civic
   service
   political
   cultural
social life, entertaining
dating
caring for pets
veterinarian

6: Personal Finances

spending money
   cash
   checks, cashing checks
   charging
   charge accounts
   credit cards
   interest costs
   loan payments

See topic 36

bank, savings and loan
planning a family budget
getting/making a loan
getting a mortgage
getting a second mortgage
home equity loan
educational loans, financial aid
planning investments
savings accounts

savings bonds
retirement accounts
buying stock, bonds
insurance
social security
work benefits
taxes
gambling
retirement

7: Education

Expectations, routines
classroom
schedules
being on time
assignments, homework
researching, writing papers
library
tests, quizzes
final exams
standardized tests
grades, records
tuition, room and board
scholarships
neatness
honesty/cheating

See topics 53, 57, 58

At school, on campus
registration
dean's office
adviser's office
   scheduling
   course change
teacher's office hours
   getting help
   planning a research paper
housing office
bursar's office
dormitory life
   rooms, roommates
   dorm rules
   laundry
off-campus housing

campus post office
book store
student center
cafeteria, dining hall
fraternity, sorority
chapel, chaplain's office
student health service
foreign student adviser
computer center
library
other campus services
gymnasium
team, coach
team spirit
locker room
drugs and sports

8: Shopping and Services

planning
making a shopping list
using the yellow pages
newspaper/magazine ads,
  junk mail
sales, come-on's
coupons, bargains
internet shopping
finding products in big stores
kinds of stores
   department store
   supermarket
   mall
   specialty shops
   main street
   boutiques
   copy center
getting advice about products
   from consumer services
   in specialty shops
    bakery
    optician
    book store
    camera store
    on the internet

*See topics 33, 34

unit pricing
asking for prices
fixed prices/bargaining
ordering from catalogues
ordering on the internet
paying for purchases
   cash
   charge
   credit cards
   time payments
   layaway plans
   lease-purchase
   rental
   getting change
   tipping
returning merchandise
choosing and getting services
   mechanic
   barber/hairdresser
   plumber
   electrician
   carpenter
   car mechanic
   doctor
   dentist
   lawyer
   accountant

tax preparation service
insurance agent
pastor/priest
real estate agent
getting help/public services
   police department
   court
   public defender/legal aid
   emergency services
   ambulance service
   hospital/emergency room
   fire department
   town offices/city hall
   local town officials
   extension agent
   post office
   state and congressional
    representatives
   school board
   IRS - internal revenue service
   INS - immigration and
    naturalization service
   public library
   childcare, eldercare
   adult center
   teen center
   YMCA

9: Recreation

Athletics
local team sports – seasonal
children's and adult leagues
    finding a team
    signing up
    schedules
exercising – working out
    walking, running
    swimming
games – tennis, golf
children's games
    capture the flag
    jumping rope
    dodge ball
    marbles/jacks
    hide and seek
    tag
    three-legged races

See topics 37–40

Social
dinner parties
cocktail/beer parties
dances
community events, socials
restaurants

Entertainment
movies
theater
opera, musicals
popular music concerts
classical music concerts
rock concerts
professional sports events
night clubs
coffee houses
dance performance/ballet

Arts and crafts
art classes
music lessons

art studios
galleries
craft shows
gift shops
museums

At home
TV, radio
games – cards, board games
    computer games,
    role playing games
parties – children's parties
    family parties
    holiday parties
special meals –
    barbecue
    picnic
    brunch
    potluck
    buffet
hobbies

10: Citizenship

town/city offices
police department
court
contacting government officials
    local and national
    getting help
    expressing opinions
election campaigns
voter registration
voting
discussing taxes
discussing immigration status
discussing work permits
discussing civil rights
discussing civil obligations
discussing national holidays
discussing historic landmarks
discussing corruption
    bribery
    protection money
    organized crime

discussing honor codes
    codes of conduct
    truth in advertising
    civic responsibility
discussing
    national anthem
    other patriotic songs
    Gettysburg address
    Dr. King's "I have a dream"
American history
  explaining important events
    leaders
    movements
    the Constitution
    functions of government
      local
      state
      national
      international
discussing the importance of
    dissent

getting involved
    an informed electorate
    The Bill of Rights
discussing what makes a
    community
    a good place to live
    a good place to work
    a good place to raise children
discussing the roles of
    organizations –
    civic
    political
    special interest
    religious
    cultural
    arts
    public and private education
    public and private/commercial
        broadcasting
local, state, federal taxes
volunteer work

See topics 34, 51, 52, 54, 59 and Culture topics 4-11, 22, 41-42 National Documents of the U.S.A. and Canada

Topical Content

The topics of human conversation are virtually endless, but it is possible to predict a general list of topics that virtually every language learner will encounter at some time or other. The following lists are an attempt at a comprehensive list of **basic** topics. Each topic is outlined as a vocabulary list of the words, phrases, and idioms that might be encountered in a general conversation about the topic. In the case of the idioms, they are included not because they might appear in the context of a conversation, but rather because they have some semantic relationship to the topic, usually at the literal level, rather than the figurative.

It will again be obvious that the vocabulary collected under each topic is influenced by the cultural context of contemporary North America.

Finally, please bear in mind that these lists are far from complete. They should be seen as basic words of fairly high frequency. You will want to add your own discoveries to our lists, and once again we welcome your additions and comments.

Topic checklist

1: Food *also see #2 Cooking and #3 Eating*

Vegetables

artichoke	endive	potato
asparagus	garlic	pumpkin
avocado	jicama	radish
bean	kale	rhubarb
beet	kohlrabi	rutabaga
bok choy	leek	salad
broccoli	lettuce	scallion
brussels sprouts	lima beans	shallot
cabbage	mushroom	snow peas
carrot	okra	spinach
cauliflower	onion	squash
celery	parsnip	summer
chard	pickle	winter
Chinese cabbage	peas	sweet potato
collard	pepper	tomato
corn	bell	turnip
cucumber	chili	yam
eggplant	plantain	zucchini

Fruit

apple	fig	pear
apricot	guava	persimmon
banana	grape	pineapple
berry	grapefruit	plum
blackberry	kiwi	pomegranate
blueberry	lemon	prune
cantaloupe	lime	raspberry
cherry	melon	raisin
coconut	orange	strawberry
cranberry	papaya	tangerine
date	peach	watermelon

Bread and Cereal

bagel	French toast	popcorn
bread	grain	potato chip
burrito	granola	rice
biscuit	grits	roll
bun	muffin	roll up
cereal	noodle	sandwich
cold	nut	spaghetti
hot	oatmeal	sweet roll
cracker	pancake	toast
Danish pastry	pasta	taco
doughnut	pita	tortilla
dumpling	pizza	tortilla chip
English muffin		waffle

85

Meat and Poultry

meat	chicken	lamb
dark	duck	pork
red	egg	ribs
white	game	sausage
bacon	goose	turkey
beef	ham	veal

Seafood

bass	mackerel	shark
catfish	mahi mahi	shellfish
caviar	mollusk	shrimp
clam	mussel	smelt
codfish	octopus	sole
crab	oyster	squid
crayfish	perch	sturgeon
fillet	pike	swordfish
fish	pollock	trout
haddock	red snapper	tuna fish
herring	salmon	walleye pike
lobster	scallop	whitefish

Dairy

butter	cream	skim/1%/2%/whole milk
cottage cheese	half and half	sour cream
cheese	margarine	whipped cream
ice cream	milk	yoghurt

Food Groups

fruits	meats, beans, fish, nuts, eggs	oils, fats
grains, breads, cereals	milk, dairy	vegetables

Dishes and Cuts

breast	hamburger	pie
chili	hash	ribs
chop	hot dog	roast
chop suey	leg	salad
cold cuts	leftover	sauerkraut
casserole	loaf	souffle
cocktail	meatball	soup
corned beef	meatloaf	steak
curry	meat patty	stew
fillet	mixed vegetables	stuffing
fondue	paté	wing

Desserts

brownie	cupcake	Jello	sherbet. ice, sorbet
cake	custard	pastry	soufflé
cheesecake	fruit	pie	sundae
cookie	ice cream	pudding	tart

Herbs, Spices, and Other Flavoring

allspice	coriander	mustard	sage
anise	clove	nutmeg	savory
basil	cocoa	oregano	salt
bay leaf	curry	paprika	syrup
cardamom seed	dill	parsley	sugar
caraway seed	fennel	pepper	brown
chervil	garlic	black	white
chive	ginger	cayenne	tarragon
chocolate	honey	chili	thyme
cilantro	marjoram	white	vinegar
cinnamon	mint	rosemary	

Condiments and Sauces

bacon bits	hollandaise sauce	mayonnaise	salad dressing
barbecue sauce	horseradish	mustard	soy sauce
butterscotch	hot sauce	pepper	steak sauce
cheese	jelly, jam	pickle	sugar
chocolate sauce	ketchup	relish	tartar sauce
chutney	marshmallow	salsa	white sauce
cocktail sauce	marmalade	salt	worchestershire sauce
gravy			

Beverages, Drinks

ale	coffee	liqueur	soda
beer	coke	liquor	soft drink
brandy	cola	milk	tea
cider	decafe coffee	mineral water	tonic water
club soda	ginger ale	punch	water
cocktail	juice	Sanka	whiskey
cocoa	lemonade	seltzer	wine

Idioms and Expressions

baker's dozen	natural/organic food	food fit for the gods	to spill the beans
baloney	to cry over spilled milk	to know which side one's	square meal
to beef about	to have one's cake	bread is buttered on	to take the cake
to beef up	and eat it, too	like two peas in a pod	upper crust
to bring home the bacon	to not know beans	Variety is the spice of life.	Hot dog!
corny	to pepper with questions	not my cup of tea	
cream of the crop	proof of the pudding	to egg on	
fast food	to put all one's eggs	fishy	
junk food	in one basket	sour grapes	

2: Cooking also see #1 Food and #3 Eating

Equipment

baking pan	casserole dish	food processor	mixer	saucepan
baster	chef's knife	frying pan	mixing spoon	sifter
blender	chopping block	grater	oven	skillet
bowl	cookbook	grill	pan	spatula
bottle opener	colander	kettle	pot	steamer
bread pan	cover	ladle	potato masher	stove
broiler	double boiler	lid	pressure cooker	strainer
burner	dutch oven	measuring cup	recipe	thermometer
can opener	eggbeater	microwave oven	rolling pin	wisk

Processes

add	broil	dice	knead	refrigerate	smoke
bake	brown	drain	mash	roast	spread
barbecue	can	dredge	marinate	roll out	sprinkle
beat	carve	dry	measure	salt	steam
blanch	chill	fold in	melt	sauce	stir
blend	chop	flour	mince	scorch	stir-fry
boil	coat	freeze	mix	season	stain
bone	combine	freeze dry	parboil	sift	steep
bottle	cook	fry	peel	simmer	toast
burn	cover	grate	pickle	skin	toss
braise	cure	grease	pour	slice	turn
brew	deep fry	grind	preserve	soak	whip

Ingredients

baking powder	butter	dressing	lard	peanut butter	stock
baking soda	corn meal	filling	loaf	roast	stuffing
batter	cornstarch	flake	leftover	salad dressing	syrup
bread crumbs	crust	flavor	molasses	sauce	vinegar
brine	dash	flour	oil	seasoning	(egg) whites
broth	dough			shell	(egg) yolks

Dishes, Measures

bread basket	gallon	pinch	platter	tablespoon
casserole	measuring spoons	pint	quart	teaspoon
cup measure	pie plate	pitcher	serving dish	tureen

Adjectives

boiled	fresh	high, hot (oven) rare	scalloped	steamed
broiled	fried	medium	raw	slow (oven)	tender
crisp	ground	moderate (oven) ripe	soft-boiled	thickened
curdled				well-done

Idioms and Expressions

a flash in the pan	half-baked	the pot calling the kettle black
take with a grain of salt	hard-boiled	watered down

3: Eating also see #1 *Food* and #2 *Cooking*

Dishes and Utensils

carving knife	glass	salad bowl
dessert dish	goblet	saucer
cup	gravy boat	serving dish
fork	knife	spoon
dessert	napkin	soup bowl
dinner	plate	soup spoon
salad	platter	tureen

Meals

appetizer	course	picnic
breakfast	dessert	smorgasbord
brunch	dinner	snack
buffet	lunch	supper

Verbs

bite	eat	ruin your appetite
chew	gobble	sip
diet	graze	snack
dine	munch	swallow
drink	nibble	taste

Adjectives

bitter	hungry	sweet
coarse	moist	tart
delicious	rich	thick
dry	sour	thin
famished	starved	thirsty
full	succulent	tough

Misc.

baker	natural food	seconds
chef	nutritious	vegan
cook	organic	vegetarian
gourmet	potluck	whole food

Idioms

to eat like a bird	to pig out	to bite off more than
a picky eater	to wolf down one's food	one can chew
to eat like a pig	to eat for two	have no appetite for

4: Housing/Housekeeping

General

building	gated community	quarter	town
city	ghetto	residence	town plan
community	home	rural	trailer park
country	house	sprawl	urban
development	housing development	subdivision	village
farm	neighborhood	suburb	zoning

Types

adobe	high-rise	palace	tenement
A-frame	houseboat	ranch house	tent
apartment	hut	row house	tepee
cape	igloo	saltbox	town house
condominium, condo	log cabin	shack	trailer
chalet	manor	skyscraper	tree house
flat	mobile home	split-level	wigwam

Construction Materials

brick	insulation	plywood	steel
cement	linoleum	roofing	stone
clapboard	log	sheetrock	tile
concrete	molding	shingles	vinyl
flooring	paneling	siding	wall board
glass			wood

Parts

addition	door	fireplace	plumbing
bay	back	floor	rafters
breaker box	front	foundation	sill
breezeway	screen	frame	stairs
bulkhead	storm	fuse box	steps
ceiling	drive(way)	garage	walk
chimney	electric outlets	heating system	wall
chimney flue	ell	light switch	window
dormer	electrical outlet	picture window	wiring

Places

attic, store room	den	lawn	porch, balcony,
basement	dining room	living room	deck, veranda
bath(room)	family room	mud room	study
bedroom	garage	nursery	sun room
breakfast room/nook	hall	pantry	toilet
cellar	kitchen	patio	utility room
closet	laundry room	play room	yard

Events and Activities

babysitting	doing the laundry	house cleaning	TV watching
cooking	home improvement	light repair work	visitors
delivery person	house guests	mail carrier	yard work

Furnishings and Equipment

ashtray	crib	iron	shelf
basin	cupboard	ironing board	sheets
bathtub	curtains	kitchen table	shower
bed	desk	lamp	sideboard
double	dining room table	laundry basket	sink
twin	dishwasher	light	sofa
bunk	draperies	linen	stereo
queen-size	dresser	linoleum	stove
king-size	dryer	love seat	table
blanket	DVD player	mircrowave oven	television
bookshelves/case	easy chair	oven	TV stand
cabinet	end table	plasma TV	toaster
carpet	electric outlet	radio	toilet bowl
chair	entertainment center	record player	towel
coffee table	fireplace	refrigerator	vacuum cleaner
computer	freezer	rug	washing machine
cot	furnace	scanner	water heater
counter	hutch	shades	

Activities

change (the linen/ sheets)	do the ironing	straighten (up)	lease
clean (up)	make the bed	sweep	let
do the dishes	paint	vacuum	mortgage
do the laundry	pick up	wash	move
dust	polish	wax	own
fix	put away	buy	renovate
fold the laundry	repair	build	remodel
hang out the laundry	scrub	furnish	rent
	set the table	insure	sub-let

Idioms and Expressions

to hit home	to hit the sack	to make a clean sweep of
on the house	spick/spic and span	to ride a broomstick
to raise the roof	to whitewash	handwriting on the wall
wet blanket	to turn the tables on	to keep up with the Joneses
on the carpet	up/down one's alley	A new broom sweeps clean.
to pull up stakes	blind alley	A house is not a home.

91

5: Lawn and Garden <small>also see #16 Plants & Trees</small>
Materials

dirt	mud	potting soil	seed starter mix
earth	mulch	fertilizer	seedling
insecticide	compost	seed	soil
manure			weed killer

Tools and Equipment

aerator	grafting tape	plant stand	shovel
bulb planter	greenhouse	plant stakes	spade
bushel basket	hedge clipper/trimmer	plant support ring/	sprayer
clipper	hoe	cage	spreader
compost bin	hose	posthole digger	sprinkler
compost heap	lawn mower	pot, flower pot	snow shovel
cultivator	lawn roller	pruner	snow blower
edger	leaf blower	pruning knife	tiller
garden cart	lopper	pruning saw	tractor
gardening glove	netting	rake	trimmer
gardening shears	pest control	rider mower	trowel
gardening scissors	pitchfork	rototiller/roto tiller	weeder
grafting knife	planter	seed tray	wheelbarrow

Procedures

broadcasting seed	harvesting	planting	splitting
clearing	heading off	potting	shoveling
clipping	grafting	pruning	tilling
composting	mowing	raking	transplanting
culling	mulching	replanting	trimming
cultivating	picking	seeding	watering
fertilizing	pinching back/off	soil testing	weeding

Miscellaneous

annual	fallow	gate	root
bouquet	fence	organic gardening	stem
branch	flower bed	overfeeding	trunk
brush	garden – types	over watering	perennial
bulb	flower	plant – parts	raised bed
bush	formal	branch	row
crop	herb	bud	scarecrow
drought	vegetable	leaf	tree

Common Flowers

bulb – types	iris	columbine	pansy
bluebell	oriental lily	geranium	peony
crocus	snowdrops	hibiscus	petunia
day lily	aster	impatiens	phlox
daffodil	buttercup	marigold	poppy
tulip	chrysanthemum	morning glory	rose
hyacinth			zinnia

6: Clothes
General

bathing suit/trunks
bathrobe
belt
blazer
blouse
bow tie
boxer shorts
bra
briefs
buckle
cap
cape
cardigan
coat
cocktail dress
dinner jacket
dress
dungarees
earmuffs
garter
girdle
gloves
gown
hat
jacket

(blue)jeans
leotard
jumpsuit
mittens
muffler
nightgown
nylons
overalls
overcoat
pajamas
panties
pants
pantsuit
pantyhose/panty hose
parka
raincoat
running shorts
scarf
shirt
  dress
  sport
shorts
ski jacket
   pants
skirt

slacks
slicker
slip
snowsuit
sport coat/jacket
stole
suit
suspenders
sweater
sweat pants
sweat suit
sweatshirt
(neck)tie
tank top
tights
trench coat
trousers
T-shirt/tee shirt
turtleneck
tuxedo
underclothes
underpants/under shorts
undershirt
vest
wig

Footwear

boots
  cowboy
  dress
  riding
clogs
flats
high heels

galoshes
gym shoes
moccasins
knee socks
overshoes
peds
rubbers

running shoes/walking shoes
shoes
shoelaces/strings
slippers
sneakers
socks
stockings

Sewing and Parts

bobbin
button
buttonhole
cloth
collar
cuff
darn

elastic
fabric
fringe
knit
hem
hemline
hood

material
mend
nap
neckline
needle
notch
patch

Sewing and Parts, continued

pattern	sewing machine	thread
pins	size	threader
pocket	sleeve	tack down
ruffle	snap	tape measure
scissors	stitch	tuck
seam	thimble	yarn
		zipper

Adjectives

brand new	knit	second-hand
checkered	large (sized)	silk
corduroy	loose	small (sized)
cotton	machine washable	striped
dress	medium (sized)	tight
dry	nylon	torn
cleanable	permanent press	velvet
flannel	plaid	washable
frayed	polka dot	worn out
hand-me-down	polyester	wool
hand washable	rayon	woven

Verbs

baste	hem	take in
cut (out)	knit	take off
darn	pin up	take up
dress	put on	tear (out)
fit	rip (out)	thread
gather	sew (up)	trace
get dressed	stitch (up)	wear
grow out of (into)	tack	wear out

Idioms and Expressions

all dressed up	to handle with kid gloves	on pins and needles
to be in someone's shoes	to hit below the belt	the shoe's on the other foot
to burn a hole in one's pocket	If the shoe fits, wear it.	to spin a yarn
to buttonhole someone	to keep one's shirt on	spit and polish
to collar someone	to look for a needle in a haystack	stuffed shirt
clothes make the man	to lose one's shirt	tied to someone's apron strings
dolled up	on a shoestring	wear and tear

7: Paraphernalia
Nouns

address book
bag
barrette
beads
beeper
billfold
bobby pin
bracelet
briefcase
brooch
calling/business card case
calculator
cane
cell phone
change purse
checkbook
chewing tobacco
choker
cigar
cigarette
coin
coin purse
comb
contact lens
credit card case
crutches
cufflinks
date book
discman/diskman CD player
earring
(eye) glasses
  bifocal
  sun
  reading

lash light
glasses case
hair pin
hair brush
hair pull
handbag
handheld PC
handkerchief
hanging bag
identification
ID bracelet
iPod
jack knife
kerchief
key chain
key ring
keys
laptop computer
lighter
lipstick, lipgloss
locket
mace
marker
matches
minidisc/minidisk player
mp3 player
nail clippers
nail file
necklace
notebook
notebook PC
organizer, pocket or palm
overnight bag
pager

pen – ball point pen
  fountain pen
  rollerball
pencil - mechanical
  wooden
pencil eraser
pencil sharpener
penknife
pen light
pillbox
pin
pipe
playing cards
pocketbook
pocket calendar
pocket computer
pocketknife
pocket watch
purse
ring
  engagement
  school
  signet
  wedding
shoulder bag
snuff
tie clip
tie pin
tissues
tobacco pouch
umbrella
wallet
walking stick
wristwatch

Idioms and Expressions

to flip a coin
to make heads or tails of
key to the city
little black book

to pick someone's pocket
pipe dream
purse snatcher
to put that in one's pipe and smoke it

rose colored glasses
up to snuff
well groomed

8: Family also see Culture #31 Family Relationship Chart

adopted child	gram	mommy
adoptive parent	gramp	mother
aunt	grandchild(ren)	(mother)-in-law
baby brother/sister	granddaughter	niece
big brother/sister	grandfather	nephew
biological parent	grandma	orphan
bride	grandmother	pa
brother	grandpa	paternal
cousin	grandson	pop
dad	great aunt/uncle	relative
daddy	great grandchild(ren)	sibling
daughter	groom	sis
dependent	guardian	sister
family dog	half-brother/sister	son
folks	husband	spouse
father	in-laws	step-brother
fiance(e)	kin, kin folks	-father
first husband/wife	kindred	-mother
foster parent	ma	-sister
foster child	maternal	uncle
genealogy	middle child	widow
godparents	mom	widower
		wife

Idioms and Expressions

all in the family	close/distant relations	one's old (man)
apples never fall far from the tree	to come by it naturally	runs in the family
	extended/nuclear family	sibling rivalry
better half	kissing cousins	spitting image
blended family	family feud	to take after
blood brother	family tree	son of a gun
blood is thicker than water	favorite son	wicked stepmother
chip off the old block	like father, like son	wife (to be)

9: Human Relationships, Qualities, and Stages

Nouns

admiration	antagonism	competition	envy	hatred	love	rivalry
affection	cooperation	friendship	hate	intimacy	marriage	sex
						teamwork

Verbs

admire	cooperate	dislike	envy	have sex	like	make love
befriend	compete	distrust	hate	ignore	love	share
						trust

People

acquaintance	colleague	crony	fiance/fi-	girlfriend	mate	party
antagonist	companion	crowd	ancee	guest	mistress	playmate
associate	company	date	follower	host	mob	relative
boyfriend	comrade	disciple	friend	leader	pal	roommate
buddy	counselor	enemy	gang	lover	partner	team
						teammate

Qualities

aloof	cooperative	fresh	insane	pretty	sexy
artistic	courageous	friendly	intelligent	quiet	shy
attractive	courteous	funny	jealous	reserved	spiteful
bashful	cowardly	gorgeous	kind	romantic	stand-offish
beautiful	crazy	greedy	lazy	rude	strong
bold	cruel	gullible	loud	ruthless	stuck up
brave	dependable	handsome	lovely	sane	studious
brazen	determined	hard-working	lovable	self-conscious	stupid
cheerful	diligent	helpful	mean	selfish	trustworthy
conceited	disciplined	humorous	plain	sensitive	ugly
cold	dumb	ill-mannered	pleasant	sentimental	up-tight
complacent	foolish	impolite	polite	serious	well-mannered

Stages

adolescent	childhood	immature	juvenile	pre-teen	teenager
age	childish	infant	mature	retired	toddler
aged	elderly	infantile	middle-age	senior citizen	young
baby	grownup	kid	old	senile	young adult
child					youth

Idioms and Expressions

to have an affair	to flip one's lid	to have a crush on	side-kick
blind date	to gang up on	living together	to sponge off
to break up	to go through the motions	old man (lady)	steady date
fair sex	to hang in there	to pull no punches	to take someone down a peg
fall-guy	to hang it all out	ringleader	every Tom, Dick and Harry

10: Travel

Places

airport	garage	parking place/space
auto rental agency	gas station/service station	passing lane
baggage check in	hotel	repair shop
baggage claim area	immigration	rest area
baggage office	inn	restaurant
bed and breakfast	information booth	security
berth	intersection	suttle bus
bus station	Interstate Highway	terminal
Chamber of Commerce	junction	train station
check-in counter	limousine	ticket office
club car	lobby	toll booth
coach (car)	motel	tourist office
customs	parking garage	travel agency
dining car	parking lot	waiting room

Some Events

arrival	delay	layover
auto accident	departure	making internet reservations
boarding	flat tire	packing
checking bags	flight cancellation	parking ticket
checking flight times	going through security	passing
checking in	hitch-hiking	speeding ticket
checking out	hailing a cab	traffic violation

Idioms and Expressions

to bump into	to hang around	to go through customs
to car pool	to hit the road	life in the fast lane
to get a move on	to catch the (bus)	jet lag
to split	to take the (bus)	to hitch a ride
to take off	to travel light	to bum a ride

11: Time

Daily

dawn	forenoon	p.m.	evening
sunrise	morning	sunset	night
sunup	noon	sundown	midnight
morning	midday	twilight	middle of the night
a.m.	afternoon	dusk	

Instruments

alarm clock	chronometer	metronome	sun dial
almanac	clock	stop watch	watch
calendar			wristwatch

Measures

second	day	month	decade
minute	week	year	century
half-hour	fortnight	leap year	millennium
hour			

General measures

instant	era	every day	yearly
moment	eon	weekly	past
period	split-second	bi-weekly	present
age	daily	monthly	future
epoch			

Seasons

spring	summer	fall	winter
		autumn	

Idioms and Expressions

behind the times	to lose time	from the first	ASAP - as soon as
for the time being	behind the times	in the beginning	possible
in the nick of time	it's high time	in the wink of an eye	PDQ - pretty darn
in time	time zones	in a jiffy	(or damn) quick
to kill time	time-and-a-half	in a minute/second	B.C. - before Christ
to pass the time	the time of one's life	the crack of doom	A.D. - *anno Domini*
on time	time will tell	doomsday	in the year of our
once upon a time	double time	to call it a day	Lord
overtime	to two-time	all the live long day	CE - in the Common/
to keep time	at no time	fly-by-night	Current/Christian
to make time	time out	to make a night of it	Era
the time is right	time-honored	to get along in years	BCE - Before the CE

12: Weather and Climate

Nouns

air	gale	snow
air mass	global warming	squall
blizzard	gust	temperature
breeze	hail	thunder
cloud	high	thunderstorm
cumulus	humidity	thunderhead
cyclone	hurricane	tornado
downpour	ice	velocity
drift	low	wind
drizzle	lightning (bolt)	wind chill factor
drought	mist	
el niño. la niña	pressure	barometer
fog	rain	hygrometer
freezing point	shower	thermometer
front	sleet	weather forecast
frost	smog	weather report

Verbs

blow (up)	hail	shine
cloud up	lift	sleet
drift	mist	snow
drizzle	pour	thaw
freeze	rain	thunder

Adjectives

breezy	hazardous	polar
chilly	hazy	rainy
cloudy	hot	scorching
cold	humid	severe
dreary	icy	slippery
dusty	inclement	smoggy
dry	lowering	snowy
foggy	mild	sunny
freezing	overcast	temperate
frigid	partly (sunny/cloudy)	tropical
frosty	pleasant	wet

Idioms & Expressions

to blow over	environmental change	to shoot the breeze
bolt from the blue	Every cloud has a silver lining.	to take the wind out of
to break the ice	to be full of hot air	one's sails
castles in the air	heat wave	three sheets to the wind
cats and dogs	to make hay while	up in the air
cold snap	the sun shines	weather the storm
come rain or shine	to rain on one's parade	windbag
environmental activist	to ride out the storm	windfall

13: Geography

Space

asteroid	falling star	moon	quasar	solar wind
black hole	galaxy	nebula	ring	star
comet	meteor	orbit	satellite	sun
constellation	meteorite	outer space	shooting star	sun spot
dark matter	meteor shower	planet	space	universe

Solar System: 8 Planets and the Dwarf Planet

The sun	Jupiter	Mercury	Saturn	Dwarf planet:
Planets:	Mars	Neptune	Uranus	Pluto
Earth			Venus	

Earth

Antarctic Circle	cliff	fault	isthmus	plain	strait
Arctic Circle	coastline	field	lake	plateau	stream
area	continent	fiord	lagoon	pole	surf
atoll	crater	forest	latitude	pond	swamp
bay	current	geyser	ledge	prairie	tide
beach	dam	glacier	longitude	range	Tropic of Cancer
bog	dale	globe	marsh	ravine	Tropic of Capricorn
brook	delta	gorge	meadow	reef	undertow
canal	desert	gulf	mountain	reservoir	valley
canyon	ditch	gully	north	rift	volcano
cape	east	hedge	ocean	river	wave
cascade	equator	hill	peak	sea	waterfall
channel	estuary	island	peninsula	south	west
chasm					woods

Material

dirt	pebble	igneous	sod	stone
earth	rock – types:	metamorphic	soil	turf
mud	sedimentary			

Events

after shock	ebb	eruption	flood	tidal wave
avalanche	erosion	flow	landslide	tremor
earthquake				tsumani

Idioms and Expressions

a stone's throw	East is East and West is West.	over the hill
babes in the woods	high and dry	to sell down the river
to bog down	to leave no stone unturned	to show true grit
dirt cheap	to make a mountain of a mole hill	spaced out
down-to-earth	once in a blue moon	to stem the tide
earthy	out of the woods	a stick in the mud
	out of this world	under the sun
	over hill and dale	to win by a landslide

101

14: Natural Resources

Ore and Minerals

aluminum	flint	lead	rock	stone
bauxite	gold	limestone	rock salt	sulphur
chromium	gravel	marble	sand	talc
clay	gypsum	nickle	salt	tin
cobalt	granite	phosphates	silicon	uranium
copper	iron	platinum	silver	zinc

Forest and Sea Products

bamboo	fertilizer	medicinal herbs	rubber	turpentine
bark	guano	mulch	sea salt	wood
coral	lumber	peat moss	seaweed	wood chips
chicle	maple syrup	reeds	sod	wood pulp

Energy-producing Products

carbon	gas	methane	petroleum	thermal energy
coal	hydrogen	natural gas	petrochemical	water
firewood	hydro power	oil	products	wind power
fuel				

Gases

helium	methane	neon	oxygen
hydrogen	natural gas	nitrogen	ozone

Gems

agate	garnet	opal	sapphire
amethyst	heliotrope	pearl	topaz
aquamarine (beryl)	jade	quartz	tourmaline
carnelian	lapis lazuli	rhinestone	turquoise
diamond	malachite	ruby	zircon
emerald			

Idioms and Expressions

All that glitters is not gold.	genetic diversity	a real gem
as good as gold	a gold rush	renewable energy
Silence is golden.	heart of stone	rub salt in a wound
between a rock and a hard place	feet of clay	silver threads among the gold
diamond in the rough	pearls of wisdom	Every cloud has a silver lining.
A diamond is forever.	a pearl of great price	You can't make bricks
fire and brimstone	platinum blond	without straw.

15: Animals

Domestic animals – common pets and farm animals

cat	elephant	guinea pig	mouse	pig
cow	ferret	hamster	mule	pony
dog	gerbil	horse	ox	sheep
donkey	goat	llama	parrot	rabbit

Wild Animals

armadillo	deer	manatee	otter	sea cow
badger	dolphin	mole	porcupine	seal
bear	dugong	moose	porpoise	skunk
beaver	elk	mountain goat	possum, opossum	squirrel
bobcat	fisher (cat)	mountain lion	prairie dog	whale
caribou	fox	mouse	rabbit	wildcat
chipmunk	groundhog	muskrat	raccoon	wolf
cougar	hare	narwhale	rat	wolverine
coyote	hedgehog	lynx	reindeer	woodchuck

Zoo Animals

alligator	cheetah	giraffe	leopard	panther
ape	chimpanzee	gorilla	lion	rhinoceros
bear	crocodile	hippopotamus	monkey	tiger
buffalo	elephant	hyena	orangutan	zebra

Reptiles and Amphibians

chameleon	lizard	salamander	tadpole	tortoise
frog	newt	snake	toad	turtle

Fish, Shellfish, Crustaceans. etc

bass	cod	lobster	salmon	snail
bluegill	eel	monk(fish)	scallop	starfish
carp	flounder	mussel	sea horse	sturgeon
catfish	goldfish	oyster	sea urchin	sunfish
clam	guppy	perch	shark	trout
crab	herring	pike	shrimp	tuna

Insects, etc

ant	caddis fly	fly, house fly	millipede	spider
aphid	caterpillar	fruit fly	mosquito	springtail
bedbug	centipede	grasshopper	moth	termite
bee	cockroach	hornet	no-see-um	thrip
beetle	cricket	knat	praying mantis	tick
blackfly	daddy longlegs	lady bug	sandflea	wasp
blowfly	dragonfly	louse	scorpion	water strider
bug	earwig	maggot	silverfish	worm
butterfly	flea	mayfly	snowflea	yellowjacket

103

Body parts

abdomen	fur	horns	paw	spot	trunk
antennae	hair	legs	scale	stripe	tusk
claw	head	muzzle	shell	tail	whiskers
fangs	hide	neck	snout	teeth	wings
feelers	hoof	nostril	spine	thorax	wool

Dwellings

aquarium	burrow	cave	nest	pen
barn	cage	hutch	pasture	tank
				trap

Groupings

band (gorillas)	colony (ants)	herd (elephants)	pod (whales)	team (horses)
bed (clams)	flock (sheep)	herd (horses)	pride (lions)	tribe (goats)
brood (hens)	flock (birds)	nest (snakes)	school (fish)	troop (monkeys)
cloud (gnats)	gaggle (geese)	pack (dogs)	swarm (bees)	yoke (oxen)

Young Animals

bunny - rabbit	cygnet - swan	fingerling - fish	kid - goat, man
calf - cattle, elephant, whale	duckling - duck	fledgling - birds	kitten - cat
chick - chicken, other fowl	eaglet - eagle	foal - horse, zebra	lamb - sheep
colt - horse (male)	fawn - deer	fry - fish	piglet - pig
cub - fox, bear, lion, whale	filly - horse (female)	gosling - goose	polliwog/tadpole - frog
			puppy- dog

Comparative Expressions

big as a whale	fat as a pig	slippery as an eel	drinks like a fish
blind as a bat	fast as a jackrabbit	slow as a turtle	eats like a horse
brave as a lion	happy as a clam	sly as a fox	eats like a bird
busy as a bee	proud as a peacock	strong as an ox	runs like a deer
crazy as a loon	quiet as a mouse	stubborn as a mule	swims like a fish
dumb as an ox	silly as a goose	wise as an owl	climbs like a monkey

Idioms and Expressions

to back the wrong horse	to get one's goat	pig-headed
black sheep	to look a gift horse in the mouth	to play possum
bull session	to go to the dogs	road hog
bum steer	to hold one's horses	to shoot fish in a barrel
to let the cat out of the bag	to horse around	to smell a rat
cock and bull story	horse of another color	snake in the grass
copycat	in the doghouse	straight from the horse's mouth
crocodile tears	to make a beeline for	to take the bull by the horns
cry wolf	to make a monkey out of	to throw the bull
darkhorse	to monkey around with	white elephant
fish out of water	monkey business	wolf in sheep's clothing

16: Birds

Kinds:

albatross
blackbird
bluebird
bobwhite
boobie
cardinal
catbird
chickadee
chicken
condor
cormorant
cowbird
crane
crow
cuckoo
duck
eagle
egret
emu
falcon
finch
flamingo
flycatcher
frigate bird
goldfinch

goose
grackle
grosbeak
grouse
gull
hawk
heron
hummingbird
jay
kingbird
kingfisher
kite
kiwi
lark
loon
magpie
meadowlark
nighthawk
nuthatch
oriole
osprey
ostrich
owl
parrot
partridge
peacock
pelican

penguin
pheasant
phoebe
pigeon
puffin
quail
raven
roadrunner
robin
sandpiper
snipe
sparrow
starling
stork
swallow
swan
tern
thrasher
thrush
titmouse
turkey
vulture
warbler
whippoorwill
woodpecker
wren

Body parts:

beak
bill
breast
claw
crest
egg
feather
feet
head
leg
nest
peck
tail
talon
waddle
wing

egg
shell
white
yolk

Nouns

brood
flock
nest

Activities

flock
fly

hatch
lay

nest
preen

Idioms and Expressions

bird in the hand
birds of a feather flock together
the bluebird of happiness
chicken
to cook one's goose

early bird
to eat crow
feather in one's cap
to kill two birds with one stone
nest egg

swan song
to talk turkey
ugly duckling
water off a duck's back
wild goose chase

105

17: Plants and Trees also see #5 Lawn and Garden

Types, etc.

arbor	field	garden	hedge	park	wilderness
bush	forest	grove	orchard	swamp	woods

Trees

ash	chestnut	elm	lilac	palm	redwood
beech	deciduous	evergreen	maple	pine	spruce
birch	dogwood	hemlock	oak	poplar	sumac
cedar					willow

Fruit trees

apple	avocado	grapefruit	lemon	orange	pear
apricot	cherry	kiwi	lime	peach	plum

Tree parts

acorn	bud	needle	ring	seed	stump
bark	flower	nut	root	seedling	thorn
branch	leaf	pine cone	sap	seed pod	trunk
graft					twig

Plants, Weeds, etc.

berry bushes	crabgrass	grass	mushroom	reed	tumbleweed
burdock	fern	milkweed	poison ivy	toad stool	vine
cattail					water lily

Wildflowers, etc.

clover	daisy	goldenrod	Indian paintbrush	sunflower
columbine	dandelion	lady's slipper	Queen Anne's lace	violet

Garden flowers

alyssum	daffodil	iris	lily of the valley	petunia	snapdragon
begonia	geranium	lily	marigold	poppy	sunflower
chrysanthemum	impatiens		pansy	rose	tulip
crocus					zinnia

Flower parts

anther	petal	pollen	seed	stamen	stigma
ovary	pistil			stem	style

Idioms and Expressions

Adam's apple	to hit the hay	to rest on one's laurels
against the grain	in a nutshell	to reap what one sows
to beat around the bush	that's just peachy	to sow wild oats
bed of roses	the last straw	to turn over a new leaf
grapevine	out on a limb	wallflower

18: Language and Literature

also see Metalinguistic Aspect #1
A Glossary of Grammatical Terms

Nouns

adjective	essay	lie	poetry	signature
adverb	etymology	linguistics	prayer	slang
article	exaggeration	literature	pronoun	speech
autograph	exclamation	meaning	pronunciation	spiel
comma	fiction	monologue	prose	statement
comprehension	grammar	narration	pun	stress
conversation	idiom	narrative	punctuation	style
definition	interview	noun	question	syntax
dialect	intonation	paragraph	quotation	title
dialogue	jargon	paraphrase	recitation	usage
diction	joke	period	semantics	verb
drama	journalism	phonology	sentence	verbiage

Verbs

abridge	discuss	lie	recite	symbolize
call	drawl	mean	relate	talk
censor	edit	mislead	report	tell
chat	elaborate	misspell	respond	title
communicate	encode	mutter	say	transcribe
comprehend	erase	narrate	scrawl	translate
converse	exaggerate	paraphrase	sign	transliterate
cry	explain	pray	speak	type
curse	explicate	print	spell	utter
debate	express	pronounce	sputter	vow
decode	gossip	punctuate	stammer	whisper
define	interpret	quote	stutter	write
dictate	interview	read	swear	

Idioms and Expressions

to call a spade a spade	double talk	neither rhyme nor reason
to call to order	gobbledygook	talk of the town
a close call	to read between the lines	tall story
far cry	to sign on the dotted line	
It's Greek to me.	to swear on a stack of Bibles	

Literary Terms

adventure story	criticism	historical fiction	novella	story, plot
autobiography	detective story	lyric	play	subject matter
biography	drama, melodrama	memoir	poem	theater
character	fantasy	meter, metrics	poetry	theme
children's books	fiction	mystery	prose	title, subtitle
classic	flash fiction	narrative	rhyme	tragedy
comedy	free verse	non-fiction	short story	verse
crime fiction	Gothic, horror story	novel	science fiction	young adult, adult

19: Thinking

Nouns

analysis	decision	intention	reason
attitude	deduction	judgement	reflection
belief	deliberation	knowledge	speculation
brains	experience	logic	stupidity
certainty	fantasy	meditation	thinking
cogitation	feeling	mind	thought
comprehension	idea	notion	truth
conception	image	observation	understanding
conclusion	impression	perception	view
contemplation	intellect	rationale	wisdom
conviction	intelligence	realization	wit

Verbs

analyze	distinguish	misconstrue	reflect
appreciate	doubt	misunderstand	remember
apprehend	experience	mull	reminisce
believe	fantasize	note	retain
brood	feel	notice	ruminate
cogitate	figure out	observe	see
comprehend	forget	perceive	sense
conceive	imagine	plan	speculate
conclude	judge	ponder	think
consider	know	question	trust
contemplate	learn	realize	understand
decide	meditate	recall	view
deliberate	memorize	reconstruct	wonder

Adjectives

analytical	cognizant	intellectual	smart
appreciative	convinced	intelligent	stupid
aware	crafty	irrational	thoughtful
brainy	decisive	knowing	trusting
brilliant	deliberate	observant	truthful
certain	dull	perceptive	understanding
clever	experiential	pensive	vague
conclusive	imaginative	rational	wise
cognitive	indecisive	reasonable	witty

Idioms and Expressions

absent minded	level-headed	pipe dream
fat headed	literal minded	narrow minded
to know the ropes	to make neither head nor tail	neither rhyme nor reason

108

20: Numbers and Math also see #22 Shapes

Nouns

addition	division	product
algebra	equation	proof
analysis	figure	quotient
angle	formula	radius
arithmetic	fraction	rate
average	function	ratio
axis	geometry	rational number
axiom	plane	relativity
calculation	solid	remainder
calculator	hypotenuse	root
calculus	infinity	set
cipher	integral	sequence
circumference	irrational number	solution
computation	logarithm	square root
computer	logic	statistics
constant	long division	straight line
corollary	mathematics	subtraction
cube	mean	sum
curve	median	term
decimal	multiplication	theorem
decimal point	numeral	theory
denominator	percentage	topology
difference	pi	trigonometry
diagram	postulate	value
diameter	prime number	variable
digit	probability	whole number
dimension	problem	

Verbs

add	double	multiply
average	equal	reduce
balance	equate	round up/down
calculate	figure	solve
compute	formulate	square
count	graph	subtract
divide		triple

Idioms and Expressions

double or nothing	math facts	second-rate
face value	multiplication tables	to see double
fifty-fifty	to play by the numbers	sixes and sevens
It doesn't add up.	to put two and two together	to be square
lump sum	sewing circle	Two's company; three's a crowd.

21: Colors

Primary

red	yellow	blue
orange	green	indigo
		violet/purple

Secondary

aquamarine	emerald	pink
beige	gold	rose
black	gray	ruby
bronze	ivory	silver
brown	khaki	slate
buff	lavender	tan
chestnut	maroon	teal
chocolate	off white	turquoise
coffee	olive	umber
copper	olive drab	white

Adjectives

bright	earth	metallic
brilliant	fluorescent	mottled
cool	glossy	pale
dark	hot	pied
dull	light	rich
flat	lurid	vivid

Miscellaneous

rainbow	spectrum	CMYK (cyan, magenta,
camouflage	RGB (red, green, and blue)	yellow, and black)

Paints, etc.

acrylic	crayons	oil
chalk	enamel	pastel
charcoal	finger	stain
colored marker	ink	tempera
colored pencil	latex	water colors

Idioms and Expressions

black and blue	in the black, in the red	red letter day
black hearted	in the pink	red tape
blue, the blues	to paint the town red	rose colored glasses
dyed in the wool	pink and blue	to be seeing red
greenhorn	red carpet	silver lining
green with envy	red cent	Silence is golden.
in black and white	red herring	yellow (cowardly)

22: Shoes also see #20 Numbers and Math

Adjectives

angular
arched
blunt
circular
concave
concentric
congruent
conical
convex
curved
crooked
cylindrical
elliptical
elongated

flat
flattened
globular
hexagonal
horizontal
irregular
linear
long
narrow
octagonal
oval
parallel
perpendicular
pointed

ragged
round
rectangular
regular
sharp
slender
slim
square
smooth
straight
triangular
twisted
warped
wide

Nouns

arc
arch
block
blob
circle
cone
cube
cylinder
diamond
disc
dome

globe
helix
heptagon
hexagon
horseshoe
mound
octagon
oval
parallelogram
peak
pentagon

point
polygon
pyramid
quadrangle
rectangle
sphere
spiral
square
surface
tip
triangle

Idioms and Expressions

round peg in a square hole
domestic triangle
vicious circle
a crooked person

odds and ends
sharp as a tack
square
straight as an arrow

to run circles around someone
the Pentagon
point of an argument
tip of an iceberg

111

23: Substances and Materials

Nouns

acid	flint	plastic
air	gas	plywood
aluminum	gasoline	powder
ashes	glue	rock
asphalt	goo	rubber
base	grease	sand
brass	gunk	sheet
bronze	kerosene	rock
cement	lubricant	smoke
cloth	moisture	soil
cloud	mud	steam
concrete	oil	steel
copper	ointment	stuff
dirt	paste	tar
dust	petroleum	water
earth	plaster	wood

Adjectives

abrasive		
corroded	impermeable	slippery
corrosive	invisible	slimy
crumbly	liquid	soft
dull	metallic	solid
durable	pliable	soluble
dusty	resilient	spongy
flammable	rough	sticky
gaseous	rubbery	strong
gooey	rusty	thick
gritty	sharp	thin
hard	shiny	tough
	slick	wet

Idioms and Expressions

to blow off steam	to go up in smoke	to scratch the surface
brass tacks	to lay it on thick	to throw cold water on
a fly in the ointment	to take a powder	to knock on wood
slick operator	greaseball	powder keg
to grease the wheel	to grease one's palm	to cement a deal
to cast in concrete	to be plastered	dull as dishwater

112

24: Containers

bag	canteen	dish	pack	snifter
barrel	carafe	file folder	package	thermos
basket	carton	flask	pail	tin
bottle	case	glass	pitcher	tray
bowl	container	jar	portfolio	tub
box	crate	jug	pot	tube
bucket	cup	keg	rack	vase
can	demitasse	mug	sack	vessel
canister	demijohn			

Idioms and Expressions

in the bag	boxed in	lock, stock and barrel
to have someone over a barrel	a drop in the bucket	soapbox
bottleneck	left holding the bag	windbag
barrel of monkeys	jug wine	ugly mug
bag lady	on the bottle	a real dish

25: Manipulations

aim	fill	mold	screw	tip
arrange	flatten	move	scratch	trip
assemble	flex	open	seal	turn
attach	flick	pick up	set	turn off
bash	flip	pick out	set down	turn on
beat	flop	pick over	slam	turn over
bend	fold	pluck	spin	turn under
bolt	hammer	plug in	start	turn around
break	hang (up)	plug up	stop	twist
close	heat	pound	strike	undo
cool off, down	hook	press	strip	unfold
crack	ignite	pull	take apart	unhook
crumble	insert	punch	take out	unplug
crush	knead	push	take up	unlatch
cut	latch	put in	take down	unlock
deposit	level	reverse	tap	unscrew
depress	light	rap	tear	untie
disassemble	load	rip	thread	unzip
detach	lock	roll	throw	weave
drain	loop	rub	thrust	wipe
drive	maneuver	sand	tie	work
empty	mix	scrape	tilt	zip

Idioms and Expressions

flop house	to put the screws to someone	spin doctor
to pull a fast one	to put a spin on information	to strike while the iron's hot

26: Emotions

Nouns

affection	bravery	fatigue	joy	rage
aggravation	cheer	fear	joviality	regret
amusement an-	courage	feeling	laughter	restlessness
ger	craziness	fright	love	sadness
anguish	dejection	gladness	mood	sorrow
annoyance	delight	glee	nervousness	tears
anxiety	depression	greed	pain	temper
awe	disappointment	happiness	passion	terror
belligerence bit-	disgust	hope	pity	tiredness
terness	embarrassment	horror	pleasure	trouble
bliss	enthusiasm	indifference jeal-	prejudice	weariness
boredom	envy	ousy	pride	zest

Verbs

abhor	bother	disgust	hate	please
aggravate	burn up	embarrass	hope	rejoice
agitate	calm	envy	laugh	sadden
amuse	cheer up	excite	lament	shake up
anger	console	fatigue	like	sob
annoy	cry	fear	love	stir
antagonize	delight in	feel	moan	tire
bewilder	depress	frighten	mope	tremble
blush	detest	fume	mourn	trouble
bore	disappoint	gladden	pain	weep

Adjectives

abhorrent	bitter	disgusted	happy	painful
abject	blissful	embarrassed	hopeful	passionate
affectionate	bored	enthusiastic	insane	pleased
afraid	bothered	envious	irritated	restless
aggravated amo-	brave	excited	jealous	sad
rous	calm	fatigued	jolly	sexy
amused	cheerful	fearful	joyful	shy
angry	cheery	flustered	jovial	sorrowful
annoyed	crazy	forlorn	loving	tearful
anxious	dejected	frightened	melancholy	timid
apprehensive bel-	delighted	gay	merry	tired
ligerent	depressed	glad	moody	troubled
berserk	disappointed dis-	gleeful	mournful	upset
bewildered	consolate	grouchy	nervous	weary

Idioms and Expressions

at wit's end	happy as a clam	method in one's madness	a heart breaker
to blow one's top	hot and bothered	love will find a way	tear jerker
fit to be tied	in a dither	out of sorts	troubled waters
to go to pieces	to make a scene	standoffish	at the end of one's rope

114

27: The Body and its Functions

External

head	hand	chest	penis	shin
hair	palm	breast	foreskin	ankle
shoulders	thumb	nipple	testes	heel
neck	finger	stomach/	testicles	instep
arm	index	belly	anus	sole
armpit	middle	abdomen	leg	foot
forearm	ring	waist	knee	toe
elbow	little	hip	thigh	big toe
wrist	knuckle	buttocks	calf	little toe
fist	fingernail			

Face

forehead	eye	eyelid	mouth	lip
eyebrow	pupil	cheek	jaw	chin
temple	white	nose	tongue	dimple
ear	eyeball	nostril	tooth	mustache
earlobe	eyelash	bridge	gums	beard
eardrum				sideburns

Bones

skull	spine	shoulder blade	pelvis	thigh bone
backbone	collarbone	ribs	hipbone	kneecap
vertebrae				skeleton

Insides

brain	liver	appendix	muscle	tonsils
windpipe	pancreas	bladder	blood	larynx
heart	kidney	vein	nerves	vagina
lung	intestines	artery	throat	rectum

Body products

urine	saliva/	perspiration/	tears	sperm
feces	spit	sweat	oil	eggs

Adjectives

pregnant	fat	pudgy	robust	tight
tall	muscular	healthy	weak	loose
short	skinny	ill	strong	supple
thin	plump	sick	athletic	lithe

115

Verbs

belch	cry	hear	run	stand
bend	defecate	hiccup	see	swallow
bite	digest	hop	sit	taste
burp	eat	jump	skip	titter
breathe	flex	laugh	smell	twist
chew	fornicate	leap	smile	urinate
choke	gasp	menstruate	spit	groan
copulate	giggle	moan	sniffle	scowl
creep	grin	nibble	sob	weep

Idioms and Expressions

after one's own heart
all ears
apple of one's eye
to give one's right arm
at arm's length
with open arms
bad blood
to beat one's brains out
to beat one's head against a
    stone wall
to bend over backwards
to bite off more than one
    can chew
in cold blood
brainstorm
to waste one's breath
to save one's breath
to take away one's breath
to breathe freely
cold feet
to cool one's heels
to cut off one's nose to
    spite one's face
to eat one's heart out
to eat one's words
to rub elbows with
elbow grease
to keep an eye on
to see eye to eye
to make eyes at
to keep a straight face
to keep one's fingers crossed
first-hand
to foot the bill

to put one's foot down
to put one's best foot forward
to put one's foot in one's mouth
on all fours
funny bone
bone headed
to get on one's nerves
to get something off
    one's chest
guts
potbelly
to let down one's hair
to split hairs
hard-hearted
hard-headed
head and shoulders above
over one's head
heart-to-heart
by heart
to have a heart
a heel
to keep a stiff upper lip
to knock one's block off
lowbrow, highbrow
to make no bones about
by word of mouth
to shoot one's mouth off
foul-mouthed
narrow-minded
to neck
neck and neck
up to one's neck
nose is out of joint
nosey

to pay lip service to
to pay through the nose
to pick a bone with
to pull one's leg
to pull the wool over
    one's eyes
to shake a leg
straight from the shoulder
a cold shoulder
a chip on one's shoulder
by the skin of one's teeth
to get under one's skin
a slap in the face
a pain in the neck
a slip of the tongue
sweet tooth
to take a load off one's feet
to set one's teeth on edge
under one's thumb
all thumbs
to toe the mark
to be on one's toes
tooth and nail
tongue in cheek
tongue tied
tongue twister
on the tip of one's tongue
to turn the other cheek
to turn up one's nose at
to turn one's back on
to turn a blind eye on
to watch one's step
to make one's mouth water
to wet one's whistle

28: Automobiles

Makes

Acura
Audi
Bentley
BMW
Buick
Cadillac
Chevrolet
Chrysler
Citroen
Daewoo
Datsun

Dodge
Ferrari
Fiat
Ford
Honda
Hummer
Hyundai
Infiniti
Isuzu
Jeep

Kia
Lexus
Lincoln
Mazda
Mercedes Benz
Mercury
Mini
Mitsubishi
Oldsmobile
Nissan

Pontiac
Rolls Royce
SAAB
Saturn
Scion
Smart Car
Subaru
Suzuki
Toyota
Volkswagen/VW
Volvo

Types

ATV (all-terrain vehicle)
camper
compact
convertible

coupe (2-door)
economy
hatchback
hybrid
minivan

pick-up
RV (recreational vehicle)
sedan (4-door)
sports car

station wagon
stock car racer
SUV (sport utility vehicle)
van

Parts (external)

back-up light
blinker
brake light
bumper
fender
fog light
gas cap
grill

headlight
  high beam
  low beam
hood
hub cap
inspection sticker
license plate
luggage rack

lug nut
moonroof
rim
sunroof
tailgate
taillight
tire

trunk
turn signal
wheel
window
windshield
windshield washer
windshield wiper

Parts (internal)

airbag
anti-lock brakes
brake pedal
CD/iPod player
child seat
clutch
coin holder
console
cup holder
dome light

EZ Pass Transponder
gas pedal
gages:
  gas
  odometer
  oil
  tachometer
  temperature
gearshift
glove compartment

GPS System
hand brake
ignition key
instrument panel
odometer
radio
rear view mirror
seat
seat belt
spare tire

speedometer
steering wheel
stick shift
tool kit:
  crowbar
  flare
  jack
  lug wrench
  snow/ice scraper
visor

Parts (engine and mechanical, etc.)

air filter/cleaner	exhaust pipe	gear shift	starter
alternator	exhaust manifold	automatic	suspension
battery	fan belt	stick	transmission
brake	fluids	generator	all-wheel drive
carburetor	antifreeze/coolant	horn	automatic
catalytic converter	brake fluid	muffler	four-wheel drive
cruise control	oil	piston	front/back wheel
dip stick	washer fluid	radiator	drive
drive belt	water	serpentine belt	standard
drive train	fuel pump	shock absorber	universal joint
engine	gas tank	spark plug	

Verbs

back up	dim (the lights)	roll down the window	stall
brake	drive	run out of gas	steer
break down	fill the tank	shift	swerve
bump into	get/have a flat tire	signal (a turn)	tow
check the oil	honk the horn	skid	turn
coast	park	slow down	turn around
crash	put on the brakes	speed (up)	U-turn

Places

back road	construction	junk yard	roundabout
barrier	exit	median	toll booth
breakdown lane	fast lane	off-ramp/on-ramp	toll road/bridge
bridge	gas station	overpass	traffic circle
car wash	garage	shoulder	travel lane
clover leaf	Interstate highway	rest area	underpass

People

backseat driver	driver	mechanic	passenger
car salesman			police officer

Directions

Caution	Keep Left/Right	No U-Turn	Speed Limit
Curves	Merge	Pedestrians	Stop Ahead
Deer Crossing	Moose	Reduce Speed	Traffic Turning and
Divided Highway	No Passing	School Zone	Entering
Exit Only	No Left/Right Turn	Signal Ahead	Two-Way Traffic
Junction			

Miscellaneous

AAA/America Auto-mobile Association	DWI	junker	road hazard
auto insurance	emergency kit	limo/limosine	rolling coffin
beater	fender bender	NASCAR	rust bucket
clunker	flare	parts car	winter beater
demolition derby	four-by-four/4X4	to total a car	wreck
	Indy 500	tow truck	

118

29: Transportation

Land

ATV (all-terrain vehicle)	chariot	rickshaw	subway
automobile, auto	coach	RV (recreational vehicle)	tanker
bus	convertible	scooter	tank
bicycle,)	el, elevated railway	sedan	truck
bike	jeep	skateboard	taxicab, taxi, cab
cable car	litter	skimobile/snowmobile	train
camper	locomotive	sled	tricycle
car	moped	sleigh	trolley
carriage	motorcycle	snowmobile	truck
cart	pickup	sports car	van
	railroad, railway	stagecoach	wagon

Animals

burro	dog (sled)	horse	pony
camel	donkey	llama	oxen
cow	elephant	mule	water buffalo

People

bus driver	driver	taxi cab driver	copilot
chauffeur	engineer	teamster	flight attendant
coachman	guide	truck driver	pilot
conductor	mechanic	aviator	steward/stewardess

General

alley	E-Z pass	rest area	timetable
bridge	gasoline	road	trail
burden	highway	schedule	tire
cargo	interstate	station	toll booth
coal	lane	steam	turnpike
diesel	oil	street	vehicle
engine	path	thruway	wheel

Air

aircraft	concourse	jet	seat assignment
airliner	control tower	light plane	security
airplane	engine	luggage	spacecraft, ship
airport	gate	propeller	space shuttle
baggage check	glider	reservation	ticket
baggage claim area	hangar	rocket	ticket counter
blimp	helicopter	runway	window
boarding pass	hot air balloon	seat	wings

Water

aircraft carrier	fleet	motorboat	sailboat
amphibian	freighter	motor launch	sea
ark	frigate	navy	shell
barge	galley	oar	ship
boat	gunboat	ocean	spar
bow	harbor	ocean liner	square rigger
buoy	helm	paddle	steamship/steamboat
canal	hovercraft	paddlewheel	steering wheel
canalboat	hull	pond	stern
canoe	jet ski	port	stream
catamaran	kayak	propeller	submarine
centerboard	keel	rapids	surfboard
channel	lake	river	trimaran
craft	landing craft	raft	tugboat/towboat
cruiser	lifeboat	rowboat	vessel
cruise ship	lighter	rudder	warship
dinghy	lighthouse	runabout	yacht
ferry/ferryboat	mast	sail	white water

Verbs

arrive	fly	park	take off
check in	glide	ride	tour
depart	hitchhike	row	tow
disembark	land	sail	trek
drive	launch	soar	travel
embark	paddle	steer	walk

Idioms and Expressions

to backfire	to miss the boat
to get on the bandwagon	to pave the way for
on the (water) wagon	water under the bridge/ over the dam
in the same boat	to fall asleep at the wheel
off the beaten track	to take a back seat to
to burn one's bridges behind one	to run around in circles
to know the ropes	slow boat to China
to lose one's way	shipshape
to make way for someone or something	up the creek without a paddle
to meet someone halfway	backseat driver

30: Community
Places and Organizations

arts council
chamber of commerce
sidewalk
park
park bench
civic center
community center
public library
Catholic church

mosque
Protestant church
Jewish synagogue
Grange
VFW - Veterans of
   Foreign Wars
DAR - Daughters
   of the American
   Revolution

Elks
Eagles
Knights of Columbus
Lions Club
Shriners
Masons
Boy/Girl Scouts
4-H Club
playground

FFA - Future Farmers
   of America
American Legion
PTA - Parent-Teachers
   Association
school board
senior center
garden club
union hall
university club

Events

auction
band concert
beauty contest
bingo
church bazaar
church supper
county fair

demonstration
farmers' market
flea market
funeral
hoedown
memorial service

parade
picket line
political rally
rodeo
rummage sale
scouting jamboree

strike
tag, yard, lawn sale
Town Meeting
voting
wake
walk-a-thon
wedding reception

31: Hotels

airport limousine,
   limo
baggage
ball room
bar
bath
bed
bellhop
bill
bureau
bed and breakfast
boarding house
call (wake-up)
cashier
currency exchange
chair
chambermaid

coffee shop
convention desk
concierge
clerk
dining room
doorman
elevator
elevator operator fit-
   ness center
flop house
gardener
guest
guest house
health club
hospitality center
housekeeper
hostel

hotel
ice machine
information desk
inn, innkeeper
key/ room key
laundry
lobby
lounge
luggage
maid
manager
meeting
motel
operator
organization
party
reservation

residential hotel
resort
room
   single
   double
room clerk
room service
restaurant
safety deposit box
security guard
suite
table
tourist
tourist cabins
tourist court
tour guide
travel desk

Verbs

call (roomservice)
check in

check out
disturb (do not)

pack
register

reserve
stay

Idioms and Expressions

bag and baggage
room and board

It's the Ritz.
stop for the night

overnight guest
overnight stay

home away from home
weekend rates

32: Restaurants

Nouns

appetizer	cup	meal	refill (of coffee)
ashtray	dessert	menu	salad bar
bar	dish	mug	salt
bowl	fork	napkin	serving spoon
booth	glass	order	table
buffet	gourmet	plate	tablecloth
chair	gratuity	platter	tax
check	knife	reservation	tip
cocktail	main course	round (of drinks)	wine cellar
course			wine list

Verbs

dine	order	prepare	tip
eat out	pay	reserve	take out

Types

automat	deli(catessen)	fast-food	pizzeria
cafe	diner	gourmet	pizza parlor
cafeteria	drive-in	luncheonette	snack bar
coffee shop	drive thru	natural foods	soda fountain
			vending machine

Personnel

baker	cook	host	pastry chef
bartender	dishwasher	hostess	prep cook
busboy	guest	maitre d'	server
cashier	headwaiter	manager	waiter
chef			waitress

Adjectives

a la carte	fresh	rare	succulent
baked	fried	raw	take-out
bland	grilled	salty	tasteless
boiled	hot	scrumptious	tasty
broiled	mashed	sliced	to go
cold	medium	spicy	vegan
delicious	overdone	steamed	vegetarian
dry			well-done

Idioms and Expressions

to wine and dine	doggy bag	to go dutch	to foot the bill
bill of fare	dutch treat	pick up the check	dine and dance
bottomless cup	room and meals tax	to take the check	specials
	chief cook and bottle washer		

33: Stores and Shops

General

browsing
chain store
department store
downtown

main street
mall
neighborhood

one-stop shopping
outlet center
specialty shops

shopping center
shopping district
window shopping
variety store

Specific

antique shop
appliance store
art gallery
arts and crafts store
auto parts store
bakery
bookstore
cafeteria
camera shop
candy store
car dealership
carpets & flooring
cellphone store
clothing store
coffee shop
comic book/game store
computer store
convenience store

country store
delicatessen
department store
discount store
dollar store
drug store
electronics store
fabric/draperies store
farmers' market
fast-food chain
fix it shop
flea market
florist
furniture store
garden center
gift shop
grocery store
hardware store

health food store
hobby shop
jewelry store
liquor store
mail-order
minimart
music store
newsstand
office supply store
optician
outlet store
paint store
pawn shop
pet shop
pizza parlor
pharmacy
photography store
printing/copy center

restaurant
Salvation Army store
service center
sewing center
shoe store
snack bar
sporting goods store
stationery store
supermarket
telephone store
thrift shop
tobacconist/cigar store
toy store
TV-radio store
used book store
used clothing store
used furniture store
vegetable stand

34: Agencies and Services

advertising agency
animal shelter/SPCA
appliance repair
auto rental agency
auto repair shop
bank/savings and loan
barber shop
beauty parlor
business consultant
cable/satellite company office
carpenter shop
certified public
   accountant office
charities
copy center
counseling office
dance studio
day-care center
dry cleaners
electrician
employment agency

fire department
funeral parlor
gardener/lawn care
health center/club
homeless shelter
insurance agency/broker
Internal Revenue Service
laundry
laundromat
law firm
loan association
martial arts studio
medical clinic
military recruiting office
moving company
newspaper office
news stand
Planned Parenthood
plumber
police department
post office

radio-TV repair
real estate agency
shoe repair service
self-storage units
service station
storage warehouse
senior citizen's center
shipping center
social security office
soup kitchen
stockbroker
tailor
tanning salon
tax consultant
travel agency
telephone company
   business office
town/city hall/offices
welding shop
welfare office
Women's Crisis Center

35: Post Office/Delivery Services

Personnel

carrier
clerk
delivery person

mail carrier
mail sorter

post office worker
    postmaster/mistress

Nouns and Adjectives

address
aerogram
airmail
booklet of stamps
book rate
box
bulk mail
cancellation
certified mail
C.O.D.
coil of stamps
commemorative stamp
customs form
dead letter
envelope
express mail
fee
first class/second, third.
franking privileges
general delivery

global priority mail
insured mail
international mail
junk mail
letter
lobby
magazine rate
mail box
media mail
money order
next day
newspaper
overnight
package
parcel post
philatelic window
postage
postage due
postage meter
postage stamp

post card
post office (P. O.) box
priority mail
registered mail
return address
return receipt
self-addressed envelope
self-adhesive stamp
service window
sheet of stamps
special delivery
special handling
stamp
stamp collecting
surface mail
U.S.P.S
weight
ZIP Code
   plus four
Zone (shipping)

Verbs

address
cancel
certify
deliver
fill out
forward
insure

lick
mail
post
pick up
receive
register

return
seal
send
ship
stamp
trace
track

Other

courier service
delivery
  afternoon/p.m.
  morning/a.m.
  next-day
  overnight
  same-day
  two-day
  three-day

handle with care
fragile
pick-up

FedEx (Federal Express)
UPS (United Parcel Service)
DHL/Airborne Express

36: Banks and Money

Verbs

apply for
authorize
balance
borrow
cancel
call in a loan
cash

change
charge
close out
convert
count
credit
debit

deposit
endorse
insure
justify
loan
lend
make change

overdraw
pay
put in
save
stop payment
take out
withdraw

Nouns

asset
automatic payment
ATM - automatic teller machine
balance
bank
bank account
bank book
bill
cash
CD - certificate of deposit
check
checking account
check register
check stub

coin
commercial loan
credit card
currency
debit card
deposit
deposit slip
deposit receipt
dime
dollar
fixed rate (interest)
half dollar, 50¢ piece
home equity loan
interest
invoice
frozen assets

line of credit
loan
loan agreement
loan payment
money
mortgage
nickel
paycheck
payment book
penny
piggy bank
principal
quarter
receipt
record book
safe

safe deposit box
savings account
savings bond
second mortgage
secured loan
silver dollar
statement
transfer
traveler's check
total
variable rate (interest)
vault
window
wire transfer
withdrawal
withdrawal slip

Personnel

drive-up teller
executive officer

loan officer
messenger

president
safe deposit clerk

secretary
security guard
teller

Idioms and Expression

to bank on something
a bear market/a bull market
to bounce a check
bottom dollar
cash in your chips
cheapskate
as good as gold
to get one's money's worth
greenback
layaway plan
to pass the buck

pretty penny
to take a rain check
rubber check
a run on the bank
bank holiday
flat broke
in the money
to corner the market
to make or break
to make a buck
to make both ends meet

I.O.U.
a man of means
a panhandler
penny wise and pound foolish
queer as a three-dollar bill
to nickel and dime to death
under the mattress
under the table
Waste not, want not.
A penny saved is a penny earned.
A fool and his money are soon parted.

37: Recreation

Games (also see 38)

backgammon	Chinese checkers	Monopoly
board games	cribbage	poker
bridge	crossword puzzle	role playing games
canasta	computer games	rummy
cards	hearts	solitaire
charades	jig saw puzzle	Scrabble
checkers	mahjong	twenty questions
chess	mankala	video games

Hobbies

aquariums/ tropical fish	embroidery	painting
butterfly collecting	flower arranging	pottery
coin collecting	gardening	rock collecting
collecting antiques, etc.	gun collecting	sewing
canning	house plants	terrariums
ceramics	miniatures	stamp collecting
cooking	model building	Sports (see List 35)
dolls/ doll houses	model railroading	Music (see List 36)

Amusements & Shows

amusement park	disco	night club
carnival	ice show	radio
circus	magic show	television
concert hall	movies	theater
dinner theater/ summer stock	pool hall	video game arcade

Arts

ballet	exhibition	photography
concert	martial arts	recital
dance	music	sculpture
drama	painting	theater

Crafts

batik	embroidery	pottery
carpentry	knitting	quilting
crewel	model making	sewing
crocheting	needlepoint	weaving

Places

amusement park	country club	racquet/racket club
aquarium	discotheque	ski resort
bar	health club	social club
beach	historical site	sports stadium
botanical garden	marina	swimming pool
campground	movie theatre	teen center
circus	museum	tennis club
cocktail lounge	national park, forest	theatre
concert hall	nightclub	zoo

Activities

backpacking	gardening	rally
badminton	golf	racquetball
ballet	gymnastics	reading
baseball	handball	roller blading
basketball	hiking	roller skating
bicycling/ cycling	hockey	sailing
birdwatching	horseback riding	sewing
board game	horse race	skating
body building	hunting	skate boarding
bowling	in-line skating	skiing
bungee jumping	jogging	sky diving
camping	kite flying	soccer
canoeing	listening to radio, stereo	softball
car race	long-distance running	squash
concert	making music	surfing
croquet	martial arts	swimming
diving	minature golf	tennis
dog race	motor boating	track and field
extreme sports	mountain climbing	video games
fishing	opera	volleyball
flying	painting	water skiing
football	paragliding	watching TV
frisbee	playing cards	weight lifting
gourmet cooking	pottery making	wrestling

Idioms and Expressions

to put one's cards on the table	drawing card	to steal the show
to put one's money on the line	to flip over something	up one's sleeve
to put up or shut up	go fly a kite	surfing the net
no dice	a flop	Do not pass Go.
dicey	to hit the jackpot	to win by a nose
an ace up one's sleeve	on the wrong track	nip and tuck

127

38: Sports and Games

archery	curling	hiking	polo	speed skating
badminton	diving	hockey	racquetball	squash
baseball	extreme sports	horseback riding	roller blading	surfing
basketball	fencing	hunting	roller skating	swimming
billiards	figure skating	jogging	running	table tennis
bowling	fishing	lacrosse	skiing	tennis
boxing	football	marathon running	downhill	track
bicycling	golf	mountaineering	cross-country	volleyball
bronco busting	gymnastics	Ping-Pong	soccer	water polo
canoeing	handball	pool	softball	weight lifting
climbing				wrestling

Equipment

arrow	fishing rod	mat	racket/racquet	soccerball
balance beam	flying rings	net	racquetball	softball
baseball bat	glove	paddle	reins	surfboard
birdie	golf ball	parallel bars	saddle	target
bow	golf clubs	Ping-Pong ball	shuttlecock	tee
bicycle	hockey stick	pole	skates	tennis ball
canoe	horse	pool cue	ski pole	tennis racket
fishing lure	indian clubs	puck	skis	trampoline

Areas

arena	course	green	pool	roller drome
coliseum	court	gymnasium	ring	stadium
country club	field	lane	rink	track
				trail

Verbs

aim	defend	kick	play	serve
attack	hike	lose	punt	tackle
catch	hit	participate	run	take part in
club	hurl	pitch	save	tie
coach	jog	place	score	throw
defeat				win

Idioms and Expressions

all part of the game	hook, line, and sinker	last lap
batting average	to keep the ball rolling	for keeps
below par	to make a hit	long shot
behind the eight ball	in the rough	to be punchy
to break the record	to rate a ten	to pull one's punches
comeback	right off the bat	to know what the score is
doubleheader	to pinch hit	second wind
to get on the ball	rain check	to have a score to settle
to get to first base	free-for-all	seventh inning stretch
to go to bat for	hit or miss	a shot in the dark
to have a lot on the ball	to jump the gun	to win hands down

128

39: Music

Nouns

album	composition	jazz	release
alto	concert	lyrics	rhythm
artist	conductor	measure	singer
ballad	concerto	melody	solo
band	disc	MP3	sonata
bar	disc jockey (DJ)	note	song
bass	folk song	piece	soprano
beat	group	program	symphony
cassette	hit	recital	tape
chorus	hymn	record	tenor
compact disc (CD)			tune

Verbs

accompany	harmonize	play	sing
compose	hum	pluck	strum
conduct	interpret	rap	toot
croon	jam	read (music)	whistle
finger	pick	record	write

Types

acoustic	classical	jazz	popular, pop
background	contemporary	light classical	rap
band	country & western	modern	religious
baroque	dance	mood music	rock and roll, rock
bebop	electronic	musical	rhythm and blues
bluegrass	folk	new age	spirituals
chamber	hard rock	opera	soul
church	hip hop	operetta	symphonic

Instruments

banjo	dulcimer	keyboard	strings
bass	electric guitar	oboe	synthesizer
bassoon	fiddle	organ	tambourine
cello	gospel	mandolin	trombone
clarinet	guitar	piano	trumpet
cornet	harp	punk	tuba
cymbals	horn	saxophone	viola
drums			violin

Idioms and Expressions

to blow your own horn	golden oldies	to pipe down	to sing for one's supper
elevator music	to play second fiddle	song and dance	music to one's ears
to face the music	to soft-pedal	for a song	the blues
to fiddle around with			to beat the band

40: Photography, Cinema, and Video

also see #55 The Media

Photography

accessory	definition	frame	over-exposed	shutter
album	depth of field	F-stop	photo(graph)	slide
aperture	developer	glossy	pixel	snapshot
automatic	digital	instamatic	Polaroid	speed
battery	dodge	lens	portrait	strap
black and white	double exposure	lens flare	pose	studio
blow up	double prints	light meter	positive	take (a picture)
burn	duplicate	load	process	telephoto
camera	enlarge	long exposure	projector	time lapse
canister	enlargement	macro	print	tone
cartridge	exposure	mailer	red eye	tripod
case	film	matte	reduce	under-exposed
color	filter	megapixel	rewind	viewer
come out	fisheye lens	memory disc	roll (of film)	viewfinder
composition	flash	mug shot	rez, resolution	washed out
contrast	focal length	negative	screen	white balance
crop	focus	out-of-focus	setting	wide-angle lens
darkroom				zoom lens

Cinema/ Movies

action	digitalization	green screen	rating	short subject
actor/actress	director	independent film	reel	show
adult	documentary	letter-box	release	sound track
adventure	drama	matinee	restricted	star
animation	dubbed	mature	reverse	sub-titled
blockbuster	entertainment	movie	romance	supporting actor
cartoon	epic	musical	running time	tear-jerker
CG/CGI/CA	fantasy	mystery	score	thriller
(computer	feature	Oscar	sci-fi (science	ticket
graphics)	film	pacing	fiction)	trailer
classic	film festival	porno(graphy)	screen	x-rated
comedy	film studio	prequel	sequel	videographer
composit	flash animation	preview	SFX (special	western
critic	gaffer	producer	effects)	wide-screen

Video

camcorder	fast forward	pan & scan	VCR (video tape	game
cassette	format(ted)	playback	recorder)	player
closed captioned	freeze	rent	video	rental
DVD (digital	home video	rewind	camera	store
video disc)	music video	tracking	disc	tape

41: Medicine and Health

Places and Areas

admitting
ambulance
assisted living
birthing room
clinic
check in
delivery room

emergency room
hospital
HMO (health
    maintenance org.)
insane asylum
intensive care unit
    (ICU)

labor room
laboratory
maternity ward
mental hospital
nursing home
operating room

out-patient clinic
pediatric ward
private room
recovery room
sanitarium
waiting room
ward

Equipment

adhesive tape
band-aid
bandage
bed
bed pan
cane
cast

crutches
gauze
heating pad
hot water bottle
operating table
oxygen tent
Q-tip (swab)

sanitary
napkins
scalpel
stethoscope
thermometer
    oral
    rectal

tongue
depressor
toothpaste
tweezers
vaporizer
walker
wheelchair
x-ray machine

People

anesthetist
candy striper
chiropractor
dermatologist
doctor (M.D.)
general practitioner
    (G.P.)
gynecologist
intern

lab technician
neurologist
nurse
nurse practitioner
nursing assistant
obstetrician
ophthalmologist
orthopedic surgeon
out-patient

pathologist
patient
pediatrician
pharmacist
physician
physician's assistant
podiatrist
practical nurse
psychiatrist

psychoanalyst
psychologist
radiologist
receptionist
registered nurse (R.N.)
specialist
surgeon
undertaker
urologist

Verbs

ache
admit
bleed
cough
deliver
diagnose

discharge
examine
faint
give birth
gargle
hurt

irritate
nurse
operate
pain
prescribe
recover

recuperate
relapse
set
swell
throb
throw up
vomit

Processes

appendectomy
blood pressure
Caesarean section
D&C
delivery (of a baby)
diagnosis
EKG

examination
heart beat
hysterectomy
implant
injection
inoculation
intensive care

MRI
observation
prognosis
pulse
sample
shot
specimen

surgery
temperature
tonsillectomy
transplant
vaccination
vasectomy
x-ray

Medicine

antacid	aspirin	eyedrops	penicillin	sedative
antidote	capsules	laxative	pill	suppository
antihistamine	contraceptive	nasal spray	the Pill	tablet
antiseptic	decongestant	ointment	prescription	vitamins

Problems/Symptoms

abscess	a cold	exhaustion	injury	sprain
accident	constipation	fever	infection	stiff
ache	cough	the flu	inflammation	strain
allergy	cut	fracture	nausea	swollen
asthma	deaf	hemorrhoids	pain	virus
blind	diarrhea	(piles)	rash	vomit
burn	dislocation	hyperthermia	runny nose	wart
chills	dumb	indigestion	sore	wound

Diseases and Conditions

AIDS	crohn's disease	herpes	multiple sclerosis	shingles
allergy	diabetes	high blood pressure	mumps	skin cancer
alcoholism	diarrhea	HIV positive	neurosis	smallpox
Alzheimer's	down syndrome	immunity	paranoia	stroke
angina	drug addiction	influenza (flu) leu-	pneumonia	syndrome
arteriosclerosis	dysentery	kemia	polio	syphilis
arthritis	emphysema	malaria	psychosis	tetanus
asthma	fetal alcohol	measles	rheumatic fever	tuberculosis (T.B.)
autism	syndrome	meningitis	rubella (German	tumor
bronchitis	gonorrhea	mental	measles)	typhoid fever
bursitis	heart attack	retardation	SARS	typhus
cancer	hepatitis	mononucleosis	scarlet fever	ulcer
chicken pox	hernia	(mono)	schizophrenia	V.D. (venereal
cholera				disease)

Idioms and Expressions

on call	over the hill	a shiner
office hours	to kick the bucket	a black eye
Say "ah."	a new lease on life	a shot in the arm
Turn your head and cough.	to give someone a dose	a sight for sore eyes
born with a silver spoon	of their own medicine	to turn one's stomach
in one's mouth	to take one's medicine	under the weather
to cough up	nuts, nutty as a fruitcake	on the wagon
chain smoker	to go off the deep end	"break a leg"
dead as a doornail	a bitter pill to swallow	An apple a day
dead to the world	in the pink	keeps the doctor away.
over one's dead body	safe and sound	skin and bones
one foot in the grave	to have a screw loose	sick and tired of
to croak	hooked on drugs	to catch a cold
to give up the ghost	monkey on your back	to come down with
hard of hearing	horrors (withdrawal)	

42: Dentistry

Places

clinic	office	waiting room

Equipment

air compressor	dental floss	drill	toothbrush
cleaning tools	dentist's chair	mirror	toothpaste
			x-ray machine

People

dentist	dental	oral surgeon	receptionist
dental assistant	hygienist	orthodontist	

Verbs

ache	drill	hurt	seal
cap	extract	pull out	x-ray
clean	fill	repair	

Miscellaneous

abscess	crown	false teeth	molar
bicuspid	canines	front tooth	nerve
braces	decay	filling	novocaine
bridge	dentures	gap toothed	pain
buck teeth	dog tooth	incisor	root
cavity	eye tooth	jaw	root canal
checkup			wisdom tooth

Idioms and Expressions

baby teeth	to cut one's teeth on	long in the tooth
one's bark is worse than one's bite	to give one's eye tooth for	toothy grin
to bite the hand that feeds one	to knock your teeth out	winning smile
to bite off more than one can chew	like pulling teeth	the tooth fairy

43: Hygiene

Nouns

antibacterial soap	dishwasher	mouthwash	soap, hand and bath
bath bathtub	feminine hygiene	shampoo	sterile
deodorant	products	shower	toothbrush, toothpaste
detergent	hand washing	shower stall	washing machine

Verbs

bathe	filter water	sanitize	sterilize
clean	do laundry	scrub	wash
clean up	purify	shower	wash up

44: Barber and Beautician

Nouns

Afro	cream rinse	hair oil	razor blade
appointment	crew-cut	hairpiece	receding hairline
bangs	curl	hairpins	redhead
barber	curler	hair style	rollers
barrette	dandruff	hair stylist	scissors
beard	depilatory	handlebar moustache	shampoo
beautician	drier	highlight	shave
blond/blonde	dye	manicure	setting lotion
bobby pin	fashion	manicurist	sideburns
bowl cut	flat top	Mohawk	split ends
braid	goatee (beard)	mousse	streak
brunette	hairbrush	moustache	tatoo
brush	haircut	page boy	tint
butch	hairdo	pedicure	towhead
carrot top	hairdresser	permanent	toupee
clippers	hair drier	pigtails	wave
comb	hair grease	ponytail	whiskers
conditioner	hairline	razor	wig
cosmetics	hair net	razor cut	

Verbs

bleach	curl	dye	shampoo
blow dry	cut	massage	shave
brush	design	rinse	tint
clip	dry	set	trim
comb			wave

Adjectives

bushy	frizzy	normal	straight
close	hairless	oily	thick
curly	hairy	over the ear	thin
dry	kinky	scraggly (beard)	unisex
dyed	long	short	wavy

Hair colors

auburn	brown	honey blonde	gray
black	brunette	flaxen blond	red
blond, blonde	dishwater blonde	strawberry blond	white

Idioms and Expressions

to get in one's hair	hairline crack	not a hair out of place	Handsome is as handsome
hairbreadth escape	long hair	one's hair stands on end	does.
hairpin turn	to put one's hair up	tall, dark, and handsome	Beauty is in the eye of the
let one's hair down	hairy	blonds have more fun	beholder.

45: Cosmetics and Toiletries

Nouns

after-shave lotion
baby shampoo
bath oil
bath salts
bath soap
beauty cream
beauty lotion
blush
body lotion
body cream
bubble bath
cold cream
cologne
comb
compact
cosmetic base
cotton balls
cotton swabs/ Q-tips
cuticle remover
deodorant
   roll-on
   soap

solid
spray
stick
dental floss
depilatory
emery board
eyebrow pencil
eye drops
eye-liner
eye-shadow
eye wash
facial cleanser
facial mask
facial soap
hand cream
hand cleanser
hand lotion
hand soap
hair brush
hair color
hair dye
hair remover

hair rinse
lip balm
lip gloss
lipstick
make up
mascara
moisturizer
mouth wash
mud pack
nail clippers
nail file
nail polish
nail polish remover
ointment
oral rinse
perfume
powder
razor
   disposable
   one-track
   safety
   two-track

razor blade
rouge
scent
septic stick
shampoo
shaver (electric)
shaving brush
shaving cream
shaving mug
shaving soap
skin cream
soap
sun block
sun screen
suntan lotion
tissues
toilet water
toothbrush
toothpaste
toothpaste gel
tooth powder
tweezers
witch hazel

Verbs

apply
beautify
blend
brush
cleanse

clip
cut
dab
deodorize

manicure
moisten
perfume
put on

shave
trim
touch up

Idioms and Common Sayings

Beauty is in the eye of the beholder.
Beauty is only skin deep.
B.O. (body odor)
Cleanliness is next to Godliness.
a close shave
five o'clock shadow
a greaser

the great unwashed
Handsome is as handsome does.
a little shaver
to look oily
a painted woman
to smell of trouble
to wash one's mouth out with soap

46: Jobs and Work

accountant	entertainer	manager	scientist
advertising agent	factory worker	mason	school administrator
artist	farmer	masseur, masseuse	secretary
assembly line worker	farm hand	mechanic	security officer
automotive engineer	field hand	merchant marine	service station
babysitter	file clerk	messenger	attendant
baggage handler	fireman, firefighter	meter reader	shipping clerk
baker	fisherman	mover	shoemaker
banker	flight attendant	musician	soldier
bank teller	food handler	news reporter	spy
barber	garbage collector	nurse	stenographer
beautician	gardener	office boy	steward(ess)
bookkeeper	glazier	ombudsman	store clerk
building contractor	guard	optician	street cleaner
bureaucrat	groundskeeper	optometrist	student
bus driver	heating contractor	painter (house)	surgeon
business consultant	hotel/motel clerk	parking lot attendant	surveyor
businessman/woman	house detective	pest exterminator	swimming pool
butcher	housekeeper	pharmacist	contractor
carpenter	housewife/ -husband	photographer	tailor
car washer	insurance agent	piano tuner	tax consultant
cashier	insurance claims	pilot	taxidermist
chambermaid	adjustor	plumber	taxi driver
chef	insurance	podiatrist	teacher, professor
chiropractor	investigator	police officer	technician
civil engineer	interpreter	politician	telephone lineman
cleaningman/ woman	illustrator	pollster	telephone operator
commercial artist	interior decorator	post office clerk	teller
computer programmer	jack of all trades	potter	translator
construction worker	janitor	priest, minister,	travel agent
cook	jeweler	rabbi, evangelist	traveling salesman
courier	journalist	nun, imam	tree surgeon
cowboy/ cowgirl	judge	press spokesperson	trucker, truck driver
crossing guard	junk dealer	printer	TV/radio repairman/
delivery person	lab technician	psychiatrist	woman
dental hygienist	landscape architect	psychologist	typesetter
dentist	laundry worker	publicist	typist
detective	lawyer	publisher	undertaker
diplomat	legislator	receptionist	upholsterer
dishwasher	librarian	real estate agent	veterinarian
doctor	life guard	red cap	volunteer
dog walker	lighting contractor	repairman/woman	waiter, waitress
doorman/woman	lobbyist	reporter	webmaster
editor	logger	research specialist	weather forecaster
electrical engineer	longshoreman	roustabout	meteorologist
electrician	machine operator	rubbish collector	window washer
employment officer	mail carrier	sailor	writer
engineer	maintenance worker	sales clerk	zoo keeper

47: Office

Nouns

adding machine
appointment
business
calculator
carbon copy
computer
   hard disc
   hardware
   mainframe
   network
   personal (PC)
   program
   server
   software
conference
copier
department
desk
desk chair

dictation
disc storage
duplicate
envelope
equipment
FAX machine
file cabinet
files
information backup
intercom
letter
letterhead
mail
meeting
modem
paper clip
pencil sharpener
postage meter
postage scales

printer
records
router
scanner
shorthand
shredder
stapler
stationery
supplies
supply cabinet
switchboard
swivel chair
telephone
telephone answering machine
tape dispenser
typewriter
voice mail
word processor
work station

Verbs

copy
dictate
input
fax

file
mail
manage
program

staple
take dictation
transmit
type

Personnel

accountant
assistant
boss
board of directors
bookkeeper
bursar
chairman/woman
clerk
chief executive officer (CEO)

chief financial officer (CFO)
director
employee
employer
executive
executive secretary
IT/internet technology specialist
manager
office manager

officer
personnel officer
president
receptionist
secretary
supervisor
treasurer
typist
vice-president (VP)

Idioms and Expressions

to take a letter
secretarial/typing pool

to be called on the carpet
right-hand man/woman

business is business
office politics

48: Business

Nouns

account
accounting software
accounts payable
accounts receivable
advertisement,
ad, advertising
annual report
asset
audit
bad debt
balance
balance sheet
benefit/benefits
    package
bid
bill
bill of lading
bond
books
bottom line
buy out
capital
capital gains
cash
cash flow
commercial
commission
common stock
computer

computer support
contract
corporate seal
corporate secretary
corporate officers
cost benefit analysis
cost of sales
credit
credit check
debit
debt
deduction
deficit
department
depletion
depreciation
Dow-Jones Average
(the) economy
equipment
equity
estimate
excise tax
expenditure
expense
expense account
fee
fiscal year
financial statement
fringe benefit

income
income tax
interest
inventory
investment
invoice
labor
labor union
labor contract
lease
ledger
leverage
liability
license
loss
maintenance
management
margin
(the) market
merger
mortgage
negotiations
offer
operations
overhead
payroll
petty cash
president
profit

pro forma invoice
purchase order
quotation (quote)
research and
    development (R&D)
receipt
rent
rental
retained earnings
royalty
sales
sales tax
securities
share (of stock)
social security
spread sheet
supplies
statement
stock
stock exchange
stock market
takeover
tax
value added tax
wage
wage scale
Wall Street
worksheet
write off

People

accountant
administrative
    assistant
agent
analyst
bookkeeper
broker
certified public
    accountant (CPA)
chairman of the board
chief executive
    officer (CEO)
chief financial
    officer (CFO)

clerk
communications
    specialist
comptroller
consultant
coworker
dealer
department head
director
employee
employer
executive
executive secretary
filing clerk

foreman
investor
lawyer
legal counsel
mail room clerk
manager
market researcher
mentor
operator
owner
partner
part-time employee
proprietor
salesman/woman

secretary
shipping clerk
specialist
supervisor
stenographer
stockholder
telemarketer
temporary worker
trader
treasurer
trustee
typist
vice president
worker

Types

agency	dealership	non-profit	partnership
chain	franchise	organization	service
company	holding company	non-governmental	subsidiary
conglomerate	industry	organization (NGO)	trust
corporation	monopoly		

Verbs

balance	fire	lease	sell
borrow	invest	loan	staff
buy	lend	merge	take over
finance	liquidate	restructure	tender an offer

Adjectives

commercial	incorporated (Inc.)	net	private
fiscal	industrial	non-commercial	public
gross	limited (Ltd.)	not-for-profit	volunteer

Idioms and Expressions

in the black	monkey business	"There's no business	employee relations
bullish	profit motive	like show business."	employment benefits
in the red	good repute	funny business	industrial wasteland
bearish	"The business of	good morale	It's none of your
black market	America is business."	customer relations	business.
the bottom line			

Employment: Getting a Job

apply for a job	work permit/	workman's	competency testing
application	Green Card	compensation	work evaluation
employment forms	probationary period	benefit packages	performance review
employment record	wages, pay, salary	reimbursement	discrimination
former employer	hours, work week	vacation	affirmative action
interview	payroll deduction	child care	classified ads
reference	W-4 form	civic duties (jury, etc.)	help wanted ads
resume	W-2 form	union membership	employment office,
skills	I9 eligibility	union dues	agency
training	verification	drug screening	

49: Agriculture

Nouns

acreage	farmer	kitchen garden	shepherd
agronomy	farmers' market	manure	sheep farm
aqua culture	feed	market	silage
baler	fence	milking equipment	silo
barn	field	milk	spreader
bulk tank	fish	processing plant	staple crops
combine	farm	mowing	subsidy
commodity	fodder	gardening	ranch
contour plowing	garden	orchard	thresher
crop	harrow	pasture	tiller
crop-dusting	harvest	pesticides	tractor
cultivation	herb garden	pitchfork	truck
cultivator	horticulture	plow	truck farming
dairy	horticulturist	produce	veterinarian (vet)
earth	hydroponics	product	wagon
fallow ground	insecticide	rotation	well
farm	irrigation	reaper	yield
	implements	seed	

Verbs

breed	graze	hoe	plant	thresh
clone	grow	inseminate	plow	water
cultivate	harvest	irrigate	raise	weed
fertilize	harrow	mow	reap	winnow
graft	hay	mulch	sow	

Livestock

bull	cow	goose	lamb	rabbits
calf	duck	hog	ox	sheep
cattle	goat	horse	pig	steer
chicken			poultry	turkey

Crops and Products

berries	dairy	grains	milk	sugar beets
citrus	eggs	legumes	organic produce	vegetables
cotton	fruit	livestock	silage	wool

Idioms and Expressions

cut and dried	40 acres and a mule	one reaps what one sows
to farm something out	The grass is always greener on	to sow one's wild oats
to make hay while the	the other side of the fence.	to separate the wheat from the
sun shines	genetically altered	chaff

50: Shops and Tools

Names of tools

ax, axe	hatchet	square
bit	level	straight edge
blow torch	mallet	staple gun
brace	plane	tape measure
calipers	pliers	tin snips
chisel	router	vise
clamp	sander	wedge
drill	saw	wire cutters
hammer	screwdriver	wrench

Verbs

bolt	nail	scribe
build	paint	solder
clamp	plane	staple
cut	pound	turn
glue	sand	varnish
hammer	saw	weld
measure	screw	wire

Miscellaneous

apprentice	paint	stain
bolt	plumber	staple
brad	plywood	steel
carpenter	polyurethane	wool
coat (of paint)	primer	tack
electrician	sandpaper	tubing
helper	screw	varnish
nail	shellac	welder
nut	spike	wire

Idioms and Expressions

to get the axe	jack of all trades	handyman
to have an axe to grind	live wire	on the level
to hit the nail on the head	nuts and bolts	to measure up
many irons in the fire		

141

51: Law

People

attorney	expert witness	minor
bailiff	Grand Jury	offender
clerk	investigating officer	parole officer
coroner	judge	plaintiff
counsel	juror	probation officer
court	jury	prosecutor
court reporter	jury foreman	prosecuting attorney
defendant	law office	public defender
defense attorney	lawyer	state's attorney
district attorney		witness

Places and Things

bar	criminal trial	probate court
bench	Family Court	public defender
civil trial	Federal District Court	session (of the court)
court	gavel	Small Claims Court
courthouse	jury box	State District Court
Court of Appeals	judge's chambers	Supreme Court
courtroom	legal aid service	witness stand

Adjectives

alleged	innocent	no contest; *nolo contendre*
hanged (criminal)	judicial	(objection) over-ruled
hung (jury)	legal	(objection) sustained
guilty	liable	pre-trial

Verbs

accuse	defend	post bail
acquit	deliberate	prosecute
allege	dissent	reverse a decision
appeal	enter a plea	sentence
argue	find	serve a sentence
award	hear a case	sue
call (a witness)	indict	swear
charge	instruct	testify
charge the jury	jump bail	throw out a case
commute	overturn	try
convict	plead	uphold

Events and Processes

accusation
aquittal
alimony
allegation
appeal
bail
case
charge
claim
conviction
court order
crime
crime scene investigation
cross-examination
damages
death penalty
decision
defense

deposition
DNA
evidence
exhibit
findings
forensics
fraud
grievance
hearing
indictment
injunction
inquiry
inquest
law
libel
litigation
manslaughter
mistrial

opinion
parole
perjury
probation
prosecution
recess
retrial
right(s)
ruling
sentence
sequester
settlement
suit
summons
testimony
trial
verdict
writ

Idioms and Expressions

to bail out
death row
to do time
to get away with murder
jailbird
to lay down the law

legalese
of age
open and shut case
out-of-court settlement
the question is mute
to take the law into one's own hands

to take the stand
to take the fifth amendment
third degree
to throw the book at
to throw out of court
under age

52: Police, Crime, and Emergencies

Good Guys

chief of police	game warden	police officer	SWAT team
constable	investigator	private eye	traffic cop
cop	meter maid	private investigator	undercoverman/woman
detective	narcotics officer (narc)	riot police	U.S. Marshal
deputy	patrolman	sergeant	vice squad
F. B. I.	plainclothesman	sheriff	victim
fireman	policeman/woman	state trooper	warden

Bad Guys

arsonist	gang	mob	second-story man
burglar	hit man	mobster	serial killer
call girl	hood	mole	street walker
child abuser/molester	inforcer	mugger	swindler
con artist	juvenile delinquent	petty thief	terrorist
con man	Ku Klux Klan (KKK)	pickpocket	thief
crook	killer	prostitute	thug
deadbeat dad/mom	loan shark	pusher	tough
drug dealer/trafficker	lynch mob	rapist	underworld
felon	madam	rioter	vandal
fence	Mafia	robber	whore

Crimes

armed robbery	domestic violence	investment fraud	scam
arson	drug trafficking	kickback	sexual molestation
assault (and battery)	drunk driving	kidnapping	skimming profits
assassination	extortion	larceny	slavery
blackmail	holdup	laundering money	smuggling
breaking and entering	homicide	libel	spousal abuse
break in	embezzlement	manslaughter	speeding
bribery	extortion	mugging	stalking
burglary	forced labor	murder	statutory rape
carjacking	forgery	narcotics smuggling	stealing
child abuse/molestation	fraud	pornography	stick up
child pornography	gambling	premeditated murder	swindling
child labor	gun running	prostitution	telemarketing fraud
computer fraud	harassment	protection racket	terrorism
con/confidence game	hijacking	purse snatching	theft
counterfeiting	identity theft	pushing dope	treason
defamation of character	insider trading	rape	vandalism
domestic assault	internet fraud	robbery	white collar crime

Places

beat	jail	prison	station
betting parlor	lockup	precinct	sweatshop
cell	penitentiary	rounds	whorehouse

144

Events

apprehension
arraignment
arrest
capture
chase
conviction

frame up
get away
investigation
line up
mug shot
pay off

racial profiling
raid
reading one's rights
round up
speed trap
traffic violation

Emergencies

accident
ambulance
blood bank
civil defense
clinic
CPR - cardiopulmonary
  resuscitation
dentist
doctor
doctor's office
drowning
drug overdose
drug store
Emergency Broadcasting
  System
emergency entrance

emergency room
emergency vehicle
evacuation
explosion
fire
fire department
fire drill
fire engine
fire horn
fireman
flashing lights
jaws of life
loud speaker
megaphone
monitor
mouth-to-mouth

natural disaster
neck brace
nuclear alert
pharmacist
pharmacy
public alarm signal
rescue
robbery
shock
siren
stretcher
tourniquet
training
transfusion
veterinarian's office
911

Things

assault weapon
badge
billy club
finger print
gun
handcuffs

knife
mace
manacles
night stick
paddy wagon
pistol

police gazette
revolver
shackles
siren
squad car
tazer
wanted posters

Idioms and Expressions

cement overshoes
close the case
cops and robbers
Cosa Nostra
crime boss
Crime doesn't pay.
deadly weapon

fuzz
the godfather
by hook or by crook
inside job
in the name of the law
the mob
organized crime

police protection
the rackets
to rub someone out
Smoky the Bear
the syndicate
ten most wanted
victimless crime

53: Communication Technology

Computers

application
back-up
banner advertising
blackberry
break in
broadband, high-speed
  internet service
cable
CD-ROM
chat room
chip
click on
cookies
CPU
crash
cyberspace
delete
desktop
dial-up connection
disk
display

distance learning
download
DSL (digital
  subscripting line)
e-commerce
EFT (electronic funds
  transfer)
email
ethernet
external hard drive
floppy disk
fire wall
fire wire
freeze
games
hack
hard disk
hardware
icon
input
internet

iPod
ISP (internet service
  provider)
keyboard
laptop
link
megabyte
memory
minidisk
modem
monitor
mouse
network
operating system
palm pilot
podcast
printer
printout
program
router
save

scanner, to scan
screen saver
search engine
server
software
spam
surf
thumb drive,
  USB flash drive
trash
undo
upgrade
URL
virus protection
web site
wireless
  communication
word processor
worm
WWW (world
  wide web)

Telephone

800 line
answering machine
answering service
call
caller ID
call forwarding
call waiting
car phone
cell phone
collect

conference call
dial
dial tone
extension
fund raising
hang up
information
local
long distance

pay phone
phonathon
phone bill
phone book
phone booth
pound sign
prepaid phone card
pulse
redial

reception
speakerphone
star
telemarketing
toll free
touchtone
trace
to transfer a call
voice mail
yellow/white pages

Other

CB (citizen's band radio)
communication tower
fax
GPS/global positioning system

intercom
internet cafe
network
pager

radar
sonar
tower
walkie-talkie
satellite

Idioms and Expressions

The computer is down.
computer freak, whiz, nerd
to crash
to cut and paste
to Google

Sorry, wrong number.
Your call cannot be
  completed as dialed.
Your call is important to us.
Can you hear me now?

a computer geek, nerd
a hacker
to surf the net
channel surfing

54: Politics and Government

See topics on Government in the Cultural Aspect section.

People

aide
alderperson
assemblyperson
attorney general
candidate
city council person
columnist
commentator

congressperson
delegate
governor
incumbent
mayor
member of congress
pollster
president

representative
secretary of state
selectperson
senator
sheriff
speaker
vice president
voter

Places, etc.

apportionment
bill
cabinet
campaign
capitol
congress
congressional district
Congressional Record
convention
district
Democrat
election

hearing
homeland security
inauguration
independent
investigation
INS (Immigration and
   Naturalization Service)
IRS (Internal Revenue
   Service)
legislation
majority

minority
negotiation
Pentagon
petition
polling place
precinct
primary
progressive
Republican
State House
voter check list
ward

Adjectives

city
conservative
county
executive
federal

judicial
legislative
liberal
libertarian
local

national
populist
radical
state
town

Verbs

campaign
debate
elect
enact
filibuster

govern
impeach
lobby
pass
preside

propose
re-elect
reform
veto
vote

Idioms, Expressions, and Issues

abortion rights
affirmative action
balanced budget
campaign contribution
civil rights
discrimination
environmental protection
equality before the law

equal rights
fiscal responsibility
graft and corruption
international security
lame-duck
machine politics
military expenditures
military-industrial complex

minority representation
minority rights
one person, one vote
political action committee (PAC)
pork barrel
rights and obligations
terrorism
undue influence

147

55: The Media

Print

ad(vertisement)	front page	newsprint	review
by-line	headline	obituary	scandal sheet
classifieds	journal	op-ed	scoop
columnist	journalist	press	subscribe
copy editor	lead story	print	subscription
correspondent	magazine	publish	(newspaper) syndicate
daily	monthly	publisher	tabloid
edition	news	quarterly	wedding announcement
editor	news magazine	reader	weekly
editorial	newspaper	reporter	writer

Television/TV *also see #40 Photography, Cinema, and Video*

ad (advertisement)	game show	pay-per-view	set
affiliate	HDTV (high definition	on-demand	show
anchorman/woman	television)	prime time	sit-com
antenna	host	premium channel	special
audience	interview	producer	sponsor
broadcast	live	program	studio
bulletin	mini-series	public access TV	syndication
cable	mute	public television	talk show
cameraman/woman	network	ratings	taped
channel	news	reality TV	televise
closed caption	newscaster	reception	TiVo
commercial	OVA (original video	remote	transmitter
coverage	animation)	satellite dish	viewer
digital television	paid programming	screen	weather channel
episode	panelist	series	

Radio

air wave	commercial	ham operator
AM (amplitude modulation)	dial	local broadcasting
antenna	DJ (disc jockey)	on-line/web radio
band	FM (frequency modulation)	NPR (National Public Radio)
broadcast	frequency	satellite radio
call letters	fund raising	short-wave
CB (Citizen's Band Radio)		station

Idioms and Expressions

"All the news that's fit to print"	the cable, cable news	late breaking story
No news is good news.	the comics/ funny papers	late night programming
Stop the presses!	hard news	letter to the editor
Don't touch that dial.	headline news	entertainment section
We'll be right back.	hot tip	top of the hour
Keeping them honest.	investigative reporting	top story

56: Religion

See the topic on Religion in the Cultural Aspect section.

Nouns

altar
baptismal font
belfry
cathedral
chapel
church
confessional
cross

hymnal
meeting house
mission
mosque
nave
synagogue
organ
parish

pew
prayer book
pulpit
Star of David
steeple
temple
transept
under croft

People

altar boy
alter guild
acolyte
archbishop
bishop
cantor
cardinal
choir
cleric/ clergy
crucifer

congregation
deacon
elder
evangelist
fundamentalist
imam
laity
lay brother/ sister/ man/ woman
minister

missionary
monk
nun
organist
pastor
Pope
priest
rabbi
reader
usher

Sacraments, Rituals, and Scriptures

baptism
Bible
bar mitzvah
call to prayer
catechism
christening
circumcision
communion
confirmation
confession
cross
funeral

Gospel
Haj
hymn
Koran
last rites
marriage
mass
New Testament
offering
Old Testament
prayer

psalm
pilgrimmage
Ramadan
ritual
scroll
seder
sermon
Sunday school
Talmud
Torah
Veda
vestments

Verbs

believe
be saved, to save
celebrate
convert

meditate
persecute
pray
preach

proselytize
shun
sing hymns
worship

Major Religions and Denominations

Baha'i Faith
Baptist Churches
Brethren (German Baptist)
Buddhism
(Roman) Catholic Church
Churches of God
Congregationalist Churches
Christianity
Eastern Orthodox Churches
Episcopal Church

Hinduism
Islam
Jehovah's Witnesses
Judaism
Lutheran Churches
Mennonite Churches
Methodist Churches
Mormon Churches (Church of
    the Latter Day Saints)
Orthodox

Pentecostal Churches
Presbyterian
Protestant
Quaker (Society of Friends)
Seventh Day Adventist
Shi'ah Moslem
Shinto
Sufism (Islamic Mysticism)
Sunni Moslem
Unitarian Universalist

Adjectives

agnostic
atheist
Buddhist
Christian
conservative
fundamentalist
Hindu

holy
Jewish
kosher
liberal
low/high church
Moslem
orthodox

reformed
religious
reverend
reverent
sacred
spiritual
strict

Important days

Ash Wednesday
Christmas
Easter Sunday
Eid
Good Friday

Hannukah
holy week
Kwanza
Lent

Palm Sunday
Passover
Ramadan
Rosh Hashana
Yom Kippur

Idioms, Expressions, and Concepts

act of God
Amen!
apocalypse
between the devil and the deep
    blue sea
Bible belt
born again
damnation,
to damn
diaspora
charity
crucifixion
end of the world is at hand
epiphany
eye for an eye
faith

fire and brimstone
good heavens
goodness gracious
God bless you
God willing
go to hell
Hallelujah!
heaven
heavens to Betsy
hell fire
Holy City
holy Moses!
holy roller
judgment day
kismet

matter of faith
messiah
month of Sundays
next year in Jerusalem
paradise
pass the hat
pass the plate
redemption
reincarnation
resurrection
revelation
to raise Cain
salvation
seventh heaven
straight and narrow
vengeance

57: Elementary, Secondary Education

Types of school

preschool programs
day care
nursery school
toddler program
head start program
kindergarten

primary school
elementary school
grade school
day school
middle school
junior high school

secondary school
high school
senior high
preparatory (prep)
school
public school
private school

parochial school
charter school
magnet school
specialized schools for:
the blind, the deaf
children with learning
disabilities
competitive athletes

Nouns

assignment
auditorium
blackboard
bulletin board
cafeteria
chalk
classroom
computer center
desk

desk work
detention
exam
grade
grading period
gymnasium, gym
high honor roll
homework
honor roll

science laboratory
language lab
learning center
lunch room
photocopier
playground
quiz
recess
report card

school
semester
study hall
teachers' room
test
textbook
vacation
voucher
workbook
worksheets

People

instructor
principal

pupil
secretary

student
superintendent

teacher
teacher's aide

Verbs

cram
enroll
evaluate

fail, flunk
grade
graduate

learn
pass
register

study
take a course
teach

Subjects

Elementary:
art
arithmetic, math
geography
music

reading
science
social studies
spelling
writing

Secondary,
the elementary
subjects plus:
chemistry
English

foreign language
history
home economics
physics
shop

Classroom Activities

manipulating objects
moving furniture
operating equipment
using the blackboard

using a tape recorder
using a typewriter
using a computer
taking dictation

spelling bee
taking attendance op-
erating a language lab
body movements

games
pencil and paper work
cutting and pasting
map work

Idioms and Expressions

to play hooky　　teacher's pet　　apple polishing　　tardy　　SAT

58: College Education

Types of schools

business school
divinity school
college
community college

graduate school
junior college
law school
medical school

on-line, distance learning
trade schools
training schools
university

Places

administration building
assembly hall
auditorium
boat house
book store
cafeteria
campus police
class room
chapel
computer center

dining hall
dormitory
field house
fraternity house
gym
housing office
lab
language lab
lecture hall
library

locker room
mail room
playing field
science lab
seminar room
sorority house
stadium
student union/center
study carrol
theater

Offices

academic dean
academic departments
accounting
admissions
athletic department
bursar
campus dean

carreer counseling
chancellor
counseling
dean
foreign student adviser
health

housing
physical education
president
registrar
R.O.T.C. headquarters
student activities
treasurer

Events

baccalaureate
convocation
drop period
examination
exam week
faculty
faculty tea
faculty meeting
fellowship
field trip
fraternity/sorority rush

games
　home
　away
　championship
graduation
hell week
homecoming
open house
orientation
party
prom

registration
reunion
semester
spring break
summer school
term
　fall
　winter
　spring
trimester
vacation

People

assistant professor
counselor
chaplain
coach
dean

department head/chair
dorm head
instructor
intern
librarian

professor
psychologist
school nurse
teaching assistant
tutor

Academic activities

academic paper
all nighter
aural exam
hand in
lecture
lab
class discussion
comprehensive exams
essay
field work

final exams
GRE (Graduate Records Exam)
grades
Law Boards
quiz
research
research paper
SAT (Scholastic Achievement Test)
scheduling

semester/study abroad
seminar
standardized test
study group
switch courses
test
thesis
TOEFL
workshop
written exam

Miscellaneous

academia
academic credit
academic freedom
academic gown
application
campus newspaper
campus radio station
certificate
cheerleader
co-education
co-ed
deadline
degree
diploma
disciplinary action

division
  humanities
  sciences
  social sciences
  interdisciplinary programs
excuse
expulsion
extracurricular
grade
grading periods
grind
humor magazine
homecoming queen
institute
late
liberal arts

literary magazine
major
marking period
minor
mortar board
pass-fail grading
plagiarism
pre-med
schedule
school newspaper
social life
suspension
student political organizations
tardy
undergraduate
year book

Academic Departments

African America/Black Studies
Anthropology
Archaeology
Art/Studio Art, Art History
Asian Studies
Biological Sciences
Chemistry
Classics
Comparative Literature
Creative Writing
Earth Sciences, Geology
Economics

Education
Engineering Sciences
English
English as a Second Language
Environmental Science
Film and Television Studies
Foreign Language, Literature
  Asian and Middle-Eastern,
  French, German, Italian,
  Russian, Spanish
Geography
History

International Studies
Linguistics, Cognative Science
Mathematics
Music
Native American Studies
Philosophy
Physics and Astronomy
Political Science. Government
Religion
Sociology
Theater
Women's and Gender Studies

Idioms and Expressions

to bone up on
to burn the midnight oil

to cram
to flunk

to hit the books
sheepskin

59: History

Periods

AD	CE	era	prehistoric
age	episode	geological time	Stone Age
BC	epoch	millennium	time
century	eon	period	

People

admiral	emperor	peasant	scout
adventurer	explorer	peon	seer
anthropologist	founder	philosopher	serf
archaeologist	frontiersman	political boss	scholar
artist	general	politician	secret agent
assassin	geographer	pope	senator
barbarian	hero	president	slave
bishop	high priest	prime minister	spy
builder	historian	prince	statesman
businessman	innovator	princess	teacher
captive	inventor	promoter	terrorist
chief	judge	prophet	trader
common man	king	queen	tradesman
counselor	knight	rabble rouser	traitor
creative genius	labor leader	rebel	tycoon
dictator	leader	representative	usurper
duke	orator	saint	warlord
engineer			warrior

Events

assassination	depression	famine	massacre
coronation	discovery	genocide	natural disasters
coup d'etat	election	holocaust	overthrow
battle	epidemic	inflation	plague
breakthrough	exploration	invention	rebellion
defeat			war

Miscellaneous

agreement	constitution	historical research	social unrest
alliance	economic growth	mob	social upheaval
biography	enemy	pact	starvation
chronicle	historical novel	saga	treaty

Idioms and Expressions

chronicle of events	history is bunk	milestone of history
history is yesterday's news	lessons of history	since the dawn of time

Those who ignore history are condemned to repeat it.

154

60: Disasters

Nouns

accidents	epidemic	plane crash
aftershock	eruption	pollution
airplane crash	evacuation	Richter scale
ambulance	explosion	relief
atomic/nuclear disaster	ethnic cleansing	rescue
avalanche	famine	riot
blizzard	fatality	shelter
bomb	fire	shipwreck
carnage	fire storm	sinking
catastrophe	first aid	starvation
civil war	flash flood	state of emergency
collision	flood	storm
conflagration	genocide	terrorism
cyclone	global warming	tidal wave
death	hurricane	tornado
deforestation	injury	tropical storm
desertification	loss of life	tsunami
devastation	mud slide	twister
disaster relief	nuclear meltdown	typhoon
drought	oil slick	victim
earthquake	oil spill	war
emergency	pestilence	wild fire
environmental destruction	plague	wreckage

Verbs

blow up	damage	freeze
blow down	destroy	injure
burn	devastate	massacre
bury	drown	rescue
collapse	evacuate	ruin
collide	explode	smash
crash	flatten	starve
crush	flood	suffocate

Idioms and Expressions

an act of God	better safe than sorry	death toll
any port in a storm	calm before the storm	loss of life

61: The Military and War

Nouns

aircraft carrier
air force
airplane
air defense
air raid
alliance
allies
armed forces
armor
armored division
armory
army
artillery
attack
battle
battleship
base
biological weapon
blackout
bomber
bomb
bomb blast
boot camp
briefing
brigade
bullet
bunker
cannon
casualty
cease fire
chain of command
chemical warfare
civil defence
cluster bomb
coalition
coast guard
collateral damage
command
cruiser
defeat
defense
depot
destroyer
disinformation

division
DMZ (demilitarized zone)
draft
field of battle
field command
field hospital
field promotion
fighter
fire storm
fleet
foot soldier
foxhole
germ warfare
grenade
guided missile
gun
headquarters
helicopter
humvee
IED (improvised explosive
     device)
infantry
intelligence
jeep
jet
logistical support
land mine
map room
marines
materiel
morale
mine
mine sweeper
missile
national alert
national guard
navy
offense
offensive
officer
peace
peacekeeper
personnel
planning session

platoon
poison gas
propaganda
promotion
reconnaissance
radioactive cloud
recruit
regiment
reserves
retreat
rocket
seabees (CB - Construction
     Battalion)
seal
shell
smart bomb
special operations
squad
staff
stealth bomber
strategy
submarine
suicide bomber
superior officer
surrender
tactics
tank
target
target practice
terrorist cell
torpedo
training camp
transport
trench
victory
volunteer
volunteer army
warfare
war games
weapon
weaponry
WMD
     (weapon of mass destruction)

People

admiral	deserter	lieutenant	petty officer
bombardier	draft dodger	liaison	private
canine officer	foot soldier	major	pilot
captain	general	marine	sailor
cavalry	G.I. (government	military adviser	sergeant
chaplain	issue)	military police (MP)	sharpshooter
chief of staff	guerrilla	navigator	sniper
colonel	gunner	officer	soldier
corporal	hostage		terrorist

Events and actions

advance	cut off	make war	sink
ambush	defeat	offensive	sortie
battle	deploy	order	skirmish
break through	dissent	overrun	surround
bombardment	infiltrate	retreat	strafe
casualty	interrogation	shell(ing)	torpedo
court-martial	invasion	shoot	wound

Peace

appeasement	defeat	peace conference	peace treaty
armistice	disengagement	peace initiative	reconciliation
cease fire	make peace	peacekeeping force	surrender
concessions	mediation	peacemaker	truce
conciliation	negotiation	peace settlement	United Nations
conscientious objector	pacification	peace talks	victory

Idioms and Expressions

All's fair in love and war.	marked man	under the gun
An army lives on its stomach.	MIA (missing in action)	USO
AWOL (absent without leave)	mutual assured destruction	War and Peace
balance of power	Nobel Peace Prize	war criminal
balance or terror	peace at any cost	the war to end all war
battle hardened	"peace in our time"	win the war but lose the peace
to bear arms	peace with honor	world war
camp follower	POW (prisoner of war)	yeoman service
concentration camp	to pull rank	Symbols:
Cowards die twice.	point blank	flags
deterrence	on the warpath	flags flown at half mast
Geneva Convention	R and R (rest and recreation)	flags in a graveyard
isolationist	scorched earth policy	hands raised over the head
4F	shell shock	white flag
a just and lasting peace	to stick to one's guns	red cross
a just war	turncoat	red poppy
make love, not war	to turn tail	yellow ribbon

62: Energy and Environment

Nouns

acid rain	extinction	oil spill
atomic wastes	filter	oil well
barrel of oil	fire	ozone
battery	fission	petroleum
catalytic converter	fossil fuel	pipeline
climate change	fuel	pollution
coal	fuel efficiency	power
combustion	fusion	propane
conservation	gas pump	reactor
consumable resources	gasoline, gas	recycling
consumption	gasoline taxes	refinery
dam	generator	regulations
deforestation	global warming	renewable energy sources
depletion	heat	resources
drilling rig	hydroelectric power	scrubbers
electricity	hydrogen power	smog
endangered species	insulation	smoke
energy costs	kinetic	solar power
energy efficiency	land fill	solar cell
energy (in)dependence	light	source
energy loss	mass transit	steam
energy taxes	motor	super conductors
engine	natural gas	tidal
environmentalist	nuclear power	turbine
environmental cleanup	nuclear reactor	utilities
environmental law	oil	waste management
environmental policy	oil drilling	water power
environmental science	oil field	wildcat operator
erosion	oil production	windmill
ethanol	oil slick	wind power

Adjectives

active	hydro-	petro-
chemical	mechanical	passive
electric(al)	nuclear	radioactive
extinct	offshore	solar
geothermal		wood-burning

Idioms and Expressions

to burn the candle at both ends	gas guzzler	sustainable growth
to carry coals to Newcastle	greenhouse effect	OPEC
energy czar	to hold a candle to	R factor
environmental catastrophe	limits to growth	unbridled consumption
environmental impact statement	population bomb	Where there's smoke there's fire.

63: Death

Nouns

ashes
autopsy
body
burial
cadaver
capital punishment
casket
catacomb
cemetery
churchyard
coffin
coroner
corpse
cremation
crypt
(the) deceased
(the) dead
death

demise
dissection
doctor-assisted suicide
effigy
elegy
epitaph
eulogy
euphemism
euthanasia
fatal illness
funeral
funeral director
funeral home
funeral parlor
funeral procession
grave
grave digger
graveside

gravestone
graveyard
hospice care
inscription
lamentation
last rites
last words
mausoleum
medical examiner
memorial
memorial contribution
memorial service
mercy killing
moaning
monument
morgue
mortician
mortuary

mourner
mourning
murder
necropolis
obituary
pall bearer
pit
plot
(the) remains
sepulcher
suicide
tomb
undertaker
urn
vault
wake
widow
widower

Verbs

bereave
bury

cremate
die

elegize
eulogize

expire
grieve

inter
mourn

Idioms and Expressions

ashes to ashes, dust to dust
to cash in one's chips
cause of death
deader than a door nail
dearly departed

to give up the ghost
in deep mourning
Irish wake
to kick the bucket
to pass away

open-casket funeral
living will
right to die
to wake the dead
RIP (rest in peace)

Of the Living Dead

ashen
apparition
to appall
banshee
bat
body snatcher
black magic
cadaverous
to conjure
demon
devil, Satan
dreadful

evil spirit
fiend
frightful
gallows
ghastly
ghost
ghost story
ghoul
gibbet
glimmer
gloom
goblin

gore
grave robber
grisly
hangman
to haunt
hell fire
hideous
horrible
horror story
loathsome
mummy
murmuring

necromancer
night walker
pact with the
    devil
pallid
phantom
resurrectionist
revolting
sorcery
seance
shade
specter

spell
spider web
spirit
spook
spooky
terrifying
undead
vampire
voodoo
werewolf
wolfman
wraith
zombie

Communicative Functions

T he sub-aspect of Communicative Functions is similar to a notional-functional syllabus. However, we have used the term communicative function to focus on the how and why of the communicative exchange. To relate this sub-aspect to the Situations and Topics, we can say that the Situation is concerned with the "where" of the exchange, the Topic the "what" and the Function the "how" and "why."

To organize the various communicative functions in some useful way, we have presented them as a kind of syllabus/check list. We have used as a sequential basis, four levels of language sophistication. These levels represent a transition from beginning language student to fully functioning bilingual person. These four levels are:

- ❏ Level 1 **Surviving** (Beginner)   161
- ❏ Level 2 **Adjusting; Settling In** (Advanced beginner)   162
- ❏ Level 3 **Participating** (Intermediate)   163
- ❏ Level 4 **Integrating** (Advanced)   164

Within each level we have organized the functions into general types as described below:

    A. **Basic Needs.** Using the language to satisfy basic physical requirements of food, shelter, and clothing.

    B. **Socializing.** Using the language to make social links with native speakers. At its lowest level it satisfies basic emotional needs.

    C. **Metalinguistic.** Using the language to deal with the language. This includes certain fundamental linguistic labels (noun, etc.) and tactics and strategies for managing communication (paraphrasing, interrupting, clarifying, etc.).

    D. **Professional.** Using the language to make a living.

    E. **Cultural.** Using the language to deal with the social and cultural milieu.

Level 1: Surviving

(Beginner)

A. Basic Needs

❑ 1. Respond physically to simple instructions such as **give, take, stand, sit, open, close, pick up, put down, put on, take off**, etc.

❑ 2. Give another person simple instructions to perform the actions above.

❑ 3. Give and understand basic warnings such as **Look out! Stop! Freeze!**

❑ 4. State basic wants and needs.

❑ 5. Request and comprehend simple information.

❑ 6. Ask for and respond to simple street directions and give simpe directions to a taxi driver.

❑ 7. Ask for assistance.

❑ 8. Get someone's attention and also use appropriate gestures.

❑ 9. Buy a small item.

❑ 10. Use a menu and order something to eat and drink.

B. Socializing

❑ 1. Greet others.

❑ 2. Take leave of another person or a group of people.

❑ 3. Arrange to meet someone.

❑ 4. Introduce yourself.

❑ 5. Identify yourself. (**I'm a ___**)

❑ 6. Use ritual apologies.

❑ 7. Reject unwanted attention firmly and simply.

❑ 8. Agree.

❑ 9. Express thanks.

❑ 10. State and comprehend simple biographical and family information.

C. Metalinguistic

❑ 1. Use and identify basic numbers.

❑ 2. Ask and tell time.

❑ 3. Use simple time expressions such as **today, yesterday, tomorrow morning, noon.**

❑ 4. Use and comprehend days of the week, months, and ways of expressing dates.

❑ 5. Control a conversation with simple phrases such as **speak slowly, please, or please repeat that.**

❑ 6. Identify and label the environment. (**What's that? It's a ___**)

❑ 7. Decipher simple signs and notices.

❑ 8. Use appropriate basic gestures.

Level 2: Adjusting; Settling In
(Advanced Beginner)

A. Basic Needs

❑ 1. State plans for the future.

❑ 2. Ask to borrow something.

❑ 3. Respond to a loan request.

❑ 4. Complain mildly.

❑ 5. Ask about the purpose of something.

❑ 6. Purchase household objects, equipment and clothing.

❑ 7. Make travel arrangements.

❑ 8. Describe a physical health problem.

❑ 9. Carry out a limited financial transaction such as cashing a check.

❑10. Fill out life forms such as a credit card application, a work permit, a school registration.

B. Socializing

❑ 1. Introduce another person.

❑ 2. Make small talk.

❑ 3. Share simple likes and dislikes.

❑ 4. Issue an invitation.

❑ 5. Decline an invitation.

❑ 6. Visit.

❑ 7. Entertain a visitor.

❑ 8. Play simple games/sports.

❑ 9. Recount past events.

❑10. Express basic emotions.

❑11. Apologize for a specific error.

❑12. Request and give permission to do something.

❑13. Compliment another person.

❑14. Accept a compliment.

❑15. Explain personal plans.

❑16. Express a personal opinion.

❑17. Express doubt.

❑18. Express irritation.

❑19. Express disappointment.

C. Metalinguistic

❑ 1. Clarify misunderstandings.

❑ 2. Use simple interjections.

❑ 3. Make a basic phone call.

❑ 4. Perform arithmetic operations aloud.

❑ 5. Spell words aloud.

❑ 6. Comprehend ads and announcements on radio and TV.

❑ 7. Read advertisements.

❑ 8. Read short notices, time tables, menus, etc.

❑ 9. Take simple dictation.

❑10. Write short informational notes.

D. Professional

❑ 1. Describe one's job.

❑ 2. Describe one's profession in general terms.

❑ 3. Explain professional objectives.

❑ 4. Express a basic professional opinion..

E. Cultural

❑ 1. Follow or sing-along with popular songs and/or folk songs.

❑ 2. Identify folk tale characters and national heroes.

❑ 3. Make general cultural comparisons in these areas:

❑ etiquette

❑ mealtimes

❑ kinship terms

❑ housing

❑ cooking

❑ gift-giving

❑ holidays and festivals

162

Level 3: Participating
(Intermediate)

A. Basic Needs

- ❑ 1. Ask for favors.
- ❑ 2. Grant favors.
- ❑ 3. Sell a personal possession.
- ❑ 4. Make arrangements with household help.
- ❑ 5. Arrange for repairs and service (household; automotive).
- ❑ 6. Make substantial purchases such as a TV or refrigerator.
- ❑ 7. Apply for specific status (insurance, citizenship, etc.)
- ❑ 8. Retrieve a borrowed item.
- ❑ 9. Dispute a bill.

B. Socializing

- ❑ 1. Plan a social event.
- ❑ 2. Attend a recreational event.
- ❑ 3. Discuss current events.
- ❑ 4. Comment on sports events.
- ❑ 5. Avoid commitments.
- ❑ 6. Sympathize.
- ❑ 7. Share personal hopes and dreams.
- ❑ 8. Tell an anecdote.
- ❑ 9. Understand jokes.
- ❑ 10. Give personal advice.
- ❑ 11. Disagree tactfully.
- ❑ 12. Ask for forgiveness.
- ❑ 13. Make an excuse.

C. Metalinguistic

- ❑ 1. Understand radio and TV news.
- ❑ 2. Break social contact with appropriate mannerisms,
- ❑ 3. Summarize.
- ❑ 4. Ask for definitions.
- ❑ 5. Make a complicated telephone call.
- ❑ 6. Translate for a new-comer.
- ❑ 7. Swear.
- ❑ 8. Use verbal gestures such as **uh-uh, hm, well, huh?**
- ❑ 9. Read newspapers.
- ❑ 10. Read professional material.
- ❑ 11. Read magazine articles.
- ❑ 12. Write social notes and letters.
- ❑ 13. Write professional reports.

D. Professional

- ❑ 1. Allow or not allow another's requests.
- ❑ 2. Give professional advice.
- ❑ 3. Give detailed instructions and explanations.
- ❑ 4. Evaluate.
- ❑ 5. Give short talks/speeches on professional matters.

E. Cultural

- ❑ 1. Explain institutions of native country.
- ❑ 2. Compare major cultural differences.
- ❑ 3. Discuss major aspects of host culture, including:

- ❑ courtship
- ❑ marriage
- ❑ sex
- ❑ family
- ❑ racial and ethnic groups
- ❑ government
- ❑ religion
- ❑ death
- ❑ mourning
- ❑ funerals
- ❑ education
- ❑ superstitions
- ❑ folklore
- ❑ hospitality
- ❑ humor

Level 4: Integrating
(Advanced)

A. Basic Needs

❑ 1. Act in emergencies.

B. Socializing

❑ 1. Share secrets.
❑ 2. Flirt.
❑ 3. Speak of personal accomplishments.
❑ 4. Tease.
❑ 5. Break off a relationship.
❑ 6. Counsel.
❑ 7. Praise.

❑ 8. Flatter.
❑ 9. Insult.
❑ 10. Plead.
❑ 11. Soften the truth.
❑ 12. Chastise another person.
❑ 13. Threaten.
❑ 14. Tell jokes.

C. Metalinguistic

❑ 1. Interpret and translate.
❑ 2. Paraphrase.
❑ 3. Play word games such as crossword puzzles.

❑ 4. Use source materials such as the Oxford English Dictionary.
❑ 5. Read books.
❑ 6. Write letters to the editor.

D. Professional

❑ 1. Debate ideas.
❑ 2. Negotiate.

❑ 3. Give professional direction.
❑ 4. Exercise leadership.

E. Cultural

❑ 1. Take and defend a stand on a current national issue.

❑ 2. Discuss, study, and critique the following aspects of the culture:
❑   arts
❑   law
❑   attitudes toward animals and nature
❑   community organization
❑   residence rules
❑   property rights
❑   status differentiation
❑   social mobility
❑   ethics

The Cultural Aspect

Language and culture are intertwined. In the previous section on the communicative aspect, North American culture makes its presence felt, especially in the lists of communicative situations and topics. To a lesser extent, communicative functions are also modified by culture. Ways of expressing thanks or extending invitations can be quite different in the English typical of Toronto, Los Angeles, Boston, or Bombay.

Because we have already listed communicative situations, topics, and functions in Part II, we will not repeat those lists here. Instead we will present cultural information that does not fit under these categories.

In other, paralinguistic ways, notably in body language and gestures, culture also impinges on communication, but we will deal with that in Part V.

And then there are all the cultural practices (customs) that can only be hinted at in a book such as this. Rather than attempt to describe North American cultural practices, we will instead present a list of Cultural Common Denominators. This list can be used as a checklist by both teacher and student to see if these areas have been adequately explored in class.

In this part of The ESL Miscellany, we will attempt to deal with the huge body of information that is commonly known by most contemporary Americans and Canadians. For example, the foreigner, unaware that the New York Yankees is a baseball team, could easily be mystified by overhearing one American ask another, "How did the Yankees do last night?" or, even more mystified when they are invited to go watch the Blue Jays play.

Obviously, it takes years to learn everything there is to know about North American culture; it is even possible that some native speakers do not know who Babe Ruth was. The capsule summaries of selected areas of North American culture contained in this section are at best a starting point for discussion, research, explanation, and study. Once again our lists should be considered only guidelines.

Cultural Common Denominators*

Every culture has customs, traditions, practices, and beliefs associated with the following cultural items. Each item in the list represents an essay, if not an entire book, but we will do no more here than suggest that the list can be used as a guideline for an orientation to North American culture. Incidentally, the list can also serve as a checklist for a series of fascinating discussions of a cross-cultural nature.

- ❏ numerals
- ❏ calendar
- ❏ personal names
- ❏ greetings
- ❏ gestures
- ❏ etiquette
- ❏ mealtimes
- ❏ kinship nomenclature
- ❏ age-grading
- ❏ athletic sports
- ❏ games
- ❏ leisure activities
- ❏ music
- ❏ dancing
- ❏ feasting
- ❏ bodily adornment
- ❏ folklore
- ❏ luck superstitions
- ❏ cooking
- ❏ food and food taboos
- ❏ family
- ❏ marriage
- ❏ kin-groups
- ❏ housing
- ❏ hospitality
- ❏ visiting

- ❏ gift-giving
- ❏ friendship customs
- ❏ courting
- ❏ joking
- ❏ sexual restrictions
- ❏ incest
- ❏ taboos
- ❏ modesty in natural functions
- ❏ funeral rites
- ❏ mourning
- ❏ medicine
- ❏ education
- ❏ law
- ❏ land-use policies
- ❏ attitude toward animals
- ❏ community organization
- ❏ residence rules
- ❏ property rights
- ❏ status differentiation
- ❏ racial and ethnic groups
- ❏ mobility
- ❏ trade
- ❏ government
- ❏ patriotism
- ❏ religious practices

*Adapted from George P. Murdock, "The Common Denominators of Culture," in *The Science of Man in the World Crisis,* ed Ralph Linton, N.Y: Columbia University Press, 1945.

1: Immigration Statistics

U.S. Immigration by Countries (1820-2000)

Germany	7,176,070	Poland	770,080
Mexico	6,138,150	Norway	758,900
Italy	5,435,830	Vietnam	744,420
United Kingdom	5,271,020	Greece	730,660
Ireland	4,782,080	Africa	689,080
Canada	4,487,570	Jamaica	598,730
Former USSR	3,906,580	Japan	530,190
Austria	1,844,450	Portugal	524,180
Hungary	1,677,140	Turkey	450,540
Philippines	1,530,600	Colombia	423,850
Central America	1,346,540	Haiti	414,400
China	1,333,490	Hong Kong	412,010
Sweden	1,259,520	Netherlands	387,540
Cuba	918,032	Denmark	376,490
Dominican Republic	845,390	Switzerland	371,280
France	823,410	Spain	302,305
India	818,780	Oceania	260,470
Korea	806,410		

Immigration – Top 20 Countries 2005

1. Mexico	161,445	11. Canada	21,878
2. India	84,681	12. El Salvador	21,359
3. China	69,967	13. United Kingdom	19,800
4. Philippines	60,748	14. Jamaica	18,346
5. Cuba	36,261	15. Russia	18,083
6. Vietnam	32,784	16. Guatemala	16,825
7. Dominican Republic	27,504	17. Brazil	16,664
8. Korea	25,562	18. Peru	15,676
9. Colombia	25,571	19. Poland	15,352
10. Ukraine	22,761	20. Pakistan	14,926

All countries   1,122,373

2. Native Americans of North America
Largest Tribes in the United States (2000 census)

Cherokee	729,533	Potawatomi	25,595	Kiowa	12,242
Navajo	298,197	Yaqui	22,412	Shoshone	12,026
Choctaw	158,774	Tlingit-Haida	22,365	Pima	11,493
Sioux	153,360	Tohono O'odham	20,087	Yakima	10,851
Chippewa	149,669	Comanche	19,376	Ottawa	10,677
Apache	96,833	Alaska Athabascan	18,838	Ute	10,385
Blackfeet	85,750	Cheyenne	18,204	Menominee	9,840
Iroquois	80,822	Aleut	16,978	Colville	9,393
Pueblo	74,085	Delaware	16,341	Yuman	8,976
Creek	71,310	Osage	15,897	Houma	8,713
Lumbee	57,868	Puget Sound Salish	14,631	Cree	7,734
Eskimo	54,761	Paiute	13,352		
Chickasaw	38,351	Crow	13,394	All others	553,560
Seminole	27,431	Other Alaska	12,675	Total	4,119,301

Largest Indian Reservations in the United States (2000 census)

Navajo	175,228	Sealaska	15,055	Cheyenne-Arapaho	10,310
Cherokee	104,482	Pine Ridge	14,484	Tohono O'odham	9,794
Creek	77,253	Doyon	14,128	Osage	9,209
Lumbee	62,327	Kiowa-		Rosebud	9,165
Choctaw	39,984	Comanche-Apache	13,045	San Carlos	9,065
Cook Inlet	35,972	Fort Apache	11.854	Blackfeet	8,684
Chickasaw	32,372	Potawatomi-		Yakama	8,193
Calista	20,353	Shawnee	10,617	Turtle Mountain	8,043
Houma	15,305	Gila River	10,578	Flathead	7,883

Canada

There are 630 Indian groups in Canada; these are referred to as First Nations and Indian Bands. Other Aboriginal peoples are called Inuit (also called Eskimos) and Métis (people of mixed heritage). This table is based on the most recent, 1996, census:

	Indians/First Nations	Métis	Inuit	Total Aboriginal
Newfoundland	5,430	4,685	4,265	14,205
Prince Edward Island	825	120	15	950
Nova Scotia	11,340	860	210	12,380
New Brunswick	9,189	975	120	10,250
Quebec	47,600	16,075	8,300	71,415
Ontario	118,830	22,790	1,300	141,525
Manitoba	82,990	46,195	360	128,685
Saskatchewan	75,205	36,535	190	111,245
Alberta	72,645	50,745	795	122,840
British Columbia	113,315	26,750	815	139,655
Yukon	5,530	565	110	6,175
Northwest Territories*	11,400	3,895	24,600	39,690
Canada (total)	**554,290**	**210,190**	**41,080**	**799,010**

3: Population by Ethnic Identity

Note: The 2000 U.S. Census asked Americans to identify themselves by race, nationality, and ethnic origin; for the first time there was an option to choose more than one category. The following information shows how they identify themselves.

Racial and National Origin for the U.S. in 2000

Origin	Population	%	% of change since 1990
Total U.S. population	281,421,906	100.0%	13.2%
White *self-identified*	216,930,975	77.1%	8.6%
Black *only or in combination with other race(s)*	36,419,434	12.9%	21.5%
American Indian and Alaska Native	4,119,301	1.5%	110.3%
Asian	11,898,828	4.2%	72.2%
Native Hawaiian and other Pacific Islander	874,414	0.3%	139.5%
Other race	18,521,486	6.6%	88.9%
Two or more races	6,826,228	2.4%	
Hispanic *may be of any race*	35,305,818	12.5%	57.9%

Black and Hispanic State Populations

BLACK *only or in combination with other race(s)*

Rank	State	Population
1	New York	3,234,165
2	Texas	2,513,041
3	Georgia	2,493,057
4	Florida	2,471,730
5	California	2,393,425
6	Illinois	1,937,671
7	North Carolina	1,776,283
8	Maryland	1,525,036
9	Louisiana	1,474,613
10	Michigan	1,468,317

HISPANIC *may be of any race*

Rank	State	Population
1	California	10,966,556
2	Texas	6,669.666
3	New York	2,867,583
4	Florida	2,682,715
5	Illinois	1,530,262
6	Arizona	1,295,617
7	New Jersey	1,117,191
8	New Mexico	765,386
9	Colorado	735,601
10	Washington	441,509

Black Proportions of State Populations

Note: During the Civil War (1860-1864), 11 slave states seceded from the nation: Mississippi, South Carolina, Louisiana, Georgia, Alabama, North Carolina, Virginia, Arkansas, Tennessee, Florida, and Texas; four slave states remained in the Union: Maryland, Delaware, Missouri, and Kentucky.

Rank	State	Percentage	Rank	State	Percentage
1	Mississippi	36.6	11	New York	15.9
2	Louisiana	32.9	12	Arkansas	15.7
3	South Carolina	29.9	13	Illinois	15.1
4	Georgia	29.2	14	Florida	14.6
5	Maryland	28.2	15	Michigan	14.2
6	Alabama	26.3	16	New Jersey	13.6
7	North Carolina	22.1	17	Texas	11.5
8	Virginia	20.4	18	Ohio	11.5
9	Delaware	20.1	19	Missouri	11.2
10	Tennessee	16.8		**United States**	**12.9**

4: Major U.S. Cities

2005 Rank	2000 Rank	City	Population 2005	
1	1	New York, NY	8,143,200	
2	2	Los Angeles, CA	3,844,800	
3	3	Chicago, IL	2,842,500	
4	4	Houston, TX	2,016,600	
5	5	Philadelphia, PA	1,463,300	
6	6	Phoenix, AZ	1,461,600	
7	9	San Antonio, TX	1,256,500	
8	7	San Diego, CA	1,255,500	
9	8	Dallas, TX	1,213,800	
10	11	San Jose, CA	912,300	
11	10	Detroit, MI	886,700	
12	12	Indianapolis, IN	784,100	
13	14	Jacksonville, FL	782,600	
14	13	San Francisco, CA	739,400	
15	15	Columbus, OH	730,700	
16	16	Austin, TX	690,300	
17	18	Memphis, TN	672,300	
18	17	Baltimore, MD	635,800	
19	27	Fort Worth, TX	624,100	
20	26	Charlotte, NC	610,900	
21	23	El Paso, TX	598,600	
22	19	Milwaukee, WI	578,900	
23	24	Seattle, WA	573,900	
24	20	Boston, MA	559,000	
25	25	Denver, CO	557,900	
26		Louisville	556,400	
27	21	Washington, DC	550,500	
28	22	Nashville-Davidson, TN	549,100	
29	32	Las Vegas, NV	545,100	
30	28	Portland, OR	533,400	
31	29	Oklahoma City, OK	531,300	
32	30	Tucson, AZ	515,500	
33	35	Albuquerque, NM	494,200	
34	34	Long Beach, CA	474,000	
35	39	Atlanta, GA	470,700	
36	37	Fresno, CA	461,100	
37	40	Sacramento, CA	456,400	
38	31	New Orleans, LA	454,900*	*After the 8/2005
39	33	Cleveland, OH	452,200	hurricane, New
40	36	Kansas City, MO	445,000	Orleans reduced to
41	42	Mesa, AZ	442,800	c. 200,000. Popu-
42	38	Virginia Beach, VA	438,400	lation returning
43	44	Omaha, NE	414,500	slowly. *Wikipedia*
44	41	Oakland, CA	395,300	*estimate 2007*
45		Miami	386,400	

Source: U.S. Census estimate, 2005

5: States of the United States

Union*	State	Seats**	Capital	Union*	State	Seats**	Capital
1819	Alabama	9	Montgomery	1889	Montana	3	Helena
1959	Alaska	3	Juneau	1867	Nebraska	5	Lincoln
1912	Arizona	10	Phoenix	1864	Nevada	5	Carson City
1836	Arkansas	6	Little Rock	1788	New Hampshire	4	Concord
1850	California	55	Sacramento	1787	New Jersey	15	Trenton
1876	Colorado	9	Denver	1912	New Mexico	5	Santa Fe
1788	Connecticut	7	Hartford	1788	New York	31	Albany
1787	Delaware	3	Dover	1789	North Carolina	15	Raleigh
1845	Florida	27	Tallahassee	1889	North Dakota	3	Bismarck
1788	Georgia	15	Atlanta	1803	Ohio	20	Columbus
1959	Hawaii	4	Honolulu	1907	Oklahoma	7	Oklahoma City
1890	Idaho	4	Boise	1859	Oregon	7	Salem
1818	Illinois	21	Springfield	1787	Pennsylvania	21	Harrisburg
1816	Indiana	11	Indianapolis	1790	Rhode Island	4	Providence
1846	Iowa	7	Des Moines	1788	South Carolina	8	Columbia
1861	Kansas	6	Topeka	1889	South Dakota	3	Pierre
1792	Kentucky	8	Frankfort	1796	Tennessee	11	Nashville
1812	Louisiana	9	Baton Rouge	1845	Texas	34	Austin
1820	Maine	4	Augusta	1896	Utah	5	Salt Lake City
1788	Maryland	10	Annapolis	1791	Vermont	3	Montpelier
1788	Massachusetts	12	Boston	1788	Virginia	13	Richmond
1837	Michigan	17	Lansing	1889	Washington	11	Olympia
1858	Minnesota	10	St. Paul	1863	West Virginia	5	Charleston
1817	Mississippi	6	Jackson	1848	Wisconsin	10	Madison
1821	Missouri	11	Jefferson City	1890	Wyoming	3	Cheyenne
				1846	District of Columbia	1	

* The date the state entered the union. The original states (1787) are listed below.

** Seats in the House of Congress . Each state (except the District of Columbia) has 2 senators and at least one representative. The number of representatives is based on the population of the state as of the 2000 census. The total number of senators and representatives is also the number of votes the state may cast for the President of the U.S. (electoral votes). The District of Columbia has only one representative, but 3 electoral votes.

The Thirteen Original States

Connecticut	New Hampshire	Pennsylvania
Delaware	New Jersey	Rhode Island
Georgia	New York	South Carolina
Maryland	North Carolina	Virginia
Massachusetts		

These states were the original 13 British colonies that established the United States of America starting with the Declaration of Independence in 1776. The dates given for entering the union are the dates they ratified the constitution between 1787 and 1790. They were the only states until the independent Republic of Vermont joined the union as the fourteenth state in 1791.

State Ranking by Population (2005 estimate)

Rank	State	Population	Rank	State	Population
1	California	36,132,000	27	Oregon	3,641,000
2	Texas	22,860,000	28	Oklahoma	3,548,000
3	New York	19,255,000	29	Connecticut	3,510,000
4	Florida	17,790,000	30	Iowa	2,966,000
5	Illinois	12,763,000	31	Mississippi	2,921,000
6	Pennsylvania	12,430,000	32	Arkansas	2,749,000
7	Ohio	11,464,000	33	Kansas	2,744,000
8	Michigan	10,121,000	34	Utah	2,470,000
9	Georgia	9,073,000	35	Nevada	2,415,000
10	New Jersey	8,718,000	36	New Mexico	1,928,000
11	North Carolina	8,683,000	37	West Virginia	1,817,000
12	Virginia	7,567,000	38	Nebraska	1,759,000
13	Massachusetts	6,349,000	39	Idaho	1,429,000
14	Washington	6,288,000	40	Maine	1,321,000
15	Indiana	6,272,000	41	New Hampshire	1,310,000
16	Tennessee	5,963,000	42	Hawaii	1,275,000
17	Arizona	5,939,000	43	Rhode Island	1,076,000
18	Missouri	5,800,000	44	Montana	936,000
19	Maryland	5,600,000	45	Delaware	844,000
20	Wisconsin	5,536,000	46	South Dakota	776,000
21	Minnesota	5,133,000	47	Alaska	663,000
22	Colorado	4,665,000	48	North Dakota	637,000
23	Alabama	4,558,000	49	Vermont	623,000
24	Louisiana	4,524,000	50	District of Columbia*	551,000
25	South Carolina	4,235,000	51	Wyoming	509,000
26	Kentucky	4,173,000		*Not a state.*	

Associated Free States

Name	Capital	Population*	Organization
Guam	Agana	171,000	Self-governing territory
Puerto Rico	San Juan	3,927,200	Commonwealth
Virgin Islands	Charlotte Amalie	108,600	Self-governing territory
American Samoa	Pago Pago	57,800	Self-governing territory
Northern Mariana Islands	Chalan Kanoa	82,500	Commonwealth

*2005 estimates

Non Self-Governing Possessions

Name	Population
Baker, Howland and Jarvis Islands	Uninhabited
Johnston Atoll	Government personnel
Kingman Reef	Military personnel
Palmyra	Privately owned
Navassa	Uninhabited
Midway Islands	Government personnel
Wake Island	Civilian contractors

6: Provinces and Major Cities of Canada
Provinces and Territories by Population (estimates 10/1/2006)*

Rank	Province	Population	Date	Capital
1	Ontario	12,721,776	1867	Toronto
2	Quebec	7,669,100	1867	Quebec City
3	British Columbia	4,327,431	1871	Victoria
4	Alberta	3,413,464	1905	Edmonton
5	Manitoba	1,178,491	1870	Winnipeg
6	Saskatchewan	985,859	1905	Regina
7	Nova Scotia	934,427	1873	Halifax
8	New Brunswick	748,439	1873	Fredericton
9	Newfoundland including Labrador	508,955	1949	St. John's
10	Prince Edward Island	138,596	1873	Charlottetown
	Territory			
11	Northwest Territories	41,929	1867	Yellowknife
12	Yukon Territory	31,151	1867	Whitehorse
13	Nunavut	30,850	1999**	Iqaluit
	Canada (total)	32,730,213	1867	Ottawa, Ontario

*These estimates are based on the 2001 census adjusted by the government for net under-coverage. **On April 1, 1999, the Northwest Territories was split and the Nunavut Territory was created. The 1996 census showed 64,120 people in the Northwest Territories. The 1999 estimate of the population of Nunavut was 24,000, 85% of whom were Inuit (Esquimo). "Nunavut" means "Our Land" in the Inuit language.

Major Cities of Canada
(estimates 7/1/2004)*

Rank	City, Province	Population
1	Toronto, Ontario	5,202,300
2	Montreal, Quebec	3,607,200
3	Vancouver, BC	2,173,100
4	Ottawa, Ontario	1,145,500
5	Calgary, Alberta	1,037,100
6	Edmonton. Alberta	1,001,600
7	Quebec City, Quebec	710,800
8	Hamilton, Ontario	710,100
9	Winnipeg, Manitoba	702,400
10	London, Ontario	459,600

Sources: Census/Statistics Canada website, www.statcan.ca 2007
CityPopulation.de/Canada.html 2005

7: Government Structure of the U.S.

also see #41 Constitution

There are three basic levels of government: local, state, and federal (national). At each level, there are three, independent branches: the legislative, the executive, and the judicial. Because each branch is independent, it can check and balance (control) the authority of the other branches. This is called the balance of powers.

The United States is a democracy; it is controlled by its citizens. As Abraham Lincoln said, it is a "government of the people, by the people, and for the people." The United States is also a republic, to be specific, a democratic republic. This means that its laws are made and administered by representatives elected by the people. (In this sense, the President, senators, and even local mayors are representatives.)

The only governments in the U.S. run directly by the people (pure democracies) are those of small towns, like those in New England, which make all basic decisions in Town Meetings, and even in those towns elected volunteers (selectpersons) run the town between Town Meetings.

Federal Government

The structure and function of the federal government are established and limited by the Constitution of the United States and its twenty-six amendments. The responsibilities of the federal government are for the common defense and the general welfare of the citizens, for the regulation of interstate commerce, and for relations with other countries and between the states. All powers not specifically given to the federal government by the Constitution or prohibited by the Bill of Rights (the first ten amendments) are left to the states.

How laws are made and used: The executive branch can suggest laws to the congress (the legislative branch) or the congress can originate laws. Laws authorizing the government to tax or spend money are written by the House of Representatives. All laws must be passed by both houses of congress and signed by the President. If the President will not sign (vetoes) a law, the congress can vote to override the veto.

The executive branch uses the laws made by congress; it spends the government's money and runs most of the functions of government following the instructions (laws) passed by congress, and it makes the people obey the law (enforces the law).

When people or the government are accused of breaking the law, the courts (the judiciary branch) judge whether the law has been broken and what the government should do if it has been. The courts interpret the laws made by congress, but they also base their decisions on previous decisions made by the courts. Under this system (called "common law"), the courts make decisions which function as new laws.

Legislative Branch

The Congress of the U.S. has two houses (a bicameral structure). The congress makes laws, advises the President, and must consent (agree with) his appointments and certain of his decisions such as treaties with other countries and declarations of war.

U.S. Senate: There are 100 senators, two from each state, elected directly by popular vote to serve six-year terms. Each senator has their own office and staff.

Officers: President of the Senate (the Vice President of the U.S.), President Pro Tempore, Majority Leader and Whip, Minority Leader and Whip.
Annual salary of a senator: $162,100.

U.S. House of Representatives: There are 435 Representatives, apportioned to the states based on the size of each state's population, elected directly by popular vote to serve two-year terms. Each representative has their own office and staff.
Officers: Speaker of the House, Majority Leader and Whip, Minority Leader and Whip.
Annual salary of a representative: $162,100

Major Offices of the Congress:
• General Accounting Office
• Government Printing Office
• Office of Technology Assessment
• Congressional Budget Office
• Library of Congress

Executive Branch

President: The President is the Chief Executive Officer of the federal government and Commander-in-Chief of the Armed Forces. He or she serves a four-year term. No president can be elected for more than two, four-year terms.

Annual salary of the President: $400,000 plus expenses.

The President is the head of the administration. The administration runs the government. The White House staff and the President's Cabinet work directly for the President. They are all political appointees; most of these appointments are then sent to the congress for its advice and consent (approval). The staff advises the President and does his planning and office work. The cabinet advises the President and runs the many departments and agencies of the federal government.

Election of the President: People who want to become President usually try to become the nominees of one of the two major political parties. They run in the primary elections held in some of the states. In these primaries, delegates to each party's national convention are elected by direct popular vote. In some states, the parties choose their delegates in political caucuses. At the national conventions, the delegates elect the man or woman who will be the nominee of their party.

During the presidential campaign, the two major party candidates and sometimes candidates representing minor, third parties or independent candidates try to win the support of the majority of voters in each state. No third party has won the presidency since the new Republican Party won its first election under Abraham Lincoln in 1860.

In the general election in November, the voters in each state elect electors to represent their state in the electoral college; these electors vote for the candidate who won the election in their state. Each state has as many electors (the electoral vote) as it has senators and representatives, which gives smaller states some extra influence. The candidate who wins the greatest number of electoral votes becomes president; this is not necessarily the candidate who gets the greatest number of popular votes nationwide. The winner of the popular vote has failed to become president three times, in 1824, 1876, and 1888

Order of presidential succession: When a President dies or leaves office for any reason during his or her term, he or she is succeeded by the Vice President, Speaker of the House, President Pro Tempore of the Senate, Secretary of State.

The President (or Vice President) can be removed from office only by being impeached by the House of Representatives and convicted by the Senate presided over by the Chief Justice of the Supreme Court. The congress also has the power to impeach, convict, and remove from office federal judges and other civil officers.

Vice President: The Vice President is the successor to the President if he or she leaves office, a member of the President's Cabinet, and the President of the Senate. Recently, he has also been an adviser on most of the President's decisions.

Annual salary of the Vice President: $208,100 plus expenses.

Election of the Vice President: After he or she is elected by the national convention of his or her party, each presidential candidate chooses a running mate, a nominee for Vice President. After he or she is elected by the convention, the candidate joins the presidential ticket for the election campaign. The President and Vice President win the election together.

Other parts of the executive branch:

The Civil Service: Most employees of the federal government are not political appointees but civil servants who stay in the government from one administration to the next.

The Diplomatic Corps: The ambassador and delegation to the United Nations, other ambassadors, their staffs, and the rest of the diplomatic service are directed by the Secretary and Department of State.

Legal Services: All the departments and agencies of the federal government have lawyers. The Department of Justice under the Attorney General reviews and coordinates all laws proposed to the congress, enforces the law, and represents the executive branch in the courts. The FBI (Federal Bureau of Investigation) is part of this department.

The Military: The Army, the Navy and Marines, and the Air Force are under the direct command of the President through the Secretary of Defense and then the Chairman of the Joint Chiefs of Staff, who is the nation's top military officer.

Judicial Branch

General: The legal system in the U.S. is Common Law rather than Civil Law. Laws are written and enacted by the legislatures of the states and by congress, but the decisions of the courts in interpreting these laws are based on precedents (earlier court decisions). Court decisions function as new laws; the courts have a powerful influence on all levels of government.

Some judges at the state and local levels are elected for specific terms in some states. Federal judges are appointed by the President and confirmed with the advice and consent of the Senate. They all serve for life or until they choose to resign; this protects them from political influence.

Criminal Law: All people accused of breaking criminal law before the state or federal courts have the right to be tried by a jury of either six or twelve citizens who will decide if they are guilty or innocent. They are indicted (formally accused) by the government, sometimes by a grand jury of citizens. In court they are prosecuted by a government prosecutor and defended by their own lawyer or a public defender. If they are found guilty, they can appeal the decision of the jury or the judge to a higher court, a court of appeals. If the verdict is innocent, the government cannot appeal. The constitution says nobody can be tried twice for the same crime.

If a defendant does not appeal a guilty verdict, punishment is decided on by the judge following the penal code (penalty law). Sometimes the judge is advised by the jury; sometimes his or her choice of judgments is limited by a uniform sentencing law enacted by the legislature. The punishment is then administered by the justice department of the executive branch (the police and prison system). Punishments may be appealed to the Supreme Court if they may be cruel or unusual because such punishments are forbidden by the Constitution's Bill of Rights.

Civil Law: All forms of business and relations between people, companies, and states are regulated (ruled) by either criminal or civil law. Conflicts between people, etc., which do not involve criminal activity, are resolved by the courts using civil law. Juries are used in some cases; others are decided by a judge or a panel of judges.

Federal and State Jurisdictions: The federal courts have authority (jurisdiction) in all criminal and civil cases involving the federal government or law, federal officers, and other countries, their officers or their citizens. The federal courts also have authority in cases between states, between any state and a citizen of another state, or between citizens of different states. This includes most cases involving big businesses. All other cases are tried in the state courts.

The U.S. District Courts: These courts are the lowest level of the federal court system. Most cases involving federal law, both civil and criminal, begin at this level.

There are 91 district courts, at least one and sometimes several in each state and in the territories of Guam, Puerto Rico, and the Virgin Islands.

The U.S. Courts of Appeals: There are eleven Circuit Courts, each covering a multistate region, plus two special courts, one for the District of Columbia and one for temporary emergencies. Each court holds court in several places which make up a circuit. These Circuit Courts hear appeals brought to them from the lower district courts and cases involving federal regulatory agencies.

The U.S. Supreme Court: There are nine justices of the Supreme Court (one Chief Justice and eight Associate Justices). They are appointed by the President and confirmed with the advice and consent of the Senate. The justices serve for life unless they choose to retire or they are impeached by the House and convicted by the Senate.

Annual salary of the Chief Justice: $208,100;

Annual salary of the Associates Justices: $199,200.

The Supreme Court is the highest court of appeals; its main function is to decide whether decisions of the lower courts and laws passed by the states or federal government are constitutional (in accord or agreement with the Constitution and the Bill of Rights.) The Supreme Court also decides cases when there is a conflict between the laws of one state and another or the federal government. It chooses the cases it will hear from among cases appealed to it from the lower courts and cases involving challenges to state and federal laws.

Because the Supreme Court interprets the Constitution and either cancels or defines the meaning of laws based on its interpretations of the Constitution, it has a great influence on the way the laws of the country are used. From the beginning of U.S. history, the Supreme Court has often used its power to change the political and social development of the country.

State Governments

There are 50 states in the U.S. and 15 associated states and possessions in the Caribbean and Pacific. Each has its own government. Although their structures vary in many ways, each of these governments has three branches like the federal government. The following descriptions are generally true for most states.

LEGISLATIVE BRANCH: The legislative branch of each state has a bicameral (two-house) structure like the federal government. There is an upper house called the senate and a lower house called the house or assembly of representatives. The state legislatures make both civil and criminal laws for their states.

EXECUTIVE BRANCH: Each state has a governor and a lieutenant governor, who are elected by the people of the state. The structure and functions of the executive branch differ from state to state. Most states have a secretary of state, a treasurer, a comptroller and an attorney general.

JUDICLAL BRANCH: The highest court is called the appellate court, the court of appeals, or the supreme court. Below it are the superior and inferior courts, which in some states include all local and municipal courts.

Local Governments

There are many variations in the structures of local governments. The smallest government structures are villages. Towns are generally larger, and cities are larger still. The whole state is divided into counties. In some states, each county is divided into several townships, each containing several towns and villages. In other states, each county is divided into towns, which may have several villages, town centers, or hamlets in them. The open (unincorporated) countryside between villages is governed by the township (town) or the county.

LEGISLATIVE BRANCH: Villages, towns, and cities (municipalities) always have some form of legislative board, which is directly elected by the local citizens. In cities and large towns it is called the town or city council or the board of alderpersons. In smaller towns and villages, the town council is sometimes called the board of selectpersons. The local legislatures make regulations and spend local tax money. To help them plan for changes, they often appoint local zoning and planning boards.

In most municipalities, the school system is run by a local school board, which is also directly elected by the people. Sometimes there is a township school board.

EXECUTIVE BRANCH: The smallest towns are run by the selectpersons with the help of an elected town clerk or manager. In larger towns and cities there is always an independent town or city manager or mayor.

JUDICIAL BRANCH: Villages and small towns have elected justices of the peace or local town magistrates. Larger towns and cities have municipal courts. In some states, these are part of the state court system; in others, they are independent.

Other Organizations

There are other organizations which govern life in the United States, usually through political and financial influence.

POLITICAL PARTIES: There are two major political parties, the Democratic Party and the Republican Party. There are also many minor, special interest, and regional and local parties including the Libertarian Party, Socialist Party, Socialist Labor Party, Communist Party, and Socialist Workers Party. Individuals may also run for political office as independents (without party support).

Other Groups With Political Influence:
- Business and trade associations
- Chambers of commerce
- Professional organizations
- Labor unions
- Public service boards
- Civil rights organizations
- Political action committees
- Veteran's and Fraternal organizations
- Alumni associations
- Consumer and public interest groups
- Churches
- Other special interest groups

177

8: U.S. Departments and Agencies

Departments and The Cabinet

Note: Each department is headed by a member of the president's Cabinet, who is given the title of secretary, with the exception of the Department of Justice, which is headed by the attorney general. The vice president is also a member of the Cabinet.

Department of Agriculture
Department of Commerce
Department of Defense
Department of Education
Department of Energy
Department of Health and Human Services
Department of Housing and Urban Development
Department of Homeland Security
Department of Justice
Department of Labor
Department of State
Department of the Interior
Department of the Treasury
Department of Transportation
Department of Veterans' Affairs

White House Staff

Chief of Staff
Assistant to the President/Deputy Chief of Staff
Assistants to the president:
    Cabinet Secretary
    Communications
    Counsel to the President
    Deputy Counsel to the President
    Counselor to the President
    Special Counsel
    Domestic Policy Council
    Intergovernmental Affairs
    Legislative Affairs
    Management and Administration
    National AIDS Policy
    National Economic Policy
    National Security
    Presidential Personnel
    Press Secretary
    Political Affairs
    Public Liaison
    Staff Secretary
    Director of Scheduling
    Director of Speechwriting
    Chief of Staff to the First Lady
    Special Projects

Executive Agencies

Council of Economic Advisers (CEA)
Council on Environmental Quality
National Security Council (NSC)
Office of Administration
Office of Management and Budget (OMB)
Office of National Drug Control Policy
Office of Science and Technology Policy
U.S. Trade Representative

Major Independent Agencies

Central Intelligence Agency (CIA)
Commission on Civil Rights
Commodity Futures Trading Commission
Consumer Product Safety Commission
Corporation for National and Community Service
Environmental Protection Agency (EPA)
Equal Employment Opportunity Commission (EEOC)
Export-Import Bank of the U.S.
Farm Credit Administration
Federal Communications Commission (FCC)
Federal Deposit Insurance Commission (FDIC)
Federal Election Commission
Federal Maritime Commission
Federal Mediation and Conciliation Service (FMCS)
Federal Reserve System
Federal Trade Commission (FTC)
Foundation on the Arts and the Humanities
General Services Administration (GSA)
Inter-American Foundation
National Aeronautics and Space Administration (NASA)
National Archives and Records Administration
National Labor Relations Board (NLRB)
National Railroad Passenger Corporation (AMTRAK)
National Science Foundation
National Transportation Safety Board
Nuclear Regulatory Commission
Occupational Safety and Health Review Commission
Office of Personnel Management
Peace Corps
Securities and Exchange Commission (SEC)
Selective Service System (SSS)
Small Business Administration (SBA)
Social Security Administration (SSA)
Tennessee Valley Authority (TVA)
Trade and Development Agency
U.S. International Trade Commission
U.S. Postal Service (USPS)

9: Government Structure of Canada

There are three basic levels of government: local, state, and federal (national). Although the legislative, the executive, and the judicial functions are done at all levels, under a parliamentary system like Canada's the executive function is dependent on the legislature.

Canada is a democracy, controlled by its citizens. On the national level, it is a federation of provinces and territories. There are ten provinces: Alberta, British Columbia, Manitoba, New Brunswick, Newfoundland (including Labrador), Nova Scotia, Ontario, Prince Edward Island, Quebec, and Saskatchewan. There are three territories: the Northwest Territories, Nuvavut, and the Yukon.

On a less formal but politically very important basis, Canada is a federation of two peoples, one English speaking and the other French. The history of the union of these two peoples has been one of political strain. The nation as a whole is officially bilingual. Although the distinct French character of Quebec culture and society have always been recognized in Canada, the increasing population, prosperity, and political power of English speaking Canada have stimulated a seperatist movement in Quebec that has been a major political factor throughout the 1970's, '80's, and '90's.

On another level, Canada is a monarchy. This is important historically and today many Canadians are loyal to Elizabeth II as Queen of Canada, as well as Great Britain. She is officially Head of State. The Queen's representative in Canada is the Governor General.

Canada gained functional independence from Great Britain with the British North America Act of 1867. The Constitution Act of 1982 formally ended the colonial control of Canada by the British Parliament. The government of Canada was transferred under the Constitution to the Canadian people.

Federal Government

The Head of State is the Queen, represented by the Governor General. This is a ceremonial and advisory position. The real leader of the country is the Prime Minister, who is the leader of the majority party in the House of Commons. The Prime Minister and his cabinet are members of the Commons. They serve as the executive branch, advising the Governor General and running the civil service. The capital city of Canada is Ottawa, Ontario.

There are two houses of parliament, the Commons with 301 members and the Senate with 104. Members of the Commons are elected by the people in elections every five years or when the Prime Minister and his government are voted down in the Commons and they decide to call for an election. The Senators are appointed for terms ending with their 75th birthdays. Laws must be passed by both houses of the legislature and signed by the Governor General in the Queen's name.

Provincial Government

Each of the ten provincial governments is officially headed by a Lieutenant Governor, appointed by the federal government. This is a largely formal, symbolic position, like that of the Governor General on the federal level. The real executive head of each province is the Premier, the leader of the majority party in the provincial legislature.

These are single-house legislative bodies elected every four years . In eight of the provinces, the legislature is called the Legislative Assembly. In Newfoundland, which became a province in 1949, it is traditionally called the House of Assemblies, and in Quebec it is significantly called the National Assembly.

179

10: U.S. Presidents

1. George Washington
(1732-1799)
Party: Federalist
Term: 1789-1797
Birthplace: Virginia

2. John Adams
(1735-1826)
Party: Federalist
Term: 1797-1801
Birthplace: Massachusetts

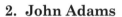

3. Thomas Jefferson
(1743-1826)
Party: Democratic-Republican
Term: 1801-1809
Birthplace: Virginia

4. James Madison
(1751-1836)
Party: Democratic-Republican
Term: 1809-1817
Birthplace: Virginia

5. James Monroe
(1758-1831)
Party: Democratic-Republican
Term: 1817-1825
Birthplace: Virginia

6. John Quincy Adams
(1767-1848)
Party: Democratic-Republican
Term: 1825-1829
Birthplace: Massachusetts

7. Andrew Jackson
(1767-1845)
Party: Democratic
Term: 1829-1837
Birthplace: South Carolina

8. Martin Van Buren
(1782-1862)
Party: Democratic
Term: 1837-1841
Birthplace: New York

9. William Harrison
(1773-1841)
Party: Whig
Term: 1841 *
Birthplace: Virginia

10. John Tyler
(1790-1862)
Party: Whig
Term: 1841-1845
Birthplace: Virginia

11. James Polk
(1795-1849)
Party: Democratic
Term: 1845-1849
Birthplace: North Carolina

12. Zachary Taylor
(1784-1850)
Party: Whig
Term: 1849-1850 *
Birthplace: Virginia

13. Millard Fillmore
(1800-1874)
Party: Whig
Term: 1850-1853
Birthplace: New York

14. Franklin Pierce
(1804-1869)
Party: Democratic
Term: 1853-1857
Birthplace: New Hampshire

15. James Buchanan
(1791-1868)
Party: Democratic
Term: 1857-1861
Birthplace: Pennsylvania

16. Abraham Lincoln
(1809-1865)
Party: Republican
Term: 1861-1865 **
Birthplace: Kentucky

Died in office
*** Assassinated in office*
§ Resigned from office

17. Andrew Johnson
(1808-1875)
Party: Union
Term: 1865-1869
Birthplace: North Carolina

18. Ulysses S. Grant
(1822-1885)
Party: Republican
Term: 1869-1877
Birthplace: Ohio

19. Rutherford B. Hayes
(1822-1893)
Party: Republican
Term: 1877-1881
Birthplace: Ohio

20. James Garfield
(1831-1881)
Party: Republican
Term: 1881 **
Birthplace: Ohio

21. Chester Arthur
(1829-1886)
Party: Republican
Term: 1881-1885
Birthplace: Vermont

22. Grover Cleveland
(1837-1908)
Party: Democratic
Term: 1885-1889
Birthplace: New Jersey

23. Benjamin Harrison
(1833-1901)
Party: Republican
Term: 1889-1893
Birthplace: Ohio

24. Grover Cleveland
(second nonconsecutive term)
Term: 1893-1897

25. William McKinley
(1843-1901)
Party: Republican
Term: 1897-1901 **
Birthplace: Ohio

26. Theodore Roosevelt
(1858-1919)
Party: Republican
Term: 1901-1909
Birthplace: New York

27. William Taft
(1857-1930)
Party: Republican
Term: 1909-1913
Birthplace: Ohio

28. Woodrow Wilson
(1856-1924)
Party: Democratic
Term: 1913-1921
Birthplace: Virginia

29. Warren Harding
(1865-1923)
Party: Republican
Term: 1921-1923 *
Birthplace: Ohio

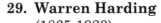

30. Calvin Coolidge
(1872-1933)
Party: Republican
Term: 1923-1929
Birthplace: Vermont

31. Herbert Hoover
(1874-1964)
Party: Republican
Term: 1929-1933
Birthplace: Iowa

32. Franklin D. Roosevelt
(1882-1945)
Party: Democratic
Term: 1933-1945 *
Birthplace: New York

33. Harry S. Truman
(1884-1972)
Party: Democratic
Term: 1945-1953
Birthplace: Missouri

34. Dwight D. Eisenhower
(1890- 1969)
Party: Republican
Term: 1953-1961
Birthplace: Texas

35. John F. Kennedy
(1917-1963)
Party: Democratic
Term: 1961-1963 **
Birthplace: Massachusetts

36. Lyndon B. Johnson
(1908-1973)
Party: Democratic
Term: 1963-1969
Birthplace: Texas

37. Richard Nixon
(1913- 1994)
Party: Republican
Term: 1969-1974 §
Birthplace: California

38. Gerald Ford
(1913-2006)
Party: Republican
Term: 1974-1977
Birthplace: Nebraska

39. Jimmy Carter
(1924-)
Party: Democratic
Term: 1977-1981
Birthplace: Georgia

40. Ronald Reagan
(1911-2004)
Party: Republican
Term: 1981-1989
Birthplace: Illinois

41. George Bush
(1924-)
Party: Republican
Term: 1989 - 1993
Birthplace: Massachusetts

42.   Bill Clinton
(1946-)
Party: Democrat
Term: 1993 - 2001
Birthplace: Arkansas

43. George W. Bush
(1946-)
Party: Republican
Term: 2001-2009
Birthplace: Connecticut

11: Canadian Governors General, Prime Ministers

Term	Governor General	Term	Prime Minister, Party
1867-1868	Viscount Monck	1867-1873	Sir John A. Macdonald, Conservative
1869-1872	Baron Lisgar	1873-1878	Alexander Mackenzie, Liberal
1872-1878	Earl of Dufferin	1878-1891	Sir John A. Macdonald, Conservative
1878-1883	Marquess of Lome	1891-1892	Sir John J. C. Abbott, Conservative
1883-1888	Marquess of Lansdowne	1892-1894	Sir John S. D. Thompson, Conservative
188-1893	Baron Stanley of Preston	1894-1896	Sir Mackenzie Bowell, Conservative
1893-1898	Earl of Aberdeen	1896	Sir Charles Tupper, Conservative
1898-1904	Earl of Minto	1896-1911	Sir Wilfrid Laurier, Liberal
1904-1911	Earl Grey	1911-1917	Sir Robert Borden, Conservative
1911-1916	Duke of Connaught	1917-1920	Sir Robert Borden, Unionist
1916-1921	Duke of Devonshire	1920-1921	Arthur Meighen, Unionist
1921-1926	Baron Byng of Vimy	1921-1926	W. L. Mackenzie King, Liberal
1926-1931	Viscount Willingdon	1926	Arthur Meighen, Conservative
1931-1935	Earl of Bessborough	1926-1930	W. L. Mackenzie King, Liberal
1935-1940	Baron Tweedsmuir	1930-1935	Richard B. Bennett, Conservative
1940-1948	Earl of Athlone	1935-1948	W. L. Mackenzie King, Liberal
1948-1952	Viscount Alexander	1948-1957	Louis S. St. Laurent, Liberal
1952-1959	Viscount Massey	1957-1963	John G. Diefenbaker, Conservative
1959-1967	Georges P. Vanier	1963-1968	Lester B. Pearson, Liberal
1967-1973	Roland Michener	1968-1979	Pierre Elliott Trudeau, Liberal
1974-1979	Jules Léger	1979-1980	Charles Joseph Clark, Conservative
1979-1984	Edward R. Schreyer	1980-1984	Pierre Elliott Trudeau, Liberal
1984-1990	Jeanne Sauvé	1984	John Turner, Liberal
1990-1995	Raymond John Hnatyshyn	1984-1993	Brian Mulroney, Conservative
1995-1999	Roméo LeBlanc	1993	Kim Campbell, Conservative
1999-2005	Adrienne Clarkson	1993-2003	Jean Chrétien, Liberal
2005-	Michäelle Jean	2003-2006	Paul Martin, Liberal
		2006-	Stephen Harper, Conservative

12: U.S. Industries

Largest U.S. Corporations (2005)

Rank	Company	Revenue
1	Exxon Mobil	$339,938,000,000
2	Wal-Mart Stores	315,654,000,000
3	General Motors	192,604,000,000
4	Chevron (petroleum)	189,481,000,000
5	Ford Motor	177,210,000,000
6	ConocoPhillips	166,683,000,000
7	General Electric	157,153,000,000
8	Citigroup	131,045,000,000
9	AIG (insurance)	108,905,000,000
10	IBM (business machines)	91,134,000,000
11	Hewlett-Packard (computers)	86,696,000,000
12	Bank of America	83,980,000,000
13	Berkshire Hathaway (insurance, etc.)	81,663,000,000
14	Home Depot	81,511,000,000
15	Valero Energy	81,362,000,000
16	McKesson (health care services)	80,514.600,000
17	J.P. Morgan Chase & co.	79,902,000,000
18	Verizon Communications	75,111,900,000
19	Cardinal Health	74,915,100,000
20	Altria Group (Kraft Food; Philip Morris Tobacco)	69,148,000,000
21	Kroger (Retail Food)	60,552,900,000
22	State Farm Insurance	59,223,900,000
23	Marathon Oil	58,958,000,000
24	Procter & Gamble (toiletries)	56,741,000,000
25	Dell (computers)	55,908,000,000

Fastest–Growing Franchises (2003)

1 Subway (sandwiches and salads)

2 Curves (women's fitness and weight loss clinics)

3 Quizno's (sandwiches, soups, salads)

4 7-Eleven (convenience stores)

5 Jackson Hewitt (tax preparation services)

6 The UPS Store

    (postal, business, communication services)

7 McDonald's (hamburgers, etc)

8 Jani-King (commercial cleaning)

9 Dunkin' Donuts (donuts, baked goods, coffee)

10 Baskin-Robbins (ice cream & yoghurt)

11 Jiffy Lube (fast oil change)

12 Intercontinental Hotels

13 Sonic Drive-in Restaurants

14 Domino's Pizza

15 Super 8 Motels

16 Kumon Math & Reading Centers

17 Chem-Dry (carpet, etc. cleaning)

18 ServiceMaster Clean

19 RE/MAX (real estate)

20 Snap-on Tools

21 Burger King (hamburgers, etc.)

22 Jan-Pro Franchising (commercial cleaning)

23 Merle Norman Cosmetics

24 Papa John's (pizza)

25 Jazzercise (dance/exercise classes)

186

13: Some Famous Americans

Before 1812

Adams, Samuel	(1722-1803)	Patriot, Boston Tea Party firebrand
Allen, Ethan	(1738-1789)	Leader of the Green Mountain Boys
Arnold, Benedict	(1741 -1801)	Treasonous Revolutionary War general
Attucks, Crispus	(c.1723-1770)	Led group that began the Boston Massacre in 1770
Boone, Daniel	(1734-1820)	Frontiersman
Clark, William	(1770-1838)	Explored the northwest with Lewis in 1804
Crockett, Davy	(1786-1836)	Frontiersman, died at the Alamo
Franklin, Benjamin	(1706-1790)	Writer, statesman, scientist
Hale, Nathan	(1755-1776)	Revolutionary War officer
Hamilton, Alexander	(1755-1894)	Statesman, author, first secretary of the treasury
Hancock, John	(1737-1793)	Statesman, Declaration of Independence signer
Henry, Patrick	(1736-1799)	Revolutionary war figure, orator
Jones, John Paul	(1747-1792)	Naval hero
LaSalle, Sieur de (R.C.)	(1643-1687)	Explored and claimed Mississippi Basin for France
Lewis, Meriwether	(1774-1809)	Explored the northwest with Clark in 1804
Pilgrims		Founded Plymouth Plantation Colony in 1720
Pocahontas	(c. 1595-1617)	Indian princess, saved explorer John Smith's life
Revere, Paul	(1735-1818)	Silversmith, hero of famous ride in 1775
Ross, Betsy	(1752-1836)	Designed and sewed first American flag
Sacagawea	(1784-1884)	Guided Lewis and Clark
Smith, Capt. John	(c. 1580-1631)	Led first colony (1607-9) in Jamestown, Virginia
Thomas Paine	(1737-1809)	Political philosopher
Turnbull, John	(1756-1843)	Historical themes painter
Whitney, Eli	(1765-1825)	Invented cotton gin and manufacture

1812-1865

Audubon, John James	(1785-1851)	Artist, ornithologist
Brown, John	(1800-1859)	Abolitionist
Carson, Kit	(1809-1868)	Scout
Clay, Henry	(1777-1852)	Political leader
Custer, George	(1839-1876)	Union general in Civil War, killed by Indians
Davis, Jefferson	(1808-1889)	President of the Confederacy
Douglass, Frederick	(1817-1895)	Author, diplomat, abolitionist
Emerson, Ralph Waldo	(1803-1882)	Philosopher, author, lecturer
Geronimo	(1829-1909)	Apache chieftain
Jackson, Thomas (Stonewall)	(1824-1863)	Confederate general in Civil War
Key, Francis Scott	(1779-1843)	Author of national anthem
Lee, Robert E.	(1807-1870)	Confederate general in Civil War
Sherman, William T.	(1820-1891)	Union general in Civil War
Sitting Bull	(1835-1890)	Dakota chief
Thoreau, Henry David	(1817-1862)	Philosopher, author, naturalist
Truth, Sojourner	(1797-1883)	Suffragette, abolitionist
Tubman, Harriet	(1820-1913)	Abolitionist, liberator
Webster, Daniel	(1782-1852)	Statesman
Webster, Noah	(1759-1843)	Lexicographer
Young, Brigham	(1801-1877)	Mormon leader, colonized Utah

1866-1916

Anthony, Susan B.	(1820-1906)	Suffragette
Barton, Clara	(1821 -1906)	Organizer of American Red Cross
Bell, Alexander Graham	(1847-1922)	Inventor of telephone, teacher of deaf
Buffalo Bill (William Cody)	(1846-1917)	Scout, showman
Carver, George Washington	(1861-1943)	Educator, botanist
Cassatt, Mary	(1845-1926)	Impressionist painter
Crazy Horse	(1849-1877)	Dakota war chief victorious at Little Bighorn
DuBois, W. E. B.	(1868-1963)	Historian, sociologist, founded NAACP
Edison, Thomas	(1847-1931)	Inventor of lightbulb, practical electric power
Ford, Henry	(1863-1947)	Industrialist, built first assembly-line cars
Homer, Winslow	(1836-1910)	Painter of marine themes
Liliuokalani, Lydia Kamekeha	(1838-1917)	Last monarch of Hawaii
Long, Huey	(1893-1935)	Politician
Peary, Adm. Robert E.	(1856-1920)	Explorer, first to reach North Pole 1909
Rockefeller, John D.	(1839-1937)	Established Standard Oil, philanthropist
Sargent, John Singer	(1856-1925)	Portrait artist
Washington, Booker T.	(1856-1915)	Educator
Wright, Orville	(1871 -1948)	Built first powered airplane with brother Wilbur

1917-1970

Bethune, Mary McLeod	(1875-1955)	Educator
Copland, Aaron	(1900-1990)	Composer
Cronkite, Walter	(1916-)	Television journalist
Disney, Walt	(1901-1966)	Film animator and producer
Earhart, Amelia	(1898-1937)	Aviatrix
Friedan, Betty	(1921 -)	Feminist, author
Goddard, Robert	(1882-1945)	Physicist, father of modern rocketry
Hearst, William Randolph	(1863-1951)	Publisher
Hopper, Edward	(1882-1967)	Painter of realistic urban scenes
Keller, Helen	(1880-1968)	Educator and writer
King Jr., The Rev. Dr. Martin Luther	(1929-1968)	Civil rights leader
MacArthur, Douglas	(1880-1964)	General in WW II, Korean War
Malcolm X	(1925-1965)	Civil rights leader
Marshall, Thurgood	(1908-1993)	Supreme Court justice, appointed 1967
McCarthy, Joseph	(1908-1957)	Anti-communist, politician
Moses, Grandma	(1860-1961)	Folk painter
O'Keeffe, Georgia	(1887-1986)	Painter of southwestern motifs
Oppenheimer, J. Robert	(1904-1967)	Physicist, father of atomic bomb
Patton, George S.	(1885-1945)	General in WW II
Pollock, Jackson	(1912-1956)	Abstract expressionist painter
Rockwell, Norman	(1894-1978)	Illustrator
Roosevelt, Eleanor	(1884-1962)	Humanitarian, UN delegate
Spock, Benjamin	(1903-1998)	Pediatrician
Steinem, Gloria	(1934-)	Feminist, author
Stevenson, Adlai	(1900-1965)	Statesman
Warhol, Andy	(1928-1989)	Pop artist
Wright, Frank Lloyd	(1867-1959)	Architect

1970-1985

Brokaw, Tom	(1940-)	Television news anchor
Brothers, Joyce	(1928-)	Psychologist
Brown, Helen Gurley	(1922-)	Publisher
Cesar Chavez	(1927-1993)	Union/civil rights activist
Child, Julia	(1912-2004)	Chef
Chung, Connie	(1946-)	Television journalist, anchor
Donaldson, Sam	(1934-)	Television journalist
Eisner, Michael	(1942-)	Chairman of Walt Disney
Falwell, Jerry	(1933-)	Televangelist
Graham, Billy	(1918-)	Evangelist, author
Graham, Katharine	(1917-2001)	Publisher of *Washington Post*
Hefner, Hugh	(1926-)	Publisher of *Playboy*
Iacocca, Lee	(1924-)	Chairman of Chrysler
Jackson, The Rev. Jesse	(1941-)	Civil Rights leader, politician
Jennings, Peter	(1938-2005)	Television news anchor
Klein, Calvin	(1942-)	Fashion designer
Landers, Ann	(1918-2002)	Advice columnist
Lauren, Ralph	(1939-)	Fashion designer
Nader, Ralph	(1934-)	Consumer advocate
O'Connor, Sandra Day	(1930-)	Supreme Court justice
Onassis, Jacqueline	(1929-1998)	Widow of John F. Kennedy
Pei, I.M.	(1917-)	Architect
Quinn, Jane Bryant	(1939-)	Economist
Rather, Dan	(1931-)	Television anchor
Ride, Sally K.	(1952-)	Astronaut
Sagan, Carl	(1934-1996)	Astronomer, author
Steinbrenner, George	(1930-)	Owner of the New York Yankees
Van Buren, Abigail	(1918-)	Advice columnist
Westheimer, Ruth	(1928-)	Sex therapist

1985-2006

Madeline Albright	(1937-)	Secretary of State
Neil Armstrong	(1930-)	Astronaut
Dick Cheney	(1925-)	Vice-President
Noam Chomsky	(1928-)	Linguist, political activist
Hillary Rodham Clinton	(1947-)	Senator
John Kenneth Galbraith	(1908-2006)	Economist
Bill Gates	(1955-)	Microsoft Chairman
John Glenn	(1921-)	Senator, astronaut
Rudi Giuliani	(1944-)	N.Y.C. Mayor
Edward Kennedy	(1932-)	Senator
Jack Kevorkian	(1928-)	Assisted suicide activist
Larry King	(1933-)	Talk show host
Henry Kissinger	(1923-)	Statesman
Estee Lauder	(1908-2004)	Cosmetics Line Founder
Rush Limbaugh	(1951-)	Radio talk show host
John McCain	(1936-)	Senator
Barack Obama	(1961-)	Senator
Colin Powell	(1937-)	General, Secretary of State
Condoleeza Rice	(1954-)	Secretary of State
Ted Turner	(1938-)	TV executive
Jody Williams	(1950-)	Nobel Prize winner

14: Entertainers

Name	Occupation	Dates
Affleck, Ben	Actor	(1972-)
Allen, Woody	Actor, director, screenwriter	(1935-)
Andrews, Julie	Actress	(1935-)
Armstrong, Louis	Jazz musician	(1900-1971)
Astaire, Fred	Actor, dancer	(1904-1983)
Baez, Joan	Singer	(1941-)
Balanchine, George	Choreographer	(1904-1983)
Ball, Lucille	Actress, comedienne	(1911-1989)
Barnum, P. T.	Circus master	(1810-1891)
Baryshnikov, Mikhail	Dancer, actor	(1948-)
Belafonte. Harry	Singer, actor	(1927-)
Bernstein, Leonard	Conductor, composer	(1918-1990)
Bogart, Humphrey	Actor	(1899-1957)
Brando, Marlon	Actor	(1924-2004)
Cage, Nicolas	Actor	(1964-)
Capra, Frank	Director	(1897-1991)
Carey, Mariah	Singer	(1970-)
Carson, Johnny	Comedian, TV entertainer	(1925-2005)
Cash, Johnny	Country musician	(1932-2003)
Charles, Ray	Blues & rock musician	(1930-2004)
Cher	Actress	(1946-)
Clark, Dick	TV entertainer	(1929-)
Close, Glenn	Actress	(1947-)
Cody, Buffalo Bill	Creator of wild west show	(1846-1917)
Como, Perry	Singer	(1912-2001)
Connery, Sean	Actor	(1930-)
Coppola, Francis Ford	Director	(1939-)
Cosby, Bill	Actor, comedian	(1937-)
Costner, Kevin	Actor, director	(1955-)
Crosby, Bing	Actor, singer	(1904-1977)
Cruise, Tom	Actor	(1962-)
Davis, Bette	Actress	(1908-1990)
Davis, Sammy Jr.	Actor, singer	(1925-1990)
De Niro, Robert	Actor	(1943-)
Denver, John	Singer	(1943-1997)
Dietrich, Marlene	Actress	(1901-1992)
Dillon, Matt	Actor	(1964-)
Disney, Walt	Director, cartoonist	(1901-1966)
Domino, Fats	Musician	(1928-)
Donahue, Phil	Talk show host	(1935-)
Douglas, Michael	Actor	(1944-)
Dunaway, Faye	Actress	(1941-)
Duvall, Robert	Actor	(1931-)
Dylan, Bob	Rock musician	(1941-)
Eastwood, Clint	Actor, director	(1930-)
Ellington, Duke	Composer, pianist, band leader	(1899-1974)
Feliciano, Jose	Singer, guitarist, song writer	(1945-)
Fiedler, Arthur	Conductor	(1894-1979)

Fields, W. C.	Actor, comedian	(1880-1946)
Fitzgerald, Ella	Jazz musician	(1918-1996)
Flynn, Errol	Actor	(1909-1959)
Fonda, Henry	Actor	(1905-1982)
Fonda, Jane	Actress	(1937-)
Fontaine, Joan	Actress	(1917-)
Ford, Harrison	Actor	(1942-)
Fosse, Bob	Director	(1927-1987)
Foster, Jodie	Actress	(1962-)
Franklin, Aretha	Soul and Gospel singer	(1942-)
Gable, Clark	Actor	(1901-1960)
Gabor, Zsa Zsa	Actress	(1917-)
Garbo, Greta	Actress	(1905-1990)
Garland, Judy	Actress	(1922-1969)
Gershwin, George	Composer	(1898-1937)
Gish, Lillian	Actress	(1896-1993)
Goldberg, Whoopi	Actress, commedienne	(1949-)
Griffin, Merv	Producer	(1925-)
Griffith, Andy	Actor	(1926-)
Guthrie, Woody	Folk singer	(1912-1967)
Hanks, Tom	Actor	(1956-)
Hayworth, Rita	Actress	(1918-1987)
Hendrix, Jimi	Rock musician	(1942-1970)
Henie, Sonja	Actress, skater	(1910-1969)
Hepburn, Audrey	Actress	(1929-1993)
Hepburn, Katharine	Actress	(1909-2003)
Heston, Charlton	Actor	(1923-)
Hines, Gregory	Actor, tap dancer	(1946-)
Hitchcock, Alfred	Director	(1899-1980)
Ho, Don	Singer	(1930-)
Hoffman, Dustin	Actor	(1937-)
Holiday, Billie	Blues singer	(1915-1959)
Hope, Bob	Comedian	(1903-2003)
Horne, Lena	Singer	(1917-)
Houdini, Harry	Magician	(1874-1926)
Huston, John	Director	(1906-1987)
Iglesias, Julio	Singer	(1943-)
Ives, Burl	Folk singer	(1909-1995)
Jackson, Michael	Rock musician	(1958-)
Jagger, Mick	Rock musician	(1943-)
John, Elton	Rock musician	(1947-)
Jolie, Angelina	Movie actress, model	(1975-)
Jones, James Earl	Actor	(1931-)
Joplin, Scott	Composer, pianist	(1868-1917)
Keaton, Diane	Actress	(1946-)
Keillor, Garrison	Writer, comedian, radio host	(1942-)
Kelly, Grace	Actress	(1929-1982)
King, B.B.	Blues musician	(1925-)
Lancaster, Burt	Actor	(1913-1994)
Landon, Michael	Actor	(1936-)
Lansbury, Angela	Actress	(1925-)
Lee, Spike	Director	(1957-)
Lennon, John	Rock musician, composer	(1940-1980)
Leno, Jay	Talk show host	(1950-)
Letterman, David	Talk show host	(1947-)
Lewis, Jerry	Comedian, Actor	(1935-)

Liberace	Pianist	(1919-1987)
Lloyd-Webber, Andrew	Composer	(1948-)
MacLaine, Shirley	Actress	(1934-)
Madonna	Rock singer, actress	(1958-)
Martin, Steve	Actor, comedian	(1945-)
Marx, Groucho	Actor,comedian	(1890-1977)
McEntire, Reba	Country musician	(1955-)
Miller, Glenn	Band leader	(1904-1944)
Monroe, Marilyn	Actress	(1926-1962)
Morrison, Jim	Rock singer	(1943-1971)
Murphy, Eddie	Actor, comedian	(1961-)
Nelson, Willie	Country singer	(1933-)
Newman, Paul	Actor	(1925-)
Nicholson, Jack	Actor	(1937-)
Nimoy, Leonard	Director, actor	(1931-)
Oakley, Annie	Sharp shooter	(1860-1926)
Orbison, Roy	Rock musician	(1936-1988)
Ozawa, Seiji	Conductor	(1935-)
Parton, Dolly	Actress, country singer	(1946-)
Peck, Gregory	Actor	(1916-2003)
Pitt, Brad	Actor	(1963-)
Poitier, Sidney	Actor	(1927-)
Porter, Cole	Composer	(1893-1964)
Presley, Elvis	Actor, rock singer	(1935-1977)
Quinn, Anthony	Actor	(1915-2001)
Redford, Robert	Actor	(1937-)
Roberts, Julia	Actress	(1967-)
Rogers, Ginger	Actress, dancer, singer	(1911-1995)
Schwarzenegger, Arnold	Actor, weigh lifter, governor	(1947-)
Scorsese, Martin	Director	(1942-)
Scott, George C.	Actor	(1927-)
Selznick, David O.	Producer	(1902-1965)
Shepard, Sam	Actor, playwright	(1943-)
Simon, Paul	Singer, musician	(1942-)
Sinatra, Frank	Singer	(1915-1998)
Sousa, John Philip	Composer	(1854-1932)
Spielberg, Steven	Director	(1947-)
Springsteen, Bruce	Rock musician	(1949-)
Stallone, Sylvester	Actor	(1946-)
Stewart, James	Actor	(1908-1997)
Stone, Oliver	Director	(1946-)
Stravinsky, Igor	Composer	(1882-1971)
Streep, Meryl	Actress	(1949-)
Streisand, Barbra	Singer, actress	(1942-)
Sullivan, Ed	Variety show host	(1901-1974)
Taylor, Elizabeth	Actress	(1932-)
Temple, Shirley	Actress	(1928-)
Tracy, Spencer	Actor	(1900-1967)
Turner, Tina	Rock musician, actress	(1939-)
Waller, Fats	Composer	(1904-1943)
Wayne, John	Actor	(1907-1979)
Welk, Lawrence	Band leader	(1903-1992)
Welles, Orson	Director	(1915-1985)
West, Mae	Actress	(1893-1980)
Williams, Hank	Country musician	(1923-1953)
Winfrey, Oprah	Talk show host, actress	(1954-)

15: Heroes

Folk Heroes and Cultural Icons

Horatio Alger
Muhammad Ali
Johnny Appleseed
Billy the Kid
Bonnie and Clyde
Buffalo Bill
Daniel Boone
John Brown
Paul Bunyan
Al Capone
Kit Carson
Cesar Chavez
Davy Crockett
James Dean
Amelia Earhart
Wyatt Earp
Thomas Edison
Benjamin Franklin
Barbara Fritchie
John Henry
Wild Bill Hickock
Jesse James

Casey Jones
Martin Luther King, Jr.
Charles Lindbergh
Malcolm X
Marilyn Monroe
Mickey Mouse
John Muir
Annie Oakley
Jessie Owens
Rosa Parks
Pecos Bill
Molly Pitcher
Pocahontas
Elvis Presley
Paul Revere
Jackie Robinson
Betsy Ross
Babe Ruth
Tom Swift
Uncle Sam
Rip Van Winkle
Sergeant York

Presidential Icons

George Washington
Thomas Jefferson
Andrew Jackson

Abraham Lincoln
Teddy Roosevelt
Franklin Roosevelt

Comic Book Heroes

Alfred E. Newman
Batman and Robin
Betty Boop
Bill the Cat
Buck Rogers
Bugs Bunny
Calvin and Hobbes
Charlie Brown
Daffy Duck
Dagwood and Blondie
Dick Tracy
Donald Duck
Elmer Fudd
Felix the Cat
Fred Flintstone
Garfield

George Jetson
Little Orphan Annie
Mickey Mouse
Mike Doonesbury
Mutt 'n' Jeff
Nancy
Opus
Popeye
Scooby Doo
Snoopy
Spiderman
Superman
Sylvester and Tweety
Wile E. Coyote and the Roadrunner
Wonder Woman
Woody Woodpecker

16: Recent Nobel Peace Prize Winners

2006 **Muhammad Yunus** and **the Grameen Bank** for their efforts to create economic and social development from below.

2005 **International Atomic Energy Agency** and **Mohamed ElBaradei** for their efforts to prevent nuclear energy from being used for military purposes and to ensure that nuclear energy for peaceful purposes is used in the safest possible way.

2004 **Wangari Maathai** for her contribution to sustainable development, democracy, and peace,

2003 **Shirin Ebadi** for her efforts for democracy and human rights.

2002 **Jimmy Carter, Jr.**, former President of the United States of America, for his decades of untiring effort to find peaceful solutions to international conflicts, to advance democracy and human rights, and to promote economic and social development

2001 **The United Nations** and **Kofi Annan,** United Nations Secretary General

2000 **Kim Dae Jung** for his work for democracy and human rights in South Korea and in East Asia in general, and for peace and reconciliation with North Korea in particular.

1999 **Doctors without Borders (Médecins sans Frontiéres),** Brussels, Belgium.

1998 **John Hume** and **David Trimble** for their efforts to find a peaceful solution to the conflict in Northern Ireland.

1997 **The International Campaign to Ban Landmines (ICBL)** and **Jody Williams** for their work for the banning and clearing of anti-personnel mines.

1996 **Carlos Felipe Ximenes Belo** and **Jose Ramos-Horta** for their work towards a just and peaceful solution to the conflict in East Timor.

1995 **Joseph Rotblat** and **the Pugwash Conferences on Science and World Affairs** for their efforts to diminish the part played by nuclear arms in international politics and in the longer run to eliminate such arms.

1994 **Yasser Arafat**, Chairman of the Executive Committee of the PLO, President of the Palestinian National Authority, **Shimon Peres** , Foreign Minister of Israel, and **Yitzhak Rabin,** Prime Minister of Israel, for their efforts to create peace in the Middle East.

1993 **Nelson Mandela,** Leader of the African National Congress, and **Fredrick Willem de Klerk,** President of the Republic of South Africa.

1992 **Rigoberta Menchu Tum,** Guatemala. Campaigner for human rights, especially for indigenous peoples.

1991 **Aung San Suu Kyi**, Burma. Oppositional leader, human rights advocate.

1990 **Mikhail Sergeyevich Gorbachev**, President of the USSR, helped to bring the Cold War to an end.

1989 **The 14th Dalai Lama (Tenzin Gyatso)**, Tibet. Religious and political leader of the Tibetan people.

1988 **The United Nations Peace-Keeping Forces.**

1987 **Oscar Arias Sanchez,** Costa Rica, President of Costa Rica, initiator of peace negotiations in Central America.

1986 **Elie Wiesel,** U.S.A., Chairman of *The President's Commission on the Holocaust.* Author, humanitarian.

1985 **International Physicians for the Prevention of Nuclear War,** Boston, MA, U.S.A.

1984 **Desmond Mpilo Tutu**, South Africa, Bishop of Johannesburg, former Secretary General South African Council of Churches (S.A.C.C.). for his work against apartheid.

1983 **Lech Walesa,** Poland. Founder of Solidarity, campaigner for human rights.

1982 **Alva Myrdal**, former Cabinet Minister, diplomat, delegate to United Nations General Assembly on Disarmament, writer, and **Alfonso García Robles**, diplomat, delegate to the United Nations General Assembly on Disarmament, former Secretary for Foreign Affairs .

1981 **Office of the United Nations High Commissioner for Refugees,**Geneva, Switzerland.

Other Nobel Prizes

Literature
Economics
Physiology and Medicine
Physics
Chemistry

Information from The Nobel Prize Internet Archive http://almaz.com/nobel/nobel.html

17: Points of Interest

State	Site
Alabama	First capital of the Confederacy in Montgomery
Alaska	Denali National Park, wildlife sanctuary surrounding Mt. McKinley
Arizona	Taliesin West in Scottsdale, home of Frank Lloyd Wright
Arkansas	Eureka Springs, resort since 1880s
California	Disneyland in Anaheim
Colorado	Mesa Verde National Park, cliff-dwelling Indians' cities
Connecticut	Mark Twain House in Hartford
Delaware	John Dickinson home in Dover, residence of "Penman of the Revolution"
Florida	Cape Kennedy, NASA Space Center
	Saint Augustine, oldest city in U.S., est. by Spanish in 1565
Georgia	Chickamauga Battlefield Park, site of decisive 1863 victory for South in Civil War
Hawaii	Iolani Palace in Honolulu, last residence of Hawaiian royalty
Idaho	Hell's Canyon, deepest gorge in North America
Illinois	Lincoln shrines in Springfield, New Salem and Sangamon
Indiana	Fort Vincennes, one of the first white settlements west of the Appalachians
Iowa	Herbert Hoover birthplace and library in West Branch
Kansas	Dodge City, frontier town on Santa Fe Trail
Kentucky	Churchill Downs in Louisville, home of Kentucky Derby since 1875
Louisiana	Mardi Gras in New Orleans
Maine	Seacoast, Acadia National Park
Maryland	U.S. Naval Academy in Annapolis
Massachusetts	Plymouth Plantation, pilgrims' first colony
	Old North Church in Boston, beginning of Paul Revere's ride
	Witch trials in Salem in 1692
Michigan	Sault Ste. Marie, French settlement est. 1668
Minnesota	Minnehaha Falls in Minneapolis, inspiration for Longfellow's "Hiawatha"
Mississippi	Vicksburg National Military Park and Cemetery
Missouri	Pony Express Museum in St. Joseph
Montana	Custer Battlefield National Cemetery at Little Bighorn River
Nebraska	Buffalo Bill Ranch State Historical Park in Nebraska City
Nevada	Legalized gambling casinos in Las Vegas, Reno and Tahoe
New Hampshire	Strawbery Banke in Portsmouth, historical buildings dating to 17th century
New Jersey	Miss America Pageant and casinos in Atlantic City
New Mexico	Carlsbad Caverns, a national park with caverns on three levels and the largest natural cave in the world
New York	Ellis Island, immigration station for East Coast
North Carolina	Kitty Hawk, Wright brothers' first flight
	Roanoke Island, first English colony in America
North Dakota	Theodore Roosevelt National Park in Badlands, contains the president's Elkhorn Ranch
Ohio	Mound City National Monuments, group of 24 prehistoric Indian burial mounds

<u>State</u>	<u>Site</u>
Oklahoma	National Cowboy Hall of Fame, Oklahoma City
Oregon	Columbia River Gorge
Pennsylvania	Valley Forge, encampment grounds for Gen. Washington and troops in 1777 Gettysburg, site of Civil War battle, turning point in war for Union
Rhode Island	John Brown House in Providence, residence of 18th century merchant
South Carolina	Fort Sumter National Monument, Union troops were overrun by Confederate soldiers to start the Civil War in 1861
South Dakota	Black Hills
Tennessee	Graceland in Memphis, home of Elvis Presley
	The Grand Ole Opry in Nashville, country music show est. 1925
Texas	The Alamo in San Antonio, fort was overrun by Santa Anna in1836
Utah	Temple Square in Salt Lake City, Mormon Church headquarters
Vermont	Bennington Battle Museum
Virginia	Monticello in Charlottesville, Jefferson's home
	Mount Vernon, Washington's home
	Appomattox, site of surrender of Gen. Lee and Confederacy in 1865
	Lexington, birthplace and tomb of Gen. Lee
Washington	Mount St. Helens, volcanic eruption in 1989
West Virginia	Harper's Ferry, John Brown led slave uprising in 1859
Wisconsin	Heritage Hill in Green Bay, museum of historical buildings and artifacts
Wyoming	Yellowstone National Park
District of Columbia	Washington Monument
	Lincoln Memorial
	Jefferson Memorial
	Franklin Delano Roosevelt Memorial
	U, S. Capitol
	White House
	World War II
	Korean War Memorial
	Vietnam War Memorial
	National Archives
	Smithsonian Institution, museums

18: National Parks

Name	Location	Est.	Features
Acadia	Maine	1916	Mt. Desert Island and adjacent mainland
Arches	Utah	1929	Stone arches and pedestals caused by erosion
Badlands	South Dakota	1929	Arid land inhabited by bison, antelope, deer
Big Bend	Texas	1935	Mountains and desert bordering Rio Grande
Biscayne	Florida	1968	Coral reef south of Miami
Black Canyon	Colorado	1999	Deep, narrow canyon of the Gunnison
Bryce Canyon	Utah	1923	Brilliantly colored eroded rocks
Canyonlands	Utah	1964	Red-rock canyons, spires and arches
Capitol Reef	Utah	1937	Sedimentary rock formations in high narrow gorges
Carlsbad Caverns	New Mexico	1923	World's largest known caves
Channel Islands	California	1938	Marine mammals, endangered species, archaeology
Congaree	South Carolina	2003	Largest old-growth flood plain, hardwood forest in N. America
Crater Lake	Oregon	1902	Lake in the heart of an inactive volcano
Cuyahoga Valley	Ohio	2000	Meandering river valley, old forests, farmland, rail journeys
Death Valley	California, Nevada	1994	Large desert: lowest point in the hemisphere
Denali	Alaska	1917	North America's highest mountain, Mt. McKinley, 20,320 ft.
Dry Tortugas	Florida	1992	Offshore islands; marine life
Everglades	Florida	1934	Subtropical swamp
Gates of the Arctic	Alaska	1978	Diverse wilderness, part of the Brooks Range
Glacier	Montana	1910	Rocky Mountains
Glacier Bay	Alaska	1925	Whales, glaciers
Grand Canyon	Arizona	1908	Mile-deep gorge, 4-18 miles wide, 217 miles long
Grand Teton	Wyoming	1929	High mountain range
Great Basin	Nevada	1922	Biological and geological attractions
Great Smoky Mts.	NC, TN	1926	Highest mountain range east of Black Hills
Guadalupe Mts.	Texas	1966	Highest peak in Texas (8,751 ft.)
Haleakala	Hawaii	1916	Dormant Haleakala volcano (10,023 ft.)
Hawaii Volcanoes	Hawaii	1916	Volcanoes, luxuriant vegetation at lower levels
Hot Springs	Arkansas	1832	47 hot springs
Isle Royale	Michigan	1931	Largest wilderness island in Lake Superior
Joshua Tree	California	1994	Desert region
Katmai	Alaska	1918	Dormant volcano, bears
Kenai Fjords	Alaska	1978	Mountain goats, marine mammals, birdlife
Kings Canyon	California	1890	Huge canyons, high mountains, giant sequoias
Kobuk Valley	Alaska	1978	Native culture and anthropology center
Lake Clark	Alaska	1978	Across Cook Inlet from Anchorage
Lassen Volcanic	California	1907	Impressive volcanic phenomena
Mammoth Cave	Kentucky	1926	Limestone labyrinth with underground river
Mesa Verde	Colorado	1906	Best-preserved prehistoric cliff dwellings in U.S.
Mount Rainier	Washington	1899	Single peak glacial system, dense forest
North Cascades	Washington	1968	Alpine landscape, glaciers, mountain lakes
Olympic	Washington	1909	Finest Pacific Northwest rainforest
Petrified Forest	Arizona	1906	Extensive natural exhibit of petrified wood
Redwood	California	1968	Coastal redwood forests, world's tallest known tree
Rocky Mountain	Colorado	1915	107 named Rocky Mountain peaks over 10,000 ft.
Saguaro	Arizona	1994	Giant cactus
Samoa	American Samoa	1988	Two rainforest preserves and a coral reef
Sequoia	California	1890	World's largest trees
Shenandoah	Virginia	1926	Scenic Skyline Drive
Theodore Roosevelt	North Dakota	1947	Roosevelt Ranch, valley of the Little Missouri River
Virgin Islands	U.S. Virgin Islands	1956	Prehistoric Caribbean Indian relics, beaches
Voyageurs	Minnesota	1971	Wildlife, canoeing, fishing, hiking
Wind Cave	South Dakota	1903	Limestone caverns in the Black Hills, buffalo herd
Wolf Trap Farm	Virginia	2003	First park for the performing arts
Wrangell-St. Elias	Alaska	1978	Second highest peak in U.S. (Mt. Elias)
Yellowstone	WY, MT, ID	1872	World's greatest geyser area, falls and canyons
Yosemite	California	1890	Giant sequoias, enormous gorges and waterfalls
Zion	Utah	1909	Multicolored gorge in southwestern Utah desert

19: Natural Features

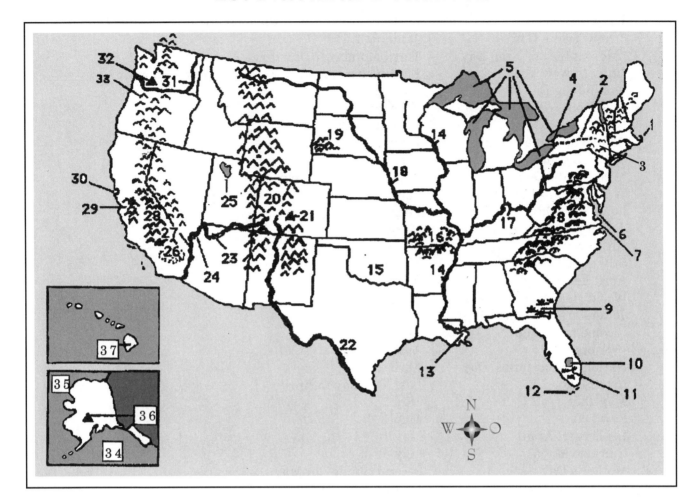

1. Cape Cod
2. Erie Canal
3. Catskill Mountains
4. Niagara Falls
5. Great Lakes
6. Chesapeake Bay
7. Cape Hatteras
8. Appalachian Mountains
9. Okefenokee Swamp
10. Lake Okeechobee
11. Everglades Swamp
12. Key West (islands)
13. Mississippi Delta

14. Mississippi River
15. Arkansas River
16. Ozark Mountains
17. Ohio River
18. Missouri River
19. Black Hills
20. Rocky Mountains
21. Pike's Peak
22. Rio Grande
23. Grand Canyon
24. Colorado River
25. Great Salt Lake

26. Death Valley
27. Mt. Whitney
28. Sierra Nevada Mountains
29. Big Sur Coastline
30. San Francisco Bay
31. Columbia River
32. Mt. St. Helens
33. Cascade Range
34. Aleutian Islands
35. Bering Strait
36. Denali (Mt. McKinley)
37. Kilauea Volcano

20: Important Days and Holidays

US Holidays	Date	*Federal legal holidays in the U.S.*
* New Year's Day	January 1	
*Martin Luther King Day	Third Monday in January	
Chinese New Year	First new moon after the sun enters Aquarius	
Groundhog Day	February 2	
Boy Scouts' Day	February 8	
Lincoln's Birthday	February 12	
Saint Valentine's Day	February 14	
Susan B. Anthony Day	February 15	
*Presidents' Day	Third Monday in February	
Washington's Birthday	February 22	
Leap Year Day	February 29	
Johnny Appleseed Day	March 11	
Girl Scouts' Day	March 12	
St. Patrick's Day	March 17	
April Fool's Day	April 1	
World Health Day	April 7	
Jefferson's Birthday	April 13	
Income taxes due	April 15	
Patriots' Day	April 19	
National Secretaries' Day	April 23	
Arbor Day	Last Tuesday in April	
May Day	May 1	
Law Day	May 1	
Lei Day (Hawaii)	May 1	
Cinco de Mayo	May 5	
Mother's Day	Second Sunday in May	
*Memorial Day	Last Monday in May	
Children's Day	June 8	
Flag Day	June 14	
Emancipation Day	June 19	
Fathers' Day	Third Sunday in June	
*Independence Day	July 4	
*Labor Day	First Monday in September	
Grandparents' Day	September 7	
Citizenship Day	September 17	
World Peace Day	September 21	
Native American Day	September 26	
Leif Erikson Day	October 9	
*Columbus Day	Second Monday in October	
Halloween	October 31	
Election Day	First Tuesday after the first Monday in November	
*Veterans' Day	November 11	
*Thanksgiving	Fourth Thursday in November	
Human Rights Day	December 10	
Bill of Rights Day	December 15	
*Christmas	December 25	
Kwanzaa	December 26 - January 1	

Canadian Federal Holidays

Victoria Day	Penultimate Monday in May	Thanksgiving Day	2nd Monday in October
Canada Day	July 1	Remembrance Day	November 11
Labour Day	1st Monday in September	Boxing Day	December 26

Major Jewish and Christian Holidays

Holiday	Religion	Date
Epiphany	Christian	January 6
Three King's Day	Christian	January 6
Eastern Orthodox Christmas	Christian	January 7
Shrove Tuesday (Mardi Gras)	Christian	Day before Ash Wednesday
Ash Wednesday	Christian	40 days (excluding Sundays) before Easter
World Day of Prayer	Inter-faith	March 7
Saint Patrick's Day	Christian	March 17
Palm Sunday	Christian	Sunday before Easter
Purim (Feast of Lots)	Jewish	14th or 15th of Hebrew month of Adar
Good Friday	Christian	Friday before Easter Sunday
Easter Sunday	Christian	The first Sunday after the full moon occurring on or after March 21
Passover (Pesach)	Jewish	15-22 of Hebrew month of Nisan
Ascension Day	Christian	Ten days before Pentecost
Pentecost	Christian	50 days after Easter
Trinity Sunday	Christian	Sunday after Pentecost
Shavuot (Feast of Weeks)	Jewish	6th or 7th of Hebrew month of Sivan
Rosh Hashanah (New Year)	Jewish	First day of Hebrew month of Tishri
Yom Kippur (Day of Atonement)	Jewish	10th day of Tishri
Sukkot (Tabernacles)	Jewish	15-21 Tishri
All Saint's Day	Christian	November 1
Advent	Christian	Four-week period before Christmas
Baha'U'Llah Birthday	Baha'i	November 12
Saint Lucia's Day	Christian	December 13
Christmas	Christian	December 25
Hanukkah	Jewish	25th of Hebrew month of Kislev

Major Islamic Holidays

Note: Because the Muslim calendar, containing only 354 days, is shorter than the Gregorian calendar Islamic holidays do not always fall on the same days of the Gregorian calendar and so are listed seperately.

Holiday	Date
Islamic New Year	First day of Islamic month of Muharram
Mawlid an-Nabi (Muhammad's Birthday)	12th of Islamic month of Rabi
Fast of Ramadan	9th month of Islamic calendar
Id al-Fitr (Festival of Fast Breaking)	29th or 30th of Ramadan to 3rd of following month of Shawwal
Beiram (The first day of spring)	10th of Islamic month of Zu'lhijjah
Id al-Adhh (The Great Festival)	10th to 13th of the Islamic month of Zu'lhijjah

21: Major Religions

Major Religious Groups in the U.S.
2004 estimates

Group	Membership
Roman Catholic	71,797,000
Baptist	47,744,000
Methodist/Wesleyan	19,970,000
Lutheran	13,520,000
Presbyterian	7,899,000
Pentecostal/Charismatic	6,220,000
Episcopal/Anglican	4,870,000
Judaism	3,995,000
Mormon/Latter Day Saints	3,806,000
Churches of Christ	3,659,000
Congregationalist	1,945,000
Jehovah's Witness	1,878,000
Assemblies of God	1,521,000
Moslem	1,558,000
Buddhist	1,527,000
Agnostic	1,399,000
Atheist	1,273,000
Hindu	1,081,000
Unitarian-Universalist	888,000

Major Religious Groups in Canada
(2001 Census)

Roman Catholic	12,793,000
No religion	4,796,000
United Church of Christ	2,839,000
Anglican	2,035,000
Baptist	729,000
Lutheran	607,000
Moslem	580,000
Other Protestant	549,000
Presbyterian	410,000
Judaism	330,000
Buddhist	300,000
Hindu	297,000
Sikh	278,000

Major World Religions
(source: www.adherents.com)

**Religions found concentrated in only one country
are indicated with the country name.**

Christianity	2.1 billion
Islam	1.3 billion
Secular/Non-religious	1.1 billion
/Agnosticism	
/Atheism	
Hindu	900 million
Chinese Traditional	394
Buddhism	376
Primal-Indigenous	300
African Traditional & Diasporic	100
Sikhism	23
Juche (North Korea)	19
Spiritism	15
Judaism	14
Baha'i	7
Jainism (India)	4.2
Shinto (Japan)	4
Cao Dai (Vietnam)	4
Zoroastrianism	2.6
Tenrikyo (Japan)	2
Neo-Paganism	1
Unitarian-Universalist	800 thousand

22: A Brief History of the U.S.

c. 1000 Leif Erikson explores North America.

1492- 1502 Columbus explores the Caribbean for Spain in four voyages and publicizes the New World.

1497 John Cabot explores the Northeast American coast to Delaware.

1513 Juan Ponce de Leon explores Florida, searches for the Fountain of Youth.

1519 Cortes conquers Mexico.

1539 Hernando de Soto explores Florida, travels past the Mississippi River.

1540 Coronado and other Spanish explorers explore Northern Mexico, the Southwest U.S. and California.

1607 English found Jamestown.

1609 Henry Hudson explores New York Harbor and the Hudson River; Samuel de Champlain explores Lake Champlain; Santa Fe, New Mexico, founded.

1619 First black laborers brought to Jamestown as indentured servants. Slavery legalized in 1650.

1620 Plymouth Plantation, Massachusetts, founded by the Pilgrims, who came on the *Mayflower.*

1626 Peter Minuet buys Manhattan Island for the Dutch; pays the Indians $24 in trinkets.

1634 Frenchman Jean Nicolet explores the Great Lakes to Lake Michigan.

1636 First college, Harvard, founded. Roger Williams founds Rhode Island with democratic rule and religious toleration.

1654 First Jewish settlers come to New Amsterdam (later New York).

1664 British seize Dutch colony of New Netherland and rename it New York.

1673 Father Jacques Marquette and Louis Jolliet explore the upper Mississippi, claiming it for France.

1682 Sieur de La Salle explores the Mississippi south to the Gulf of Mexico.

1692 Witchcraft trials in Salem, Massachusetts.

1704 First regular newspaper, *Boston News Letter,* founded.

1741 Capt. Vitus Bering discovers Alaska for Russia.

1744-1763 French lose Canada and Ohio Valley to British after 20 years of war. Indians fight on both sides

1754-1776 British attempts to tax and control the colonies cause resentment and rebellion.

1773 Boston Tea Party.

1775 Battles of Lexington and Concord—"The shot heard 'round the world." Capture of Fort Ticonderoga, New York, and the Battle of Bunker Hill in Massachusetts are colonial victories. Gen. George Washington takes charge of the colonial army in Boston.

1776 Colonies declare independence from Britain on July 4.

1777 First constitution (Articles of the Confederation) adopted.

1781 British lose Revolutionary War

1784 Peace treaty signed with British.

1787 New constitution written and adopted.

1791 Bill of Rights enacted.

1793 Eli Whitney's invention of the cotton gin makes slavery profitable for the Southern states.

1797 Navy started with three ships.

1803 U.S. under President Thomas Jefferson buys Louisiana from Napoleon.

1804-1806 Lewis and Clark, with Sacagawea, an Indian woman guide, explore the Louisiana Purchase.

1808 Slave importation outlawed. Illegal imports continue until 1860.

1812 War with Britain.

1814 In Washington, D.C., the new Capitol and White House are burned by British. Peace treaty of Ghent.

1815 British are defeated in Battle of New Orleans.

1818 Troops under Gen. Andrew Jackson invade Florida to attack the Seminole Indians and weaken the Spanish government.

1819 Spain, whose American empire from Chile and Argentina in the south to Mexico and Florida in the north is collapsing, gives Florida to the U.S.

1823 Monroe Doctrine opposes any new colonies or any European intervention in the Americas.

1825 The Erie Canal, stretching from the Great Lakes to the Hudson River, is completed. The settlement of the MiddleWest and the growth of its towns and industries is stimulated. New York, New York, the largest city in the U.S. since 1790, expands rapidly.

1828   "Jacksonian Revolution." The new Democratic Party under Andrew Jackson wins the presidency and takes power in Washington. This first major political change, staged without violence, proves the stability of the government.

1836   Mexican-U.S. struggle for Texas. Mexican Gen. Santa Anna takes the Alamo in San Antonio and is then captured by Sam Houston at San Jacinto.
First wagon train of settlers travels from Missouri to California.

1848   Gold discovered in California. Development of the West is accelerated.

1853   Commodore Matthew C. Perry opens trade with Japan for U.S. ships.

1860   Abraham Lincoln elected.

1861   Seven Southern states withdraw from the U.S., set up the Confederate States of America and start the Civil War.

1863   Lincoln legally frees the slaves. Battle of Gettysburg. Lincoln's Gettysburg address.

1865   Civil War ends with Northern victory. Lincoln is re-elected and then assassinated. Thirteenth Amendment abolishes slavery.

1866   Reconstruction of the South. Ku Klux Klan formed secretly.

1867   U.S. buys Alaska from Russia.

1869   Transcontinental railroad completed. Knights of Labor founded.

1871   Fire burns the center of Chicago.

1872   Amnesty Act restores civil rights to the South.

1876   U.S. Centennial celebrated. Gen. Custer's last stand: 265 soldiers killed by Dakota Indians. Reconstruction ended in the South.

1886   Haymarket riot and other labor unrest. (AFL) American Federation of Labor formed.

1890   "Battle" of Wounded Knee; 200 Indian men, women, and children, and 29 U.S. soldiers killed in last major conflict of the Indian wars. Sherman Antitrust Act begins to curb big business monopolies.

1898   U.S. begins to take an aggressive interest in international affairs. Spanish-American War fought to aid independence of Cuba. U.S. annexes Hawaii.

1899   U.S. attempts to save Chinese independence and make China an international market by declaring the Open Door Policy.

1903   U. S. fosters Panama's independence from Colombia to get treaty to build Panama Canal. Wright brothers fly first airplane at Kitty Hawk.

1906   San Francisco earthquake. Pure Food and Drug and Meat Inspection acts.

1911   Supreme Court breaks up Rockefeller's Standard Oil Co. monopoly.

1914   Henry Ford raises pay of his workers from $2.40 for a nine-hour day to $5 for an eight-hour day so they can afford to buy a car. The sales of Ford cars booms.

1915   The Great War starts in Europe. U.S. remains neutral. Clayton Antitrust Act spurs anti-monopoly suits by federal government. U.S. frees Haiti to make it a "protectorate." U.S. actively supports various factions in Mexican Revolution of 1913-1916. U.S. hegemony expands in Caribbean.

1917   U.S. declares war on Germany. Prohibition amendment submitted; enacted 1919-1933.

1918   World War I ends November 11.

1919   First transatlantic flight.

1920   U.S. refuses to join the League of Nations.

1921   Congress curbs immigration and sets national quotas. Ku Klux Klan revives terror against blacks and Jewish Americans.

1924   Indians are made U.S. citizens.

1925   Scopes Monkey Trial dramatizes the changing understanding of evolution, science versus religion, and education in the U.S.

1926   Robert Goddard fires first fuel rocket.

1927   Marines are sent into China to protect U.S. interests during civil war. Charles Lindbergh crosses Atlantic solo.

1929   St. Valentine's Day Massacre dramatizes the power and violence of gangsters. Stock market crash begins the Great Depression.

1932   Roosevelt initiates new federalist approach to solving the crisis in the economy. To give Americans a "New Deal" and try to end the Depression, Roosevelt rapidly increases the size and spending of the federal government over the next eight years.

1935   Committee for Industrial Organization (CIO) forms, promoting stronger unions in auto, steel and other heavy industry. Congress passes the Social Security Act.

1939   World War II begins in Europe. U.S. remains neutral but rearms and supports Britain more and more actively through 1941.

1941   Japan attacks Pearl Harbor December 7. U.S. declares war on Axis Powers (Japan, Germany and Italy).

1945   Germany surrenders May 7. First atomic bomb dropped on Hiroshima August 6. Second atomic bomb destroys Nagasaki August 9. Japan surrenders August 15. United Nations founded.

1946	Philippines given independence by U.S. on July 4.	1963	President John F. Kennedy is assassinated.
1947	Truman Doctrine combats communism. The Marshall Plan aids reconstruction in Europe. Congress passes the Taft-Hartley Labor Relations Act over President Truman's veto to curb strikes.	1964	Major civil rights legislation is proposed. President Johnson and Congress begin a great increase in government spending on social welfare programs to create Johnson's "Great Society."
1948	U.S.S.R. blockades West Berlin. British and U.S. break blockade with a massive airlift. Organization of American States founded.	1965	President Johnson orders continuous bombing in South Vietnam and sends 184,300 troops. Riots in Watts section of Los Angeles, California.
1949	NATO founded for mutual protection of West Europe, Canada and U.S. People's Republic of China established under Mao Tse-tung; U.S. refuses recognition and maintains relations with the Nationalist government in exile in Taiwan (Formosa).	1966	U.S. fights in North Vietnam and Cambodia.
		1967	Riots in Newark, New Jersey, and Detroit, Michigan. 475,000 troops in Vietnam.
		1968	Vietnam War peace talks begin in Paris. Martin Luther King, Jr., and Robert Kennedy are assassinated.
1950	Korean War begins; UN (including U.S.) sides with South Korea against Communist China-backed North Korea. U.S. agrees to give economic and military support to South Vietnam.	1969	President Nixon expands the peace talks and begins phased withdrawal of U.S. troops from Vietnam. Neil Armstrong walks on the moon.
		1970	U.S. and South Vietnamese fight in Cambodia.
1951	Senate investigations, led by Estes Kefauver, expose the power of the Mafia and organized crime. Popular Gen. Douglas MacArthur is fired from his command in Korea.	1972	President Nixon reopens relations with China.
		1973	Vietnamese peace pacts signed.
1953	Peace is declared in Korea. U.S. supports anti-communists with massive aid in Indochina War.	1974	President Nixon resigns when threatened with impeachment for covering up evidence on the 1972 break-in at the Democratic National Committee offices in Watergate in Washington.
1954	Anti-communist investigations by Senator Joseph McCarthy end in his condemnation by Senate.	1975	South Vietnam, without U.S. military support, falls to North Vietnam.
1955	AFL-CIO formed. Rosa Parks refuses to give up her bus seat, beginning a citywide boycott in Birmingham, Alabama, led by Martin Luther King, Jr. Federal court overturns bus segregation law. Civil Rights movement gains strength.	1978	The U.S. agrees to hand the Panama Canal over to Panama in 1999.
		1979	90 hostages are taken in Iran as the Shah's U.S.-backed government falls in a popular uprising. The crisis continues for 444 days.
1956	Supreme Court requires schools to desegregate.	1981	President Reagan's tax cuts are passed by Congress. The economy grows for nine years, but so does the national debt.
1957	Congress passes the first civil rights bill on voting rights since Reconstruction.	1982	The Equal Rights Amendment, guaranteeing women and others equal rights, fails to be ratified by enough states to change the Constitution. The Space Shuttle *Columbia* successfully returns from space.
1958	U.S.S.R.'s successful launch of the first man-made satellite, *Sputnik,* spurs U.S. scientific efforts and the space race. U.S. *Explorer I* launched.		
1959	Alaska and Hawaii become states. St. Lawrence Seaway opens.	1983	281 U.S. and French military personnel serving in a UN peacekeeping force in Lebanon are killed by terrorist bombs. President Reagan and six Caribbean nations send troops into Grenada to restore democratic government.
1960	Congress passes a stronger voting rights bill.		
1961	Cuban exiles, with help from the CIA, invade Cuba at the Bay of Pigs; they fail to inspire a revolt and withdraw against Fidel Castro.	1984	Marines are withdrawn from Lebanon; civil war continues.
1962	Military advisors sent to Vietnam are permitted to "fire if fired upon." John Glenn is the first American in space.	1985	President Reagan and Soviet leader Mikhail Gorbachev hold their first summit. Congress passes Gramm-Rudman bill to try to reduce government spending.

1986   Space Shuttle *Challenger* explodes while the world watches on TV. U.S. war planes attack Libya in response to terrorism. AIDS is acknowledged as an international health emergency.

1989   President Bush sends troops into Panama and ousts Gen. Manuel Noriega. U.S., U.S.S.R. and their allies declare the end of the Cold War.

1990   U.S. sends troops to Saudi Arabia to protect Middle East allies after Iraqi leader Saddam Hussein seizes Kuwait.

1991   U.S. and other UN forces bomb Iraq and reclaim Kuwait.

1992   Bill Clinton elected president. U.S. with U.N. enters Somalia.

1993   World Trade Center bombed. Great flood in the Midwest. Brady Bill (gun law) signed. Clinton attacks Iraq with missiles for alleged assassination attempt against ex-President Bush. 18 U.S. soldiers killed in ambush in Somalia; U.S. withdraws.

1994   NAFTA takes effect. Earthquake in L.A. Republican party gains control of congress.

1995   U.S. with the U.N. enters Haiti. Truck bomb destroys federal building in Oklahoma City. Diplomatic relations with Vietnam re-established. War ends in Bosnia; U.S. sends peacekeepers. Partial government shutdown as Clinton forces Congress to cut budget.

1996   TWA flight 800 crashes. Bomb explodes at the Olympics in Atlanta. Clinton reelected.

1997   Madeline Albright becomes 1st woman Secretary of State. Tobacco companies agree to settlements in antismoking suits.

1998   Clinton sex scandal erupts. House votes to impeach Clinton. Senate does not remove Clinton from office. Terrorists bomb embassies in Kenya and Tanzania. U.S. retaliates with missiles against terrorists in Sudan and Afghanistan. U.S./British air strikes against weapon sites in Iraq.

1999   Computer system disruption, "Y2K bug," and millennium terrorist attacks, expected at the New Year, don't occur. Violence in several schools around the country. U.S. economic expansion, prosperity, and budget discipline reduce national debt. Explosive growth in the use of the internet, 3rd-world population, and AIDS continue.

2000   The presidential election between Al Gore (Democratic Vice President) and Texas Governor George W. Bush, son of President George Bush, was a virtual tie. Gore won the popular vote, but the final decision on who would get Florida's electors was delayed for weeks while Florida recounted votes. The Supreme Court stopped the recount; Bush won Florida, the majority of the Electoral College, and the presidency.

2001   Bush appointed popular General Colin Powell as Secretary of State, but some of his more conservative cabinet appointments caused controversy. The new President's budget provided a $1.35 trillion tax cut over ten years to stimulate the U.S. economy. The economy, particularly technology stocks, continued a drop begun in 2000. Projected budget surpluses changed to deficits. On September 11 terrorists destroyed the World Trade Towers in New York City and one side of the Pentagon in Virginia using three full commercial airliners, about 3000 people were killed. In retaliation, the U.S. and U.K. attacked Afghanistan where the Taliban government was sheltering the al-Qaeda terrorists. The Taliban government in Kabul fell in November. In October a terrorist sent anthrax through the mails. In December Enron, an energy company, filed for the largest bankruptcy in U.S. history.

2002   The war continued in Afghanistan. A new U.S. Department of Homeland Security was organized. The stock market hit a new five-year low. WorldCom declared bankruptcy. Congress passed the McCain-Feingold Campaign Finance Reform bill. Several priests of the Catholic Church were accused of pedophilia, causing an international scandal.

2003   The Bush and British administrations failed to pressure the U.N. to invade Iraq. They attacked in a "preemptive strike," claiming the Saddam Hussein was working with al-Qaeda and readying weapons of mass destruction (chemical, biological, and nuclear) for use by terrorists. The Iraq regime fell. Bush declared an end of major action; but a guerrilla war continued and neither Saddam nor weapons of mass destruction were found. The administration was accused of giving misleading information before the war. The space shuttle Columbia, damaged during takeoff, disintegrated re-entering the atmosphere. The U.S. faced the largest budget deficit in history. Bush signs a $350 billion tax cut. In December Saddam Hussein was captured.

2004   The budget deficit reached $412 billion. The cost of energy, health care, and education increased. Iraqi sovereignty was returned to an interim government, but terrorism against civilians, partisan violence, and Iraqi and U.S. casualties increased. Contractors supporting the troops and rebuilding Iraq were accused of corruption. In the presidential campaign, Senator John Kerry failed to convince the majority of voters that the Bush administration had mismanaged the economy, the wars in Iraq and Afghanistan, and the "war on terrorism." The Republicans focused on Kerry's personality and on "moral values" and won the presidency by a narrow margin.

2005   President Bush claimed electoral support for his policies, but his popularity declined as the public learned of the administrations use of domestic wiretapping, torture of military prisoners, and "signing statements" by which the President signed a law saying he would not obey it. Secretary of State Colin Powell resigned, and later admitted that he had been misled by the administration into supporting the war. Insisting that he should "stay the course" on tax-cut economics and Iraq, Bush ignored mounting evidence of global warming and political scandals. Then the administration ignored warnings that Hurricane Katrina might hit New Orleans and flood the city. It did on August 29th. The government at all levels was unprepared and responded very slowly. The administration was widely blamed. In Iraq, Saddam Hussein went on trial in a special Iraqi court. The political and military situation in the Middle East in general continued to decline.

2006   In Darfur, Sudan, the death toll from the government suppression of the people of Darfur reached 200,000, with 2.5 million refugees. North Korea tested an atomic bomb. Iran announced plans to enrich uranium for atomic power, ignoring U.N. mandates. The anti-Israel Hamas won Palestinian elections, taking over the government. Hezbollah guerillas attacked Israel from Lebanon, and Israel was badly hurt militarily, politically, and diplomatically in stopping them. The Taliban regained strength in Afghanistan. In Iraq civil war deepened. Saddam was found guilty and hanged. Al-Qaeda leaders continued to plan and execute terrorist strikes worldwide from safe headquarters in Pakistan. In the "off-year" elections, the Democrats regained control of both houses of Congress and many other offices nationwide. Corruption and a perceived lack of effective domestic and foreign policy seem to have been the cause. A bipartisan Iraq Study Group, set up by Congress and led by George Bush Sr.'s Secretary of State, James Baker, and foreign policy expert, retired Congressman Lee Hamilton, began meeting right after the election and reported to the president 12/6 suggesting major policy changes.

2007   President Bush, after carefully considering the commission's advice and consulting widely, decided not to take much of the advice involving finding a diplomatic solution. Instead he decided to escalate the military commitment by sending 20,000 more troops to secure Baghdad. The New York Stock Market reaches a new, all-time high.

23: Folk Songs

Places

The Banks of the Ohio
Dixie
Down in the Valley
The Eyes of Texas
Home on the Range
My Old Kentucky Home
Red River Valley
The Sidewalks of New York
The Streets of Laredo

Traveling

Five Hundred Miles
Freight Train
The Golden Vanity
Sloop John B.
The Wabash Cannonball

Work

Blow the Man Down
Drill, Ye Tarriers, Drill
The Erie Canal
Git Along Little Dogies
Goodbye, Old Paint
I've Been Working on the Railroad

Children's Songs

Bingo
Hush Little Baby
This Old Man
Pop Goes the Weasel
Rock-a-Bye Baby
Row, Row, Row Your Boat
Skip to My Lou
Old MacDonald
Three Blind Mice

People

Barbara Allen
Casey Jones
Clementine
Dan Tucker
Go Tell Aunt Rhodie
Jeanie with the Light Brown Hair
John Henry
Oh, Susanna
She'll Be Coming 'Round the Mountain
Sweet Betsy from Pike
Tom Dooley

Love

Black Is the Color of My True Love's Hair
Goodnight Irene
House of the Rising Sun
In the Good Old Summertime
My Bonnie Lies over the Ocean
On Top of Old Smokey

Animals

Blue Tail Fly
The Fox
Froggie Went A-Courtin'
The Old Gray Mare

Play

A Bicycle Built for Two
Camptown Races
For He's a Jolly Good Fellow
Happy Birthday
Mountain Dew
Turkey in the Straw

Spirituals

Amazing Grace
Joshua Fought the Battle of Jericho
Kum Bay Yah
Nobody Knows the Trouble I've Seen
Old Folks at Home
Rock of Ages
Rock-a My Soul
Swing Low, Sweet Chariot
When the Saints Go Marching In

Patriotism

The Battle Hymn of the Republic
When Johnny Comes Marching Home Again
Yankee Doodle

Modern

Blowin' in the Wind
Brother, Can You Spare a Dime?
City of New Orleans
If I Had a Hammer
Old Man River
We Shall Overcome

24: Nursery Rhymes

Common Nursery Rhymes

Humpty Dumpty
Humpty Dumpty sat on a wall,
Humpty Dumpty had a great fall.
All the king's horses and all the king's men
Couldn't put Humpty together again.

There Was an Old Woman
There was an old woman
Who lived in a shoe,
She had so many children
She didn't know what to do.
She gave them some broth,
Without any bread,
Whipped them all soundly,
 And sent them to bed.

The Cat and the Fiddle
Hey diddle diddle,
The cat and the fiddle,
The cow jumped over the moon.
The little dog laughed to see such sport,
And the dish ran away with the spoon.

Old Mother Hubbard
Old Mother Hubbard went to the cupboard
To get her poor dog a bone.
But when she got there, the cupboard was bare,
And so the poor dog had none.

Jack and Jill
Jack and Jill went up the hill
To fetch a pail of water.
Jack fell down and broke his crown
And Jill came tumbling after.

Baa, Baa, Black Sheep
Baa, baa, black sheep, have you any wool?
Yes, sir, yes, sir, three bags full.
One for my master and one for my dame
And one for the little boy who lives down the lane
Baa, baa, black sheep, have you any wool?
Yes, sir, yes, sir, three bags full.

Hickory Dickory Dock
Hickory dickory dock,
The mouse ran up the clock
The clock struck one,
The mouse ran down,
Hickory dickory dock.

Mary Had a Little Lamb
Mary had a little lamb,
Little lamb, little lamb,
Mary had a little lamb
Its fleece was white as snow.
And everywhere that Mary went,
Mary went, Mary went,
Everywhere that Mary went
The lamb was sure to go.

Old King Cole
Old King Cole was a merry old soul,
And a merry old soul was he.
He called for his pipe
And he called for his bowl
And he called for his fiddlers three.
Every fiddler had a very fine fiddle
And a very fine fiddle had he.
Oh, there's none so rare as can compare
With King Cole and his fiddlers three.

Rain, Rain, Go Away
Rain, rain, go away,
Come again some other day.

Rock-a-bye Baby
Rock-a-bye, baby, on the treetop
When the wind blows the cradle will rock.
When the bough breaks, the cradle will fall,
And down will come baby, cradle and all.

Thirty Days
Thirty days hath September,
April, June and November.
All the rest have thirty-one,
Save February which alone
Has twenty-eight and one day more
When Leap Year comes one year in four.

Solomon Grundy
Solomon Grundy,
Born on Monday,
Christened on Tuesday,
Married on Wednesday,
Sick on Thursday,
Worse on Friday,
Died on Saturday,
Buried on Sunday.
That was the end
Of Solomon Grundy.

One, two, buckle my shoe,
Three, four, shut the door,
Five, six, pick up sticks,
Seven, eight, lay them straight.
Nine, ten, a big fat hen,
Eleven, twelve, dig and delve,
Thirteen, fourteen, maids a-courting,
Fifteen, sixteen, maids a-stitching,
Seventeen, eighteen, maids a-waiting,
Nineteen, twenty, food's a-plenty,
My plate is empty.

There was an old woman lived under a hill,
And if she's not gone, she's living there still.

If wishes were horses, beggers would ride;
if turnips were watches, I'd wear one by my side.

Three wise men from Gotham went to sea in a bowl.
If the bowl had been stronger, my song 'd been longer.

One misty, moisty morning,
When cloudy was the weather,
I chanced to meet an old man
Clothed all in leather.
He began to compliment
And I began to grin.
How do you do? And how do you do?
And how do you do, again?

A,b,c,d,e,f,g,
H,i,j,k,l,m,n,o,p,
Q,r,s,t,u,v,
W and x, y, z.
Now I know my ABCs,
Next time won't you sing with me?

Others

Barber, Barber, Shave a Pig	Jack Be Nimble	Sing a Song of Sixpence
Birds of a Feather Flock Together	Jack Sprat	The Man in the Moon
Bow, Wow, Wow,	Little Bo Peep	The Queen of Hearts
Whose Dog Art Thou?	Little Boy Blue	There Was a Crooked Man
Bye, Baby Bunting	Little Jack Horner	There Was a Little Girl
Cock-a-doodle Doo	Little Miss Muffet	This is the House that Jack Built
Cock Robin	Mistress Mary, Quite Contrary	Three Blind Mice
Diddle, Diddle, Dumpling,	Now I Lay Me Down to Sleep	Three Little Kittens
My Son John	Old Mother Goose	Tom, Tom, the Piper's Son
Ding dong bell. Doctor Foster	Pat-a-cake, Pat-a-cake,	To Market, to Market,
Went to Gloucester	Baker's Man	to Buy a Fat Pig
Georgie Porgie	Pease Porridge Hot	Tweedle Dumb and Tweedle Dee
Goosey Goosey Gander	Peter, Peter, Pumpkin Eater	Twinkle, Twinkle, Little Star
Hark, Hark, the Dogs Do Bark	Pussy Cat, Pussy Cat	Wee Willie Winkie
Here We Go Round	The Queen of Hearts	Willy Boy, Willy Boy,
the Mulberry Bush	Ride a Cock Horse	Where Are You Going
Hot Cross Buns	Ring around the Roses	Will You Walk Into My Parlor?
It's Raining, It's Pouring	Simple Simon	What Are Little Boys Made of?

Tongue Twisters

Peter Piper picked a peck of pickled peppers,
A peck of pickled peppers, Peter Piper picked.
If Peter Piper picked a peck of pickled peppers,
Where's the peck of pickled peppers
   Peter Piper picked?

She sells sea shells by the seashore.
The shells she sells are seashore shells.

Rubber baby buggy bumpers

The sixth sheik's sixth sheep's sick.

A tutor who tooted a flute
Tried to teach two tooters to toot.
Said the two to the tutor,
"Is it harder to toot or
To tutor two tooters to toot?"

*For a more complete collection of rhymes, visit the supplemental **ESL Miscellany** material
at **ProLinguaAssociates.com***

25: Light Verse

Light Verse

The Owl and the Pussy-cat

The Owl and the Pussy-cat went to sea
    In a beautiful pea-green boat.
They took some honey, and plenty of money,
    Wrapped up in a five-pound note.
The Owl looked up to the stars above,
    And sang to a small guitar,
"O lovely Pussy! O Pussy, my love,
    What a beautiful Pussy you are,
        You are,
        You are!
    What a beautiful Pussy you are!

Pussy said to Owl, "You elegant fowl!
    How charmingly sweet you sing!
O let us be married! too long we have tarried:
    But what shall we do for a ring?"
They sailed away, for a year and a day,
    To the land where the Bong-tree grows
And there in a wood a Piggy-wig stood
    With a ring at the end of his nose,
        His nose,
        His nose,
    With a ring at the end of his nose.

"Dear Pig, are you willing to sell for one shilling
    Your ring?" Said the Piggy, "I will."
So they took it away, and were married next day
    By the Turkey who lives on the hill.
They dined on mince, and slices of quince,
    Which they ate with a runcible spoon;
And hand in hand, on the edge of the sand,
    They danced by the light of the moon,
        The moon,
        The moon,
    They danced by the light of the moon.
        —*Edward Lear, 1851*

Wynken, Blynken, and Nod

Wynken, Blynken, and Nod one night
    Sailed off in a wooden shoe,—
Sailed on a river of crystal light
    into a sea of dew.
"Where are you going, and what do you wish?"
    The old moon asked the three.

"We have come to fish for the herring-fish
    That live in this beautiful sea;
Nets of silver and gold have we,"
    Said Wynken,
        Blynken,
            And Nod.

The old moon laughed and sang a song,
    As they rocked in the wooden shoe;
And the wind that sped them all night long
    Ruffled the waves of dew;
The little stars were the herring-fish
    That lived in the beautiful sea.
"Now cast your nets wherever you wish,—
    Never afraid are we!"
So cried the stars to the fishermen three,
    Wynken,
        Blynken,
            And Nod.

All night long their nets they threw
    To the stars in the twinkling foam,—
Then down from the skies came the wooden shoe,
    Bringing the fishermen home:
'Twas all so pretty a sail, it seemed
    As if it could not be;
And some folk thought 'twas a dream they'd dreamed
    Of sailing that beautiful sea;
But I shall name you the fishermen three:
    Wynken,
        Blynken,
            And Nod.

Wynken and Blynken are two little eyes,
    And Nod is a little head,
And the wooden shoe that sailed the skies
    Is a wee one's trundle-bed;
So shut your eyes while Mother sings
    Of wonderful sights that be,
And you shall see the beautiful things
    As you rock in the misty sea
Where the old shoe rocked the fishermen three:—
    Wynken,
        Blynken,
            And Nod.
        —*Eugene Field*

212

As I Was Going to Saint Ives

As I was going to Saint Ives
I met a man with seven wives.
Every wife had seven sacks,
Every sack had seven cats,
Every cat had seven kits.
Kits, cats, sacks and wives,
How many were going to Saint Ives?

Paul Revere's Ride

Listen my children, and you shall hear
Of the midnight ride of Paul Revere,
On the eighteenth of April in Seventy-five;
Hardly a man is now alive
Who remembers that famous day and year . . .
—*Henry Wadsworth Longfellow*

Nonsense Verse

Jabberwocky

'Twas brillig, and the slithy toves
    Did gyre and gimble in the wabe;
All mimsy were the borogroves,
    And the mome raths outgrabe.

"Beware the Jabberwock, my son!
    The jaws that bite, the claws that catch!
Beware the Jubjub bird, and shun
    The frumious Bandersnatch!"

He took his vorpal sword in hand;
    Long time the manxome foe he sought—
So rested he by the Tumtum tree,
    And stood awhile in thought.

And, as in uffish thought he stood,
    The Jabberwock, with eyes of flame,
Came whiffling through the tulgey wood,
    And burbled as it came!

One, two! One, two! And through and through
    The vorpal blade went snicker-snack!
He left it dead, and with its head,
    He went galumphing back.

"And hast thou slain the Jabberwock?
    Come to my arms, my beamish boy!
O frabjous day! Callooh! Callay!"
    He chortled in his joy.

'Twas brillig, and the slithy toves
    Did gyre and gimble in the wabe;
All mimsy were the borogroves,
    And the mome raths outgrabe.
    —*Lewis Carroll, 1871*

As I was going up the stair

As I was going up the stair,
    I met a man who wasn't there.
He wasn't there again today –
    I wish that he would go away!

    —*Anonymous*

The Jumblies

They went to sea in a sieve, they did;
    In a sieve they went to sea;
In spite of all their friends could say,
On a winter's morn, on a stormy day,
    In a sieve they went to sea.

And when the sieve turned round and round,
    And everyone cried, "You'll be drowned!"
They called aloud, "Our seive ain't big,
But we don't care a button, we don't care a fig—
    In a seive we'll go to sea!"

Far and few, far and few,
    Are the lands where the Jumblies live.
Their heads are green, and their hands are blue;
    And they went to sea in a sieve.
    —*Edward Lear, 1871*

The Crocodile

How doth the little crocodile
    Improve his shining tail,
And pour the waters of the Nile
    On every golden scale!

How cheerfully he seems to grin,
    How neatly spreads his claws,
And welcomes little fishes in,
    With gently smiling jaws.
    —*Lewis Carroll, 1871*

The Common Cormorant

The common cormorant or shag
    Lays eggs inside a paper bag.
The reason you will see no doubt
    It is to keep the lightning out.
But what these unobservant birds
    Have never noticed is that herds
Of wandering bears may come with buns
    And steal the bags to hold the crumbs.
    —*Anonymous*

26: American Literature and Cinema

1776-1830

Cooper, James Fenimore	(1789-1851)	The Last of the Mohicans
Franklin, Benjamin	(1706-1790)	Poor Richard's Almanack
Irving, Washington	(1783-1859)	"Rip Van Winkle," "Legend of Sleepy Hollow"
Paine, Thomas	(1737-1809)	Common Sense, The Crisis

The American Rennaissance (1830-1870)

Alcott, Louisa May	(1832-1888)	Little Women
Emerson, Ralph Waldo	(1803-1882)	Essays, Nature
Fuller, Margaret	(1810-1850)	Woman in the Nineteenth Century
Hawthorne, Nathaniel	(1804-1864)	The Scarlet Letter
Melville, Herman	(1819-1891)	Moby Dick, Billy Budd
Poe, Edgar Allen	(1809-1849)	The Fall of the House of Usher
Stowe, Harriet Beecher	(1811-1896)	Uncle Tom's Cabin
Thoreau, Henry David	(1817-1862)	Walden

Modern Literature (1870-1940)

Anderson, Sherwood	(1876-1941)	Winesburg, Ohio
Cather, Willa	(1876-1947)	Death Comes for the Archbishop
Chopin, Kate	(1851-1904)	The Awakening
Crane, Stephen	(1871-1900)	The Red Badge of Courage
Dreiser, Theodore	(1871-1945)	Sister Carrie
Faulkner, William	(1897-1962)	The Sound and the Fury
Fitzgerald, F. Scott	(1896-1940)	The Great Gatsby
Hemingway, Ernest	(1899-1961)	The Sun Also Rises
Henry, O.	(1862-1910)	The Gift of the Magi
James, Henry	(1843-1916)	Portrait of a Lady, The Bostonians
Lewis, Sinclair	(1885-1951)	Babbit, Main Street, Arrowsmith
London, Jack	(1876-1916)	The Call of the Wild, Sea Wolf
Mitchell, Margaret	(1900-1949)	Gone with the Wind
Porter, Katherine Ann	(1890-1980)	Flowering Judas; Pale Horse, Pale Rider
Sinclair, Upton	(1878-1968)	The Jungle
Stein, Gertrude	(1874-1946)	Three Lives
Steinbeck, John	(1902-1968)	The Grapes of Wrath
Tarkington, Booth	(1869-1946)	Seventeen, Penrod
Twain, Mark	(1835-1910)	Huckleberry Finn, Tom Sawyer
Wharton, Edith	(1862-1937)	Ethan Frome, The Age of Innocence
Williams, William Carlos	(1883-1963)	Tempers
Wodehouse, P.G.	(1881-1975)	Anything Goes
Wolfe, Thomas	(1900-1938)	You Can't Go Home Again
Wright, Richard	(1908-1960)	Native Son, Black Boy

Contemporary Literature (1940-)

Angelou, Maya	(1928-)	I Kow Why the Caged Bird Sings
Baldwin, James	(1924- 1987)	The Fire Next Time
Bellow, Saul	(1915-)	Herzog

Bradbury, Ray	(1920-)	Farenheit 451
Capote, Truman	(1924-1984)	In Cold Blood
Cheever, John	(1912-1982)	The Wapshot Chronicle
Doctorow, E. L.	(1931-)	Ragtime
Ellison, Ralph	(1914-1994)	The Invisible Man
Heller, Joseph	(1923-1999)	Catch-22
Hersey, John	(1914-1993)	A Bell for Adano
Lee, Harper	(1926-)	To Kill a Mockingbird
Mailer, Norman	(1923-)	The Naked and the Dead
Malamud, Bernard	(1914-1986)	The Fixer, The Natural
McCullers, Carson	(1917-1967)	The Heart is a Lonely Hunter
McMurtry, Larry	(1936-)	Lonesome Dove, Leaving Cheyenne
Michener, James	(1907-1998)	Tales of the South Pacific
Morrison, Toni	(1931-)	Tar Baby, Beloved
Oates, Joyce Carol	(1938-)	Do with Me What You Will
Pynchon, Thomas	(1937-)	Gravity's Rainbow
Rand, Ayn	(1905-1982)	Atlas Shrugged
Roth, Philip	(1933-)	Portnoy's Complaint, Zuckerman Unbound
Salinger, J. D.	(1919-)	Catcher in the Rye
Tan, Amy	(1952-)	The Joy Luck Club
Updike, John	(1932-)	Rabbit, Run
Vonnegut, Kurt	(1922-)	Slaughterhouse Five, Jailbird
Walker, Alice	(1944-)	The Color Purple
Warren, Robert Penn	(1905-1989)	All the King's Men
Welty, Eudora	(1909-2001)	The Optimist's Daughter

Poets

Benet, Stephen Vincent	(1898-1943)	John Brown's Body
Bradstreet, Anne	(c.1612-1672)	The Tenth Muse Lately Sprung up in America
Brooks, Gwendolyn	(1917-)	The Bean Eaters, "Malcolm X"
cummings, e. e.	(1894-1962)	Tulips and Chimneys
Dickinson, Emily	(1830-1886)	"There's a Certain Slant of Light"
Eliot, T. S.	(1888-1965)	"The Waste Land," "Four Quartets"
Frost, Robert	(1874-1963)	"Birches," "Mending Wall"
Ginsberg, Allen	(1926-1998)	"Howl"
Jeffers, Robinson	(1887-1966)	"Shine Perishing Republic," "Hurt Hawks"
Longfellow, Henry W.	(1807-1882)	"Evangeline," "Hiawatha"
Nash, Ogden	(1902-1971)	I'm a Stranger Here Myself
Parker, Dorothy	(1893-1967)	Laments for the Living
Plath, Sylvia	(1932-1963)	The Colossus
Poe, Edgar Allen	(1809-1849)	"The Raven"
Pound, Ezra	(1885-1972)	The Cantos
Riley, James Whitcomb	(1849-1916)	"When the Frost is on the Pumpkin"
Robinson, Edward Sand-	(1869-1935)	"Richard Cory"
berg, Carl	(1878-1967)	Chicago Poems
Teasdale, Sara	(1884-1933)	"Helen of Troy"
Millay, Edna St. Vincent	(1892-1950)	A Few Figs from Thistles
Warren, Robert Penn	(1905-1989)	"Brother to Dragons"
Whitman, Walt	(1819-1892)	"Song of Myself"

Playwrights

Albee, Edward	(1928-)	Who's Afraid of Virginia Woolf?
Baraka, Imamu Amiri	(1934-)	Dutchman, The Slave
Hart, Moss	(1904-1961)	Once in a Lifetime
Hellman, Lillian	(1904-1984)	The Little Foxes
Hughes, Langston	(1902-1967)	Shakespeare in Harlem
Mamet, David	(1947-)	American Buffalo
Miller, Arthur	(1915-)	Death of a Salesman
Odets, Clifford	(1906-1963)	Waiting for Lefty, The Golden Boy
O'Neill, Eugene	(1888-1953)	Long Day's Journey into Night
Saroyan, William	(1980-1981)	The Human Comedy
Shepard, Sam	(1943-)	True West, Buried Child
Sherwood, Robert	(1896-1955)	The Petrified Forest
Simon, Neil	(1927-)	Barefoot in the Park
Wilder, Thornton	(1897-1975)	Our Town
Williams, Tennessee	(1911-1983)	A Streetcar Named Desire

Academy Awards (Oscars) - Best Films

1960	The Apartment		1984	Amadeus
1961	West Side Story		1985	Out of Africa
1962	Lawrence of Arabia		1986	Platoon
1963	Tom Jones		1987	The Last Emperor
1964	My Fair Lady		1988	Rainman
1965	The Sound of Music		1989	Driving Miss Daisy
1966	A Man for All Seasons		1990	Dances with Wolves
1967	In the Heat of the Night		1991	The Silence of the Lambs
1968	Oliver!		1992	Unforgiven
1969	Midnight Cowboy		1993	Schindler's List
1970	Patton		1994	Forrest Gump
1971	The French Connection		1995	Braveheart
1972	The Godfather		1996	The English Patient
1973	The Sting		1997	Titanic
1974	The Godfather, Part II		1998	Shakespeare in Love
1975	One Flew Over the Cuckoo's Nest		1999	American Beauty
1976	Rocky		2000	Gladiator
1977	Annie Hall		2001	A Beautiful Mind
1978	The Deer Hunter		2002	Chicago
1979	Kramer vs. Kramer		2003	The Lord of the Rings: The Return of the King
1980	Ordinary People		2004	Million Dollar Baby
1981	Chariots of Fire		2005	Crash
1982	Ghandi		2006	The Departed
1983	Terms of Endearment			

27: A Few Famous Quotations

Early to bed and early to rise, makes a man healthy, wealthy and wise.

Nothing is certain but death and taxes.

There never was a good war or a bad peace.

Benjamin Franklin, *Poor Richard's Almanack*, 1732-1757

Taxation without representation is tyranny.   **James Otis, 1761**

By uniting we stand, by dividing we fall.   **John Dickinson, 1775**

Give me liberty or give me death.   **Patrick Henry, 1775**

Don't one of you fire until you see the whites of their eyes.   **William Prescott, 1775**

We must all hang together, else we shall all hang seperately.   **Benjamin Franklin, 1776**

I only regret that I have but one life to give for my country.   **Nathan Hale, 1776**

I have just begun to fight.   **John Paul Jones, 1779**

These are the times that try men's souls.   **Thomas Paine, 1785**

To be prepared for war is one of the most effectual means of preserving peace.   **George Washington, 1790**

There is always room at the top.   **Daniel Webster**

Be sure you are right, then go ahead.   **Davy Crockett, 1812**

Don't give up the ship.   **Capt. James Lawrence, 1813**

Go West, young man.   **John L. B. Soule, 1851**

The mass of men lead lives of quiet desperation.   **Henry David Thoreau, 1854**

It is well that war is so terrible—we would grow too fond of it.   **Robert E. Lee, 1862**

You can fool all of the people some of the time and some of the people all of the time,
but you can't fool all of the people all of the time.   **Abraham Lincoln, 1863**

The true republic—men, their rights and nothing more; women, their rights and nothing less.

Susan B. Anthony, 1868

There's a sucker born every minute.   **P.T. Barnum**

Politics makes strange bedfellows.   **Charles Dudley Warner, 1871**

There's many a boy here today who looks on war as all glory, but, boys, it is all hell.

Gen. William T. Sherman, 1888

Everybody talks about the weather, but nobody does anything about it.   **Charles Warner, 1890**

Some Famous Quotations (Continued)

The report of my death was an exaggeration.   **Mark Twain, 1897**

Speak softly and carry a big stick; you will go far.   **Theodore Roosevelt, 1901**

Win one for the Gipper.   **Knute Rockne, 1921**

You are all a lost generation.   **Gertrude Stein, 1926**

What this country really needs is a good five-cent cigar.   **Thomas Riley Marshall**

Never give a sucker an even break.   **W. C. Fields**

I tell you, folks, all politics is apple sauce.   **Will Rogers, 1932**

I never forget a face, but in your case I'll make an exception.   **Groucho Marx**

The only thing we have to fear is fear itself.   **Franklin D. Roosevelt, 1933**

A radical is a man with both feet firmly in the air.   **Franklin D. Roosevelt, 1939**

Here's looking at you, kid.   **Humphrey Bogart, *Casablanca*, 1943**
Play it again, Sam.

You can never be too rich or too thin.   **Wallis Simpson, Duchess of Windsor**

The world is run by C students.   **Harry S. Truman, 1945**
The buck stops here.

Fasten your seat belts; it's going to be a bumpy night.   **Bette Davis, *All About Eve*, 1950**

Ask not what your country can do for you; ask what you can do for your country.   **John F. Kennedy, 1961**

You win some, you lose some, and some get rained out.   **C. E. Wood**

One small step for a man, one giant step for mankind.   **Neil Armstrong, 1969**

I cried all the way to the bank.   **Liberace, 1973**

Nice guys finish last.   **Leo Durocher, 1975**

Sometimes when I look at my children, I say to myself, "Lillian, you should have   **Lillian Carter, 1980**
stayed a virgin."

How do I know why there were Nazis? I don't even know how to work   **Woody Allen,**
the can opener.   ***Hannah and Her Sisters*, 1986**

Sources: The Harper Book of American Quotations, Gordon Carruth and Eugene Ehrlich, eds. Harper & Row, New York , 1988
Wit and Wisdom of Famous American Women, Evelyn Beilenson and Ann Tenenbaum, eds. Peter Pauper Press, Inc., White
  Plains, 1986

28: Proverbs

Note: The list of proverbs has been correlated with the list of Topics (pp. 55-135); not all the topics are covered. The assignment of a proverb to a particular semantic category can be done according to several different criteria. We have assigned the proverbs mostly on the basis of their literal, rather than figurative, meaning.

Food

Half a loaf is better than none.
Variety is the spice of life.
The bread is buttered on both sides.

Cooking

Too many cooks spoil the broth.
The pot calls the kettle black.
Out of the frying pan and into the fire.

Eating

Don't bite the hand that feeds you.
You can't eat your cake and have it too.
First come, first served.

Housing/Housekeeping

There's no place like home.
People in glass houses shouldn't throw stones.
Walls have ears.

Clothing

Too big for their britches.
If the shoe fits, wear it.
A stitch in time saves nine.

Relationships

Every man for himself.
A friend in need is a friend indeed.
Familiarity breeds contempt.
Live and let live.
It takes one to know one.
Two is company, three is a crowd.
Spare the rod and spoil the child.

Human Qualities

He who hesitates is lost.
Honesty is the best policy.
Haste makes waste.
Where there's a will, there's a way.
Beauty is only skin deep.
Beggars can't be choosers.

Human Stages

A sucker is born every minute.
Don't throw out the baby with the bath water.
Boys will be boys.
Never say die.
Dead men tell no tales.

Time

Time heals all wounds.
Never put off 'til tomorrow what you can do today.
Rome was not built in a day.
Better late than never.
Here today, gone tomorrow.
Last but not least.

Weather

Save it for a rainy day.
Make hay while the sun shines.
It never rains but it pours.
Red sky at morning, sailors take warning;
    Red sky at night, sailor's delight.

Animals

You can't make a silk purse out of a sow's ear.
Don't throw pearls before swine.
His bark is worse than his bite.
Let sleeping dogs lie.
You can't teach an old dog new tricks.
Curiosity killed the cat.
Let the cat out of the bag.
There are many ways to skin a cat.
When the cat's away the mice will play.
You can lead a horse to water but you can't
    make it drink.
Don't look a gift horse in the mouth.

Birds

The early bird catches the worm.
Kill two birds with one stone.
 A bird in the hand is worth two in the bush.
Birds of a feather flock together.
Don't count your chickens before they hatch.

Language

Easier said than done.
No sooner said than done.
Ask me no questions and I'll tell you no lies.
Actions speak louder than words.

Thinking

Seeing is believing.
Out of sight, out of mind.
Necessity is the mother of invention.
Let your conscience be your guide.
Two heads are better than one.

Numbers/ Measures
Six of one and half-dozen of another.
Give them an inch and they'll take a mile.
One picture is worth a thousand words.

Substances and Materials
A rolling stone gathers no moss.
All that glitters is not gold.
Good riddance to bad rubbish.
Every little bit helps.

Containers
Don't put all your eggs in one basket.
One rotten apple spoils the barrel.

Emotions
Love makes the world go 'round.
Absence makes the heart grow fonder.
It's no use crying over spilled milk.
Better safe than sorry.
Misery loves company.
Once bitten, twice shy.
He who laughs last, laughs best.

The Body
In one ear and out the other.
Don't cut off your nose to spite your face.
Blood is thicker than water.
Look before you leap.

Transportation
Don't put the cart before the horse.
Like carrying coals to Newcastle.
Time and tide wait for no man.

Money
Money doesn't grow on trees.
Money talks.
Money is the root of all evil.
A fool and his money are soon parted.
A penny saved is a penny earned.
The best things in life are free.
Easy come, easy go.

Recreation
All work and no play makes Jack a dull boy.
The more the merrier.
Thank God it's Friday.
All work and no play makes Jack a dull boy.

Sports and Games
Slow and steady wins the race.
Sink or swim.
It's not whether you win or lose,
    but how you play the game.
If you can't beat 'em, join 'em.
Practice makes perfect.

Medicine and health
An apple a day keeps the doctor away.
An ounce of prevention is worth a pound of cure.
One man's food is another man's poison.
What's good for the goose is good for the gander.

Business
Nothing ventured, nothing gained.
Everyone has their price.
Business before pleasure.
The customer is always right.

Shops and Tools
Jack of all trades, master of none.
Hit the nail on the head.
Give me the right tool, I will move the world.

Law
Truth will out.
Two wrongs don't make a right.
The end justifies the means.

Media
Bad news travels fast.
No news is good news.
The pen is mightier than the sword.
Don't judge a book by its cover.

Education
Practice what you preach.
Do as I say, not as I do.

War
Don't give up the ship.
All is fair in love and war.
War is hell.

Energy
Where there's smoke, there's fire.
Burn the candle at both ends.
Fight fire with fire.

Source: The Dictionary of American Proverbs, David Kin, ed. Philosophical Library.

29: Bumper Stickers

These sayings were collected off of bumpers around the United States in 2005 and 2006.
This is a kind of folk wisdom and humor, but we will gladly acknowledge the authors if contacted.

Kids in sports stay out of courts.

Happy childhoods last a lifetime –
Prevent child abuse.

It's never OK to hit a child.

School's open. Drive carefully.

"Failure is impossible" – *Susan B. Anthony*

If you can read this, you're too damned close.

"It is not our differences that divide us,
it's our inability to recognize, accept, and
celebrate those differences." – *Andre Lorde*

Fight TV addiction.

Ignore your rights, and they'll go away.

Darwin lives.

Defunding education is defeating the future.

Remember you're UNIQUE, like everyone else.

Don't treat your soil like dirt.

I owe, I owe, It's off to work I go.

If only closed minds came with closed mouths.

War is costly. Peace is priceless.

Keep your temper. No one else wants it.

Real women drive trucks.

Politicians and diapers need to be changed –
often for the same reason.

The best way to predict the future
is to help create it,

Do not meddle in the affairs of dragons
for you are crunchy and good with ketchup.

Not all who wander are lost.

I started with nothing and
I have most of it left.

Better to build school rooms for boys
than prisons for men.

Those who are truly educated
never graduate.

I'm for the separation of church and hate.

Commit random acts of kindness
and senseless beauty.

Live simply that others may simply live.

Good planets are hard to find.

Minds are like parachutes.
They only function when open.

Urban Sprawl: Where they tear out the trees
and name streets after them.

Lord help me to be the man
my dog thinks I am.

Humans are not the only creatures on Earth.
We just act like it.

One people, one planet, one future.

Sow justice / Reap peace.

Your kids are watching.

Allow prejudice to grow
and violence will follow.

The problems we face will not be solved
by the minds that created them.

Answer my prayer: steal this car.

Never trust a skinny cook.

"What is a weed? A plant whose virtue is yet
to be discovered." – Emerson

War doesn't decide who's right, only who's left.

It's easier to make a baby than raise a child.

Well behaved women rarely make history.

30: Superstitions

The **ace of spades** is a sign of death.

Getting out of **bed** on the wrong side means you will have a bad day.

Letting a **black cat** cross your path brings bad luck.

The **bride** should not see the **husband** on the morning before the wedding.

Cattle lying down indicate rain.

A four-leaf **clover** brings good luck.

A **cricket** in the house is good luck.

Hanging a **horseshoe** over the door, points up, brings good luck.

Passing under a **ladder** brings bad luck.

Killing a **ladybug** beetle brings bad luck.

Lightning never strikes twice in the same place.

Lighting three cigarettes from one **match** brings bad luck or pregnancy to the third person.

Breaking a **mirror** brings seven years of bad luck.

Finding a **penny** brings good luck ("see a penny, pick it up, all day long you'll have good luck").

Carrying a **rabbit's foot** brings good luck.

Spilling **salt** brings bad luck, but a pinch of the spilled salt thrown over your right shoulder will keep away evil spirits.

Killing a **spider** brings rain.

If you make a wish on a falling **star,** your wish will come true.

The number **thirteen** brings bad luck.

Opening an **umbrella** in the house brings bad luck.

31: Family Relationships Chart

also see Communicative Aspect #8 Family

great great grandmother = great great grandfather*

great great aunt/uncle – great gandmother = great grandfather – great great uncle/aunt

great aunt/uncle – grandmother = grandfather – great aunt/uncle

aunt – uncle – mother = father – uncle – aunt

big (older) sister – *big* brother – **YOU** – *little (younger)* brother – *little* sister

YOU = husband** or wife** (*or* partner)   **spouse

son-in-law = daughter   son = daughter-in-law   *(your)* children

granddaugher/son   grandchildren

great granddaughter/son   great grandchildren

great great granddaughter/son   great great grandchildren

(your) brother = sister-in-law   *(your)* sister = brother-in-law

*(you have)
**2 parents –
mother = father
4 grandparents
8 great
grandparents
16 great great
grandparents**
*(2 of each are shown
on the chart)*

niece   nephew

great niece/nephew

(your) uncle = aunt

(your) first cousin = cousin

(your child's) second cousin *or (your)* first cousin once removed

(your) mother-in-law = father-in-law (*informally* in-laws)

(your) husband *or* wife

godparents *or* godmother, godfather

(your) late or ex-wife or husband ≠*** YOU = wife (*your children's* stepmother) ≠ ex-husband

(your) children   *(your children's)* step-brothers/sisters

***no longer married: death or divorce

223

32: Names
Most Common First Names (2000-2005)

Girls	Madison	Emma	Alexis	*Boys*	Matthew	Joseph	Andrew
Emily	Ashley	Abigail	Elizabeth	Jacob	Joshua	Daniel	Nicholas
Hannah	Samantha	Olivia		Michael	Christopher	Ethan	

Other Common Women's Names 1990-1999 (ranked)

Christine	Caitlin	Stephanie	Jasmine	Victoria	Morgan	Jacqueline	Olive
Mary	Megan	Taylor	Rebecca	Danielle	Gabriella	Heather	Erin
Jesse	Amanda	Nicole	Courtney	Julia	Tiffany	Laura	Caroline
Alice	Alexandra	Angel	Amber	Jane	Kelly	Shelby	Jordan
Sarah	Kay	Jennifer	Michelle	Erica	Kimberly	Crystal	Keri
Catherine	Rachel	Lauren	Haley	Milicent	Lindsey	Andrea	Amy
Britney	Brianna	Ann	Chelsea	Kelsy	Casandra	Natalie	

Other Common Men's Names 1990-1999 (ranked)

John	Ryan	Austin	Richard	Dylan	Patrick	Kenneth	Trevor
James	William	Kyle	Jordan	Timothy	Jason	Caleb	Dustin
Alexander	Zachary	Kevin	Eric	Adam	Jesse	Carlos	Edward
Tyler	Justin	Thomas	Benjamin	Jeremiah	Derek	Jared	Evan
David	Anthony	Nathan	Aaron	Lewis	Juan	Taylor	Gabriel
Brandon	Stephen	Cody	Mark	Charles	Cameron	Logan	Ian
Robert	Brian	Shawn	Samuel	Jeffrey	Travis	Paul	

The Sixty Most Common Surnames (ranked)

Smith	Moore	Thompson	Walker	Hill	Mitchell	Edwards	Morgan
Johnson	Taylor	Garcia	Hall	Scott	Perez	Collins	Bell
Williams	Anderson	Martinez	Allen	Green	Roberts	Stewart	Murphy
Jones	Thomas	Robinson	Young	Adams	Turner	Sanchez	Bailey
Brown	Jackson	Clark	Hernandez	Baker	Phillips	Morris	
Davis	White	Rodriguez	King	Gonzalez	Campbell	Rogers	
Miller	Harris	Lewis	Wright	Nelson	Parker	Reed	
Wilson	Martin	Lee	Lopez	Carter	Evans	Cook	

(Source for the information above: Social Security Administration)

Common Irregular Nicknames

Nicknames in English are typically abbreviations of the full form of the name. Thus, Benjamin becomes Ben, Samuel > Sam, Andrew > Andy, Christine > Chris, Patricia > Pat/Patty, and Victoria > Vicky, Vickie, or Vicki.

Becky (Rebecca)	Jack (John)	Maggie, Meg (Margaret)	Babe	Lefty
Bess, Beth, Betsy,	Jim (James)	Micky, Mike (Michael)	Bud, Buddy	Mack
Betty, (Elizabeth)	Kate, Kathy (Katherine)	Marjie (Marjorie)	Buba	Missy
Bill, Billy (William)	Kit (Christopher)	Peg (Margaret)	Buck, Bucky	Red, Rusty
Bob, Bobby (Robert)	Kit, Kitty, Tina (Christine)	Sally (Sarah)	Butch	Shorty, Slim
Chuck (Charles)	Larry (Lawrence)	Ted (Theodore)	Chip	Sis, Sissy
Dick, Rick (Richard)	Lex (Alexander)	Tom, Tommy (Thomas)	Doc	Sonny
Hank (Henry)	Liz, Lizzy (Elizabeth)	Tony (Anthony)	Dusty	Tex
Harry (Harold)	Mandy (Amanda)	Trish (Patricia)	Junior	Tiger

224

33: Place Names

Common Place Names

Washington	Brookfield	Elkton	New Haven
Jefferson	Deerfield	Evanston	Riverdale
Madison	Fairfield	Hampton	Troy
Monroe	Greenfield	Lexington	Hanover
Jackson	Springfield	Princeton	Salem
Lincoln	Longmeadow	Wheaton	Richmond
Franklin	Edgewood	Guilford	London
Lafayette	Elmwood	Stratford	Dover
Leesburg	Pleasantville	Portland	Plymouth
Libertyville	Summerville	Columbia	Highland Park
Independence	Bloomington	Lebanon	Newport
	Canton		

English Elements of Common Place Names in the U.S. and Canada

Note: In both Canada and the United States, Indian and French place names are common; Spanish place names are very common in the Western and Southern United States. Some examples are: Indian – Saskatchewan, Ottawa, Massachusetts, Mississippi, Illinois; French – Montreal, New Orleans, Vermont, Louisiana; Spanish – Santa Fe, San Francisco, Florida, Nevada. Many places in Canada and the U.S. are also named after places in England: Boston, MA; London, ON. However, one of the most common ways of creating North American place names has been the practice of building the names from standard elements prefixed and/or suffixed to family names or animal names. This is typically English, and done mostly with English names. For example, using the family name Hart, East Hartford Junction. Using an animal, Little Deerfield Falls.

North-	- town	- City
East-	- ton	- Village
South-	- ville	- Park
West-	- apolis	- Valley
New-	- burg	- Junction
Old-	- bury	- Hills
Great-	- boro(ugh)	- Heights
Big-	- minster	- Mills
Little-	- stead	- Locks
Fort-	- sex	- Lake
Port-	- ford	- Beach
Brook-	- land	- Point
Glen-	- wood	- Haven
Mount-	- forest	- Harbor
Saint-	- field	- Shores
Oak-	- vale	- Rock
Elm-	- dale	- Bluffs
Pine-	- crest	- Falls
Maple-	- port	- Creek
Cedar-	- side	- Rapids
	- view	- Springs
	- bridge	- Ferry

34: Sports Teams in the U.S. and Canada
Major League Baseball
American League

Eastern Division		Central Division		Western Division	
Baltimore	Orioles	Chicago	White Sox	Los Angeles	Angels
Boston	Red Sox	Cleveland	Indians	Oakland	Athletics
New York	Yankees	Detroit	Tigers	Seattle	Mariners
Tampa Bay	Devil Rays	Kansas City	Royals	Texas	Rangers
Toronto	Blue Jays	Minnesota	Twins		

National League

Eastern Division		Central Division		Western Division	
Atlanta	Braves	Chicago	Cubs	Arizona	Diamondbacks
Florida	Marlins	Cincinnati	Reds	Colorado	Rockies
New York	Mets	Houston	Astros	Los Angeles	Dodgers
Philadelphia	Phillies	Milwaukee	Brewers	San Diego	Padres
Washington	Nationals	Pittsburgh	Pirates	San Francisco	Giants
		St. Louis	Cardinals		

National Hockey League
Eastern Conference

Atlantic Division		Northeast Division		Southeast Division	
New Jersey	Devils	Boston	Bruins	Atlanta	Thrashers
New York	Islanders	Buffalo	Sabres	Carolina	Hurricanes
New York	Rangers	Montreal	Canadiens	Florida	Panthers
Philadelphia	Flyers	Ottawa	Senators	Tampa Bay	Lightning
Pittsburgh	Penguins	Toronto	Maple Leafs	Washington	Capitals

Western Conference

Central Division		Pacific Division		Northwest Division	
Chicago	Black Hawks	Anaheim	Mighty Ducks	Calgary	Flames
Detroit	Red Wings	Dallas	Stars	Colorado	Avalanche
Nashville	Predators	Los Angeles	Kings	Edmonton	Oilers
St. Louis	Blues	Phoenix	Coyotes	Vancouver	Canucks
Columbus	Blue Jackets	San Jose	Sharks	Minnesota	Wild

Major League Soccer

Eastern Conference		Western Conference	
Chicago Fire	Kansas City Wizards	Chivas USA	Los Angeles Galaxy
Columbus Crew	MetroStars	Colorado Rapids	Real Salt Lake
D.C. United	New England Revolution	FC Dallas	San Jose Earthquakes

National Football League
National Conference

East	South	North	West
Dallas Cowboys	Atlanta Falcons	Chicago Bears	Arizona Cardinals
New York Giants	Carolina Panthers	Detroit Lions	San Francisco 49ers
Philadelphia Eagles	New Orleans Saints	Green Bay Packers	Seattle Seahawks
Washington Redskins	Tampa Bay Buccaneers	Minnesota Vikings	St Louis Rams

American Conference

East	South	North	West
Buffalo Bills	Houston Texans	Baltimore Ravens	Denver Broncos
Miami Dolphins	Indianapolis Colts	Cincinnati Bengals	Kansas City Chiefs
New England Patriots	Jacksonville Jaguars	Cleveland Browns	Oakland Raiders
New York Jets	Tennessee Titans	Pittsburgh Steelers	San Diego Chargers

National Basketball Association
Eastern Conference

Atlantic Division	Southeastern Division	Central Division
Boston Celtics	Atlanta Hawks	Chicago Bulls
New Jersey Nets	Charlotte Bobcats	Cleveland Cavaliers
New York Knicks	Miami Heat	Detroit Pistons
Philadelphia 76ers	Orland Magic	Indiana Pacers
Toronto Raptors	Washington Wizards	Milwaukee Bucks

Western Conference

Southwest Division	Northwest Division	Pacific Division
Dallas Mavericks	Denver Nuggets	Golden State Warriors
Houston Rockets	Minnesota Timberwolves	Los Angeles Clippers
Memphis Grizzlies	Portland Trail Blazers	Los Angeles Lakers
New Orleans Hornets	Seattle Supersonics	Phoenix Suns
San Antonio Spurs	Utah Jazz	Sacramento Kings

Women's National Basketball Associaton

Eastern Conference		Western Association	
Charlotte Sting	Indiana Fever	Houston Comets	Sacramento Monarchs
Chicago Sky	New York Liberty	Los Angeles Sparks	San Antonio Silver Stars
Connecticut Sun	Washington Mystic	Minnesota Lynx	Seattle Storm
Detroit Shock		Phoenix Mercury	

35: Sports Legends

Hank **Aaron** *(baseball)* 1934-
Kareem **Abdul-Jabbar** *(basketball)* 1947-
Andre **Agassi** *(tennis)* 1970-
Muhammad **Ali** *(boxing)* 1942-
Mario **Andretti** *(auto racing)* 1940-
Eddie **Arcaro** *(horse racing)* 1916-97
Lance **Armstrong** *(bicycling)* 1971-
Arthur **Ashe** *(tennis)* 1943-1993
Ernie **Banks** *(baseball)* 1931-
Elgin **Baylor** *(basketball)* 1934-
Patty **Berg** *(golf)* 1918-2006
Yogi **Berra** *(baseball)* 1925-
Larry **Bird** *(basketball)* 1956-
Bonnie **Blair** *(speed skating)* 1964-
Ray **Bourque** *(ice hockey)* 1960-
Jim **Brown** *(football)* 1936-
Dick **Button** *(ice skating)* 1929-
Paul "Bear" **Bryant** *(football)* 1913-1983
Roy **Campanella** *(baseball)* 1921-1993
Wilt **Chamberlain** *(basketball)* 1936-1999
Roger **Clemens** *(baseball)* 1962-
Roberto **Clemente** *(baseball)* 1934-1972
Ty **Cobb** *(baseball)* 1896-1991
Nadia **Comaneci** *(gymnastics)* 1961-
Bob **Cousy** *(basketball)* 1928-
Buster **Crabbe** *(swimming)* 1908-1983
Jack **Demssey** *(boxing)* 1895-1983
Joe **Dimaggio** *(baseball)* 1914-1999
Dale **Earnhardt** *(auto racing)* 1951-2001
Julius **Erving** *(basketball)* 1950-
Phil **Esposito** *(ice hockey)* 1942-
Chris **Evert** *(tennis)* 1954-
Bob **Feller** *(baseball)* 1918-
Peggy **Fleming** *(ice skating)* 1948-
Lou **Gehrig** *(baseball)* 1903-1941
Althea **Gibson** *(tennis)* 1927-
Pancho **Gonzalez** *(tennis)* 1928-1995
Evonne **Goolagong** *(tennis)* 1951-
Steffi **Graf** *(tennis)* 1969-
Red **Grange** *(football)* 1904-1991

Wayne **Gretzky** *(ice hockey)* 1961-
Lefty **Grove** *(baseball)* 1900-1975
Dorothy **Hamill** *(ice skating)* 1956-
Scot **Hamilton** *(ice skating)* 1958-
Mia **Hamm** *(soccer)* 1972-
Eric **Heiden** *(speed skating)* 1958-
Sonja **Henie** *(ice skating)* 1912-1969
Ben **Hogan** *(golf)* 1912-1997
Gordon **Howe** *(ice hockey)* 1928-
Bobby **Hull** *(ice hockey)* 1939-
Reggie **Jackson** *(baseball)* 1946-
Bruce **Jenner** *(track & field)* 1949-
Earvin "Magic" **Johnson** *(basketball)* 1959-
Randy **Johnson** *(baseball)* 1963-
Marion **Jones** *(track & field)* 1975-
Michael **Jordan** *(basketball)* 1963-
Florence **Joyner** *(track)* 1959-1998
Jackie **Joyner-Kersee** *(track)* 1962-
Duke **Kahanamoku** *(swimming, surfing)* 1890-1968
Jean-Claude **Killy** *(skiing)* 1943-
Billie-Jean **King** *(tennis)* 1943-
Olga **Korbut** *(gymnastics)* 1955-
Sandy **Koufax** *(baseball)* 1935-
Michelle **Kwan** *(ice skating)* 1980-
Guy **LaFleur** *(ice hockey)* 1951-
Rod **Laver** *(tennis)* 1938-
Mario **Lemieux** *(ice hockey)* 1965-
Sugar Ray **Leonard** *(boxing)* 1956-
Carl **Lewis** *(track & field)* 1961-
Vince **Lombardi** *(football)* 1913-1970
Nancy **Lopez** *(golf)* 1957-
Joe **Louis** *(boxing)* 1914-1981
Mickey **Mantle** *(baseball)* 1931-1995
Diego **Maradona** *(soccer)* 1960-
Rocky **Marciano** *(boxing)* 1923-1969
Dan **Marino** *(football)* 1961-
Willie **Mays** *(baseball)* 1931-
John **McEnroe** *(tennis)* 1959-
Joe **Montana** *(football)* 1956-

Stan **Musial** *(baseball)* 1920-
Joe **Namath** *(football)* 1943-
Ilie **Nastase** *(tennis)* 1946-
Jack **Nicklaus** *(golf)* 1940-
Hakeem **Olajuwon** *(basketball)* 1963-
Bobby **Orr** *(ice hockey)* 1948-
Jesse **Owens** *(track & field)* 1913-1980
Satchel **Paige** *(baseball)*1906-1982
Arnold **Palmer** *(golf)* 1929-
Walter **Payton** *(football)* 1954-1999)
Pele *(soccer)* 1940-
Maurice **Richard** *(ice hockey)* 1921-2000
Cal **Ripken** *(baseball)* 1960-
Frank **Robinson** *(baseball)* 1935-
Jackie **Robinson** *(baseball)* 1919-1972
Knute **Rockne** *(football)* 1988-1931
Wilma **Rudolph** *(track & field)* 1940-1994
Bill **Russell** *(basketball)* 1934-
Babe **Ruth** *(baseball)* 1895-1948

Nolan **Ryan** *(baseball)* 1947-
Tom **Seaver** *(baseball)* 1949-
Emmit **Smith** *(football)* 1969-
Sam **Snead** *(golf)* 1912-2002
Warren **Spahn** *(baseball)* 1921-2003
Mark **Spitz** *(swimming)* 1950-
Bart **Starr** *(football)* 1934-
Casey **Stengel** *(baseball)* 1991-1975
Lynn **Swann** *(football)* 1952-
Joe **Theisman** *(football)* 1946-
Jim **Thorpe** *(track & field, football, baseball)* 1888-1953
Lee **Trevino** *(golf)* 1939-
John **Unitas** *(football)* 1933-2002
Jersey Joe **Walcott** *(boxing)* 1914-1994
Tom **Watson** *(golf)* 1949-
Ted **Williams** *(baseball)* 1918-2002
Katarina **Witt** *(ice skating)* 1965-
Babe **Zaharias** *(golf)* 1911-1956

Contemporary Sports Heroes

David **Beckham** *(soccer)*
Tom **Brady** *(football)*
Kobe **Bryant** *(basketball)*
Reggie **Bush** *(football)*
Johnny **Damon** *(baseball)*
Oscar **De La Hoya** *(boxing)*
Tim **Duncan** *(basketball)*
Ernie **Els** *(golf)*
Brett **Favre** *(football)*
Marshall **Faulk** *(football)*
Roger **Federer** *(tennis)*
Nomar **Garciaparra** *(baseball)*
Ken **Griffey**, Jr. *(baseball)*
Martina **Hingis** *(tennis)*
Ichiro Suzuki *(baseball)*
Alan **Iverson** *(basketball)*
LeBron **James** *(basketball)*
Derek **Jeter** *(baseball)*
Andruw **Jones** *(baseball)*
Anna **Kournikova** *(tennis)*
Tara **Lupinski** *(ice skating)*

Peyton **Manning** *(football)*
Pedro **Martinez** *(baseball)*
Donovan **McNabb** *(football)*
Phil **Mickelson** *(golf)*
Yao **Ming** *(basketball)*
Rafael **Nadal** *(tennis)*
Shaquille **O'Neal** *(basketball)*
David **Ortiz** *(baseball)*
Albert **Pujols** *(baseball)*
Manny **Ramirez** *(baseball)*
Mariano **Rivera** *(baseball)*
Andy **Roddick** *(tennis)*
Alex **Rodriguez** *(baseball)*
Vijay **Singh** *(golf)*
Annika **Sorenstam** *(golf)*
Diana **Taurasi** *(basketball)*
Frank **Thomas** *(baseball)*
Joe **Thornton** *(ice hockey)*
Serena **Williams** *(tennis)*
Venus **Williams** *(tennis)*
Tiger **Woods** *(golf)*

36: U.S. School System Chart

Name of School	Grade	Age of Students	Subjects
Nursery School		3-5	Games, songs, creative play
Kindergarten	K	4-6	Games, drawing, crafts, beginning reading, writing
Elementary School 1-5 or 1-6	1 2 3	5-7 6-8 7-9	Reading, writing, spelling, adding, drawing, music Language arts, subtraction, spelling, drawing, music Language arts, social studies, multiplication, music
Middle School 5-9 or 6-9	4 5 6	8-10 9-11 10-12	Language arts, social studies, division Language arts, social studies, fractions Language arts, social studies, decimals, science
Junior High School	7 8	11-13 12-14	Language arts, social studies, math, science, foreign language Language arts, social studies, math, science, foreign language
High School Freshman	9	13-15	**Core Courses:** English, algebra, civics, biology, foreign language **Electives:** Music, art, typing, bookkeeping, economics, technical education, home economics
Sophmore	10	14-16	**Core Courses:** English, geometry, history, chemistry, foreign language **Electives:** Music, art, bookkeeping, economics, consumer education, computer applications
Junior	11	15-17	**Core Courses:** English, advanced math, history, physics, foreign language **Electives:** Music, art, bookkeeping, economics, consumer education, computer applications
Senior	12	16-18	**Core Courses:** English, calculus, history, foreign language **Electives:** Music, art, bookkeeping, economics, consumer education, computer programming

College and University

Undergraduate College	Age	Degree	Length of time required
Junior College	17-	AA	2 years
Four-Year College	18-	BA, BS	4-5 years
University Graduate School	21-	MA, MS	2-3 years plus thesis
Graduate school		PhD, LHD, Litt. D., DCL	3 years plus thesis
Medical school		MD, DDS	2 years plus residency
Law school		JS	3 years

37. Currencies: U. S. Coins and Bills

1 cent/penny	5 cents/nickel	10 cents/dime	25 cents/quarter	50 cents/half dollar	1 dollar

(1¢) Lincoln	(5¢) Jefferson	(10¢) Roosevelt	(25¢) Washington	(50¢) Kennedy	($1) Sacajawea

$1.00 Washington
The dollar bill
A "buck"

$2.00 Jefferson
Two dollar bill
(rare)

*Signing of the
Declaration of
Independence*

$5.00 Lincoln
Five dollar bill
A "fiver" or "fin"

Lincoln
Memorial

$10.00 Hamilton
Ten dollar bill
A "sawbuck" or
"ten spot."

U. S. Treasury
Building

$20.00 Jackson
Twenty dollar bill

The White
House

$50.00 Grant
Fifty dollar bill

U. S. Capitol
Building

$100.00 Franklin
One hundred
dollar bill

Independence
Hall,
Philadelphia

Federal Reserve notes are printed and issued in denominations of $1, $2, $5, $10, $20, $50, and $100. The $500, $1,000, $5,000, and $10,000 denominations have not been printed since 1946.

Between 1999 and 2008 the Federal Reserve is issuing 5 new quarters each year, each commemorating one of the 50 states. The coins are being released in the order in which the states joined the Union beginning with Delaware and ending with Hawaii.

*See page 95:
Banks and Money.*

U.S. 25¢ coin is called "two bits."
Older U.S. $1 coins were called "silver dollars."

U.S. bills are called paper money and "green backs."

Canadian Coins and Bills

1¢/penny	5¢/nickel	10¢/dime	25¢/quarter	50¢/half dollar	$1/Loonie	$2/Toonie	$2/Vootie/Noonie	Face

Maple Leaf	Beaver	Schooner	Caribou	Coat of Arms	Loon	Polar Bear	Nunavut	Eliz-
abeth II								

$5.00
Sir Wilfred Laurier
Back:
Children at Play

$10.00
Sir John Macdonald
Back:
Rememberance Day
and Peace Keeping

$20.00
Queen Elizabeth II
Back:
Common Loon

$50.00
William L. M. King
Back:
Snowy Owl

$100.00
Sir Robert L. Borden
Back: Exploration
and Innovation

$1000.00
Queen Elizabeth II
Back:
Pine Grosbeak
(rare)

231

38: Television

Traditional Programming

Morning   Game shows
Daytime talk shows
Cartoons (weekends)
News programs/weather
Religious programs (Sunday)
Children's/educational programs

Afternoon   Movies
Game shows
Daytime talk shows
Afternoon soap operas
Sports events (weekends)
News programs/weather/sports
Children's/educational programs

Evenings   Movies
Documentaries
Special reports
Drama programs
Situation comedies
Evening soap operas
News programs/weather/sports

Late night   Movies
Talk shows
News programs

Television Sets

	Percent of households:
Total TV Households:	98%
Homes with:	
Color TV sets	100%
2 or more sets	81%
Basic cable/satellite	86%
VCR	89%
Remote control	98%

Favorite TV Shows

1950s
A. Godfrey's Talent Scouts
I Love Lucy
You Bet Your Life
Dragnet
The Jack Benny Show
A. Godfrey and Friends
Gunsmoke
The Red Skelton Show
December Bride
I've Got a Secret
$64,000 Question
Disneyland
The Ed Sullivan Show
Have Gun—Will Travel
The Danny Thomas Show

1960s
Bonanza
The Red Skelton Show
The Andy Griffith Show
The Beverly Hillbillies
The Ed Sullivan Show
The Lucy Show/Here's Lucy
The Jackie Gleason Show
Bewitched
Gomer Pyle
Candid Camera
The Dick Van Dyke Show
The Danny Thomas Show
Family Affair
Laugh-in
Rawhide

1970s
All in the Family
M*A*S*H
Hawaii Five-O
Happy Days
The Waltons
The Mary Tyler Moore Show
Sanford & Son
One Day at a Time
Three's Company
60 Minutes
Maude
Gunsmoke
Charlie's Angels
The Jeffersons
Laverne & Shirley

1980s
Bill Cosby Show
Cheers
Dallas
Roseanne
A Different World
America's Funniest Home Videos
Golden Girls
Wonder Years
Empty Nest
60 Minutes
Dynasty
Roseanne
Unsolved Mysteries
L.A. Law
Who's the Boss?
Grand
Murder, She Wrote
NBC Sunday Night Movie

1990s
Cheers
60 Minutes
Home Improvement
Seinfeld
E.R.
Oprah Winfrey
Veronica's Chest
Touched by an Angel
Friends
NYPD Blue
The Simpsons
Everybody Loves Raymond

2000-2006
Friends
The Simpsons
The O.C.
American Idol
House
Charmed
Sex and the City
Desperate Housewives
CSI: Miami
Arrested Development
The West Wing
Dancing with the Stars
Grey's Anatomy

233

39: U.S. Publications
U.S. Magazines Circulation

Rank Magazine, Circulation

Rank	Magazine, Circulation
1	*AARP the Magazine,* 22,675,655
2	*AARP Bulletin,* 22,075,011
3	*Reader's Digest,* 10,111,773
4	*TV Guide,* 8,211,581
5	*Better Homes & Gardens,* 7,620,932
6	*National Geographic,* 5,403,934
7	*Good Housekeeping,* 4,634,763
8	*Family Circle,* 4,296,370
9	*Ladies' Home Journal,* 4,122,460
10	*Woman's Day,* 4,048,799
11	*Time,* 4,038,508
12	*People,* 3,734,536
13	*AAA Westways,* 3,676,058
14	*Prevention,* 3,338,450
15	*Sports Illustrated,* 3,289,656
16	*Newsweek,* 3,158,988
17	*Playboy,* 3,060,676
18	*Cosmopolitan,* 2,969,952
19	*Southern Living,* 2,745,663
20	*Guideposts,* 2,640,471
21	*American Legion Magazine,* 2,528,853
22	*Maxim,* 2,517,450
23	*O, the Oprah Magazine,* 2,513,318
24	*AAA Going Places,* 2,450,540
25	*Via Magazine,* 2,435,904
26	*Redbook,* 2,412,882
27	*Glamour,* 2,371,986
28	*AAA Living,* 2,167,800
29	*Parents,* 2,049,100
30	*Smithsonian,* 2,048,322
31	*Seventeen,* 2,034,062
32	*U. S. News & World Report,* 2,028,167
33	*Parenting,* 1,972,595
34	*Money,* 1,968,211
35	*Martha Stewart Living,* 1,950,482
36	*Game Informer Magazine,* 1,934,859
37	*Real Simple,* 1,900,676
38	*ESPN the Magazine,* 1,876,136
39	*Entertainment Weekly,* 1,803,793
40	*Home & Away,* 1,801,441
41	*In Style,* 1,783,235
42	*FamilyFun,* 1,781,451
43	*Men's Health,* 1,774,558
44	*Cooking Light,* 1,732,001
45	*Country Living,* 1,723,740
46	*Endless Vacation,* 1,716,213
47	*US Weekly,* 1,668,135
48	*Shape,* 1,655,330
49	*Golf Digest,* 1,582,770
50	*Woman's World,* 1,575,214

Top U.S. Daily Newspapers

Rank City   State Newspaper   Circulation

Rank	Entry
1	Arlington,VA, *USA Today*, 2,528,437
2	New York, NY, *Wall Street Journal*, 2,058,437
3	New York, NY, *Times*, 1,683,855
4	Los Angeles, CA, *Times*, 1,231, 318
5	Washington, DC, *Post*, 960,684
6	Chicago, IL, *Tribune*, 957,212
7	New York, NY, *Daily News*, 795,153
8	Philadelphia, PA. *Inquirer*, 705,965
9	Denver, CO, *Post/Rocky Mountain News*, 704,806
10	Houston, TX, *Chronicle*, 692,557
11	New York, NY, *Post*, 691,420
12	Detroit, MI, *News/Free Press*, 669,3415
13	Dallas, TX, *Morning News*, 649,709
14	Minneapolis, MN, *Star Tribune*, 606,698
15	Boston, MA, *Globe*, 604,068
16	Newark, NJ, *Star-Ledger*, 599,628
17	Atlanta, GA, *Constitution Journal*, 561,405
18	Phoenix, AZ, *Arizona Republic*, 556,465
19	Long Island, NY, *Newsday*, 488,825
20	San Francisco, CA, *Chronicle*, 451,504
21	Cleveland, OH, *Plain Dealer*, 450,875
22	Seattle, WA, *Times/Post-Intelligencer*, 435,581
23	St. Louis, MO, *Post-Dispatch*, 423,291
24	St. Petersburg, FL, *Times*, 422,410
25	San Diego, CA, *Union-Tribune*, 408,392
26	Milwaukee, WI, *Journal Sentinel*, 404,355
27	Baltimore, MD, *Sun*, 401,918
28	Miami, FL, *Herald*, 390,171
29	Portland, OR, *Oregonian*, 384,729
30	Pittsburgh , PA, *Post-Gazette*, 373,980
31	Kansas City, MO, *Star*, 367,712
32	Orange County, CA, *Register*, 354,632
33	Columbus, OH, *Dispatch*, 352,510
34	Indianapolis, IN, *Star*, 347,217
35	San Antonio, TX, *Express-News*, 342,709
36	Orlando, FL, *Sentinel*, 341,025
37	Fort Lauderdale, FL, *South Florida Sun-Sentinel*, 339,728
38	Sacramento, CA, *Bee*, 330,993
39	Fort Worth, TX, *Star-Telegram*, 322,824
40	Tampa, FL, *Tribune & Times*, 309,916
41	Cincinnati, OH, *Enquirer/Post*, 293,151
42	Oklahoma City, OK, *Daily Oklahoman*, 287,505
43	Little Rock, AR, *Democrat-Gazette*, 275,991
44	Charlotte, NC, *Observer*, 274,125
45	Buffalo, NY, *News*, 273,177
46	Hartford, CT, *Courant*, 272,918
47	Louisville, KY, *Courier-Journal*, 271,920
48	San Jose, CA, *Mercury News*, 263,373
49	St. Paul, MN, *Pioneer Press*, 251,565
50	Des Moines, IA, *Register*, 240,912

40: Leading U.S. Advertisers

Rank	Advertiser
1	Procter & Gamble
2	General Motors Corp.
3	Time Warner
4	Verizon Communication
5	AT & T
6	Ford Motor Company
7	Walt Disney
8	Johnson & Johnson
9	GlaxoSmithKline
10	DaimlerChrysler.
11	Pfizer
12	General Electric
13	Toyota Motor Corp.
14	Sony
15	Sears Holding Corp.
16	Sprint Nextel Corp
17	McDonalds
18	Unilever
19	Viacom
20	Altria Group
21	Pepsico
22	L'Oreal
23	Federated Department Stores
24	Nissan Motor Company
25	Honda Motor Company

Ad Spending by Categories

Rank	Category	Rank	Category
1	Automotive	17	Household Equipment
2	Retail	18	Beer & Wine
3	Business, Consumer Svcs	19	Soaps & Cleansers
4	Entertainment	20	Jewelry, Optical
5	Food	21	Cigarettes
6	Drugs & Remedies	22	Miscellaneous
7	Toiletries/Cosmetics	23	Building Materials
8	Travel & Hotels	24	Pets & Pet Foods
9	Computers, Office Equip.	25	Gasoline, Lubricants
10	Direct Response Cosmetics	26	Household Furnishings
11	Candy, Snacks, Soft Drinks	27	Horticulture, Farming
12	Insurance & Real Estate	28	Liquor
13	Publishing & Media	29	Freight, Industrial
14	Apparel, Footwear	30	Industrial Materials
15	Sporting goods, Toys	31	Business Propositions
16	Electronic Equipment	32	Airplanes

41. U.S. National Documents

The U.S. National Anthem
The Star-Spangled Banner
Francis Scott Key, 1814

O say, can you see, by the dawn's early light,
What so proudly we hail'd at the twilight's last gleaming?
Whose broad stripes and bright stars, thro' the perilous fight,
O'er the ramparts we watch'd, were so gallantly streaming?
And the rockets' red glare, the bombs bursting in air,
Gave proof thro' the night that our flag was still there,
O say, does that star-spangled banner yet wave
O'er the land of the free and the home of the brave?

Declaration of Independence
Thomas Jefferson, 1776

When in the Course of human Events, it becomes necessary for one People to dissolve the Political Bands which have connected them with another, and to assume among the Powers of the Earth, the separate and equal Station to which the Laws of Nature and of Nature's God entitle them, a decent Respect to the Opinions of Mankind requires that they should declare the causes which impel them to the Separation.

We hold these Truths to be self-evident, that all Men are created equal, that they are endowed by their Creator with certain unalienable Rights, that among these are Life, Liberty and the Pursuit of Happiness — That to secure these Rights, Governments are instituted among Men, deriving their just Powers from the Consent of the Governed, that whenever any Form of Government becomes destructive of these Ends, it is the Right of the People to alter or to abolish it, and to institute new Government, laying its Foundation on such Principles, and organizing its Powers in such Form, as to them shall seem most likely to affect their Safety and Happiness. Prudence, indeed, will dictate that Governments long established should not be changed for light and transient Causes; and accordingly all Experience hath shewn, that Mankind are more disposed to suffer while Evils are sufferable, than to right themselves by abolishing the Forms to which they are accustomed. But when a long Train of Abuses and Usurpations, pursuing invariably the same Object, evinces a Design to reduce them under absolute Despotism, it is their Right, it is their Duty, to throw off such Government, and to provide new Guards for their future Security.

The Preamble of the Constitution, 1787

We the People of the United States, in order to form a more perfect Union, establish Justice, insure domestic Tranquility, provide for the common Defense, promote the general Welfare, and secure the Blessings of Liberty to ourselves and our Posterity, do ordain and establish this Constitution for the United States of America.

U.S Constitution: A Brief Summay
as amended
also see #7 *Government Structure of the U.S.*

Article I – The Legislature

1. All laws are made by Congress: the Senate and the House of Representatives.
2. A representative must be 25 years old, a U.S citizen for 7 years, and a resident of the state he or she represents. Representatives serve for 2 years. The rest of Section 2 and the amendments related to it explain how many representatives each state gets. The House chooses its own officers and has the sole power of impeachment.
3. A senator must be 30 years old, a U.S. citizen for 9 years, and a resident of the state he or she represents. Each state gets two senators and they serve for 6 years.
   The Vice President is President of the Senate, but only votes to break a tie vote. The other officers of the Senate are chosen by the Senate. The Senate tries officials impeached by the House and can remove them from office.
4. Congress shall meet once a year.
5. Each house of Congress judges the election and qualifications of its members and sets its own rules. Members can be expelled by a 2/3 vote of that house.
6. Members of Congress are paid by the U.S. Treasury. They are not allowed to have any other government job. They cannot be arrested during their term in office except for treason, a felony, or a breach of the peace. They can only be questioned about what they say in Congress while they are in Congress.
7. All bills raising money originate in the House. The Senate may amend the bill. It then goes to the President. If he signs it, or holds it for 10 days without signing it, the bill becomes law. If he vetoes it, the bill goes back to the Congress. They can rewrite it, or if they vote on it again and it passes by a 2/3 majority, it becomes law.
8. Congress has the power to tax and set other duties, but all taxes and duties must be the same in all the states. It can borrow money, regulate trade with other countries and among the states, make laws regulating naturalization and bankruptcy, coin money, set its value, and set standards of weights and measures. It can set punishment for counterfeiting, set up a post office, and set up rules for patents and copyright. It can set up courts below the Supreme Court. It can define and punish piracy and felony at sea and offenses against international law. Only Congress can declare war or raise and support and make rules for regulating an army and navy. To enforce its laws, suppress insurrections, and repel invasions, Congress can also call up, organize, arm, and discipline a militia, although each state trains its militia and appoints its officers. Congress has authority over Washington, D.C., and all government property.
9. The writ of Habeas Corpus shall not be suspended except in cases of rebellion or invasion. Congress cannot favor one state over another in matters of taxes or duties. No money can be spent by the government unless Congress provides it. The government shall not grant titles of nobility, nor shall anyone working for the government accept anything of value from another country.
10. States cannot have treaties with other states or countries nor make laws or collect taxes which conflict with the rights of the federal government, without permission of Congress.

Article II – The Executive

1. Section 1 describes the 4-year term of the President, the way he or she is elected, and how he or she is paid. It explains that the Vice President takes over if the Presidency is vacant. It gives the oath of office: *I do solemnly swear (or affirm) that I will faithfully execute the Office of President of the United States, and will to the best of my ability, preserve, protect, and defend the Constitution of the United States.*
2. The President is the Commander-in-Chief of the Armed Forces, including the Malitia when it is serving the Federal Government. He also runs the executive departments, and he or she has the right to grant pardons, except in cases of impeachment.
   With the advice and consent of the Senate, if 2/3 of the Senate agrees, the President can make treaties with other countries and appoint ambassadors, judges of the Supreme

Court, and all other officers of the government not mentioned in the Constitution, Congress may by law give the President the right to make these appointments or give that right to the courts or department heads. If offices need to be filled when the Senate is not in session, the President may appoint someone to serve until the end of that session of Congress.

3. From time to time the President must give Congress information on the State of the Union and recommend actions for their consideration. He or she can call either or both houses of Congress into a special session, and if they cannot decide when to adjourn, he may adjourn them until a date of his choice. The President receives ambassadors and other public ministers, commissions officers of the United States, and runs the country under law.

4. The President, Vice President, and all civil officers of the U.S. shall be removed from office only if they are impeached for and convicted of treason, bribery, or "other high crimes and misdemeanors."

Article III – The Courts

1. The judicial power is vested in one Supreme Court and other courts set up by Congress. Judges hold their appointments for life as long as they are not removed by Congress for bad behavior. Their pay cannot be cut.

2. The federal courts decide all national and international cases, in law and equity, relating to the Constitution and treaties, involving the government and other nations or maritime law, or controversies between the states or between individuals and states other than their own, or between individuals in different states or involving property in different states. Cases involving any state or officers of other countries start in the Supreme Court. All other cases, unless Congress makes exceptions, go to lower courts but can be appealed to the Supreme Court. Trials of crimes are held in the state where the crime was committed, and they are jury trials. When a crime is not committed in a state, the site of the trial is set by the Congressional law.

3. The only crime considered to be treason is participation in a war against the U.S. or giving aid and comfort to its enemies. At least two witnesses of an overt act are necessary to prove treason. Congress can punish a traitor

physically and financially, but only while living.

Article IV – The States

1. The laws, records, and legal decisions of each state must be accepted by the others. Conflicts must be settled by laws passed by Congress.

2. Citizens of every state have the privileges and are protected by the laws of the U.S.

3. Persons charged with treason, felonies, or other crimes, when caught in another state, shall be returned to the state with jurisdiction over the crime, if that state requests it.

4. Congress can make new states, but if the new state includes territory of other states, the legislatures of those states must consent. Congress makes the rules and regulations for all territories and other properties of the U.S.

5. The U.S. guarantees a Republican form of government for every state and must protect every state from invasion or domestic violence.

Article V – Amendments

A convention may be called to amend this Constitution if either 2/3 of both houses of Congress or 2/3 of the states vote that it is necessary. Once called, though the Congress or the states may have proposed specific amendments, the convention can propose any amendments to the Constitution. However, these amendments must then be ratified by the legislatures of or conventions in 3/4 of the states, the choice of legislatures or conventions being a Congressional decision. No amendment can deprive any state of its equal representation in the Senate without its consent, not shall the legislative power of the Congress nor the rights of individuals and states given in Article 1, section 9, be changed in any way before 1808.

Article VI – The Constitution

All agreements and debts made by the U.S. under the old Articles of Confederation are valid under this Constitution.

This Constitution and all laws and treaties made under it shall be the supreme law of the land, overruling any laws or judges in the states. All officers of the U.S. and the states must be bound to support the Constitution, and no religious test may ever be required as qualification for such U.S. or state offices.

Article VI – Ratification

9 states were needed to ratify the Constitution. The Constitutional Convention passed it on 17 September, 1787. It was ratified by all 13 states.

The Bill of Rights
The Ten Original Constitutional Amendments, 1791

First Amendment
Congress shall make no law respecting an establishment of religion, or prohibiting the free excercise thereof; or abridging the freedom of speech, or of the press; or the right of the people peaceably to assemble, and to petition the Government for a redress of grievances.

Second Amendment
A well-regulated militia, being necessary to the security of a free State, the right of the people to keep and bear arms, shall not be infringed.

Third Amendment
No soldier shall, in time of peace be quartered in any house, without the consent of the owner, nor in time of war, but in a manner to be prescribed by law.

Fourth Amendment
The right of the people to be secure in their persons, houses, papers, and effects, against unreasonable searches and seizures, shall not be violated, and no warrants shall issue, but upon probable cause, supported by oath or affirmation, and particularly describing the place to be searched, and the persons or things to be seized.

Fifth Amendment
No person shall be held to answer for a capital, or otherwise infamous crime, unless on a presentment or indictment of a Grand Jury, except in cases arising in the land or naval forces, or in the militia, when in actual service in time of war or public danger; nor shall any person be subject for the same offense to be twice put in jeopardy of life or limb; nor shall be compelled in any criminal case to be a witness against himself, nor be deprived of life, liberty, or property, without due process of law; nor shall private property be taken for public use without just compensation.

Sixth Amendment
In all criminal prosecutions, the accused shall enjoy the right to a speedy and public trial, by an impartial jury of the State and district wherein the crime shall have been committed, which district shall have been previously ascertained by law, and to be informed of the nature and cause of the accusation; to be confronted with the witnesses against him; to have compulsory process for obtaining witnesses in his favor, and to have the assistance of counsel for his defense.

Seventh Amendment
In suits at common law, where the value in controversy shall exceed twenty dollars, the right of trial by jury shall be preserved, and no fact tried by a jury shall be otherwise reexamined in a court of the United States, than according to the rules of the common law.

Eighth Amendment
Excessive bail shall not be required, nor excessive fines imposed, nor cruel and unusual punishments inflicted.

Ninth Amendment
The enumeration in the Constitution, of certain rights, shall not be construed to deny or disparage others retained by the people.

Tenth Amendment
The powers not delegated to the United States by the Constitution, nor prohibited by it to the States, are reserved to the States respectively, or to the people.

The Gettysburg Address
Abraham Lincoln, 1863

Fourscore and seven years ago our fathers brought forth on this continent a new nation, conceived in liberty and dedicated to the proposition that all men are created equal.

Now we are engaged in a great civil war, testing whether that nation or any nation so conceived and so dedicated can long endure. We are met on a great battlefield of that war. We have come to dedicate a portion of that field, as a final resting place for those who here gave their lives that that nation might live. It is altogether fitting and proper that we should do this.

But, in a larger sense, we cannot dedicate—we cannot consecrate—we cannot hallow—this ground. The brave men, living and dead, who struggled here, have consecrated it, far above our poor power to add or detract. The world will little note, nor long remember, what we say here, but it can never forget what they did here. It is for us the living, rather, to be here dedicated to the great task remaining before us—that from these honored dead we take increased devotion to that cause for which they gave the last full measure of devotion—that we here highly resolve that these dead shall not have died in vain—that this nation, under God, shall have a new birth of freedom—and that government of the people, by the people, for the people, shall not perish from the earth.

Statue of Liberty Inscription
The New Colossus
Emma Lazarus

Not like the brazen giant of Greek fame,
With conquering limbs astride from land to land;
Here at our sea-washed, sunset gates shall stand
A mighty woman with a torch, whose flame
Is the imprisoned lightning, and her name
Mother of Exiles. From her beacon-hand
Glows world-wide welcome; her mild eyes command
The air-bridged harbor that twin cities frame.
"Keep ancient lands, your storied pomp!" cries she
With silent lips. "Give me your tired, your poor,
Your huddled masses yearning to breathe free,
The wretched refuse of your teeming shore.
Send these, the homeless, tempest-tost to me,
I lift my lamp beside the golden door!"

America the Beautiful
Katherine Lee Bates, 1893

O beautiful for spacious skies,
For amber waves of grain,
For purple mountain's majesties
Above the fruited plain.
America! America!
God shed his grace on thee,
And crown thy good with brotherhood
From sea to shining sea.

"I Have a Dream"
Martin Luther King, 1963

Five score years ago, a great American, in whose symbolic shadow we stand, signed the Emancipation Proclamation. This momentous decree came as a great beacon of hope to millions of Negro slaves who had been seared in the flames of withering injustice. It came as a joyous daybreak to end the long night of captivity.

But one hundred years later, we must face the tragic fact that the Negro is still not free.

I say to you today, my friends, that in spite of difficulties and frustrations of the moments, I still have a dream. It is a dream deeply rooted in the American dream.

I have a dream that one day this nation will rise up and live out the true meaning of its creed: "We hold these truths to be self evident; that all men are created equal."

I have a dream that one day on the red hills of Georgia the sons of former slaves and the sons of former slave owners will be able to sit down together at the table of brotherhood.

I have a dream that one day even the state of Mississippi, a desert state sweltering with the heat of injustice and oppression, will be transformed into an oasis of freedom and justice.

I have a dream that my four little children will one day live in a nation where they will not be judged by the color of their skin but by the content of their character.

I have a dream today.

I have a dream that one day the state of Alabama, whose governor's lips are presently dripping with the words of interposition and nullification, will be transformed into a situation where little black boys and girls will be able to join hands with little white boys and white girls and walk together as sisters and brothers.

I have a dream today.

I have a dream that one day every valley shall be exalted, every hill and mountain shall be made low, the rough places will be made plain, and the crooked places will be made straight, and the glory of the Lord shall be revealed, and all flesh shall see it together.

This is our hope. This is the faith with which I return to the South. With this faith we will be able to hew out of the mountain of despair a stone of hope. With this faith we will be able to transform the jangling discords of our nation into a beautiful symphony of brotherhood. With this faith we will be able to work together, to pray together, to struggle together, to go to jail together, to stand up for freedom together, knowing that we will be free one day.

This will be the day when all God's children will be able to sing with new meaning:

> My country, 'tis of thee,
> Sweet land of liberty,
> Of thee I sing:
> Land where my fathers died,
> Land of the pilgrims' pride,
> From every mountain side
> Let freedom ring.

And if America is to be a great nation, this must become true. So let freedom ring from the prodigious hilltops of New Hampshire. Let freedom ring from the mighty mountains of New York. Let freedom ring from the heightening Alleghenies of Pennsylvania. Let freedom ring from the snow capped Rockies of Colorado. Let freedom ring from the curvaceous peaks of California. But not only that; let freedom ring from Stone Mountain of Georgia. Let freedom ring from Lookout Mountain of Tennessee. Let freedom ring from every hill and molehill of Mississippi. From every mountainside, let freedom ring.

When we let freedom ring, when we let it ring from every village and every hamlet, from every state and every city, we will be able to speed up that day when all of God's children, black men and white men, Jews and Gentiles, Protestants and Catholics, will be able to join hands and sing in the words of the old Negro spiritual, "Free at last, free at last, thank God almighty, we are free at last!"

Pledge of Allegiance

I pledge allegiance to the flag of
the United States of America and
to the republic for which it stands,
one nation under God, indivisible,
with liberty and justice for all.

42. Canadian National Anthem

Official Lyrics in English

O Canada! Our home and native land!
True patriot love in all thy sons command.
With glowing hearts we see thee rise,
The True North strong and free
From far and wide, O Canada,
We stand on guard for thee.
Chorus.
God keep our land glorious and free!
O Canada, we stand on guard for thee.
O Canada, we stand on guard for thee.

Official Lyrics in French

O Canada! Terre de nos aïeux,
Ton front est ceint de fleurons glorieux.
Car ton bras sait porter l'épée,
Il sait porter la croix!
Ton histoire est une épopée
Des plus brillants exploits.
Chorus.
Et ta valeur, de foi trempée!
Protègera nos foyers et nos droits.
Protègera nos foyers et nos droits.

English Translation of the Official French Lyrics

O Canada! Land of our forefathers,
Thy brow is wreathed with a glorious garland of flowers.
As is thy arm ready to wield the sword,
So also is it ready to carry the cross!
Thy history is an epic
Of the most brilliant exploits.
Chorus.
And thy valour steeped in faith!
Will protect our homes and our rights.
Will protect our homes and our rights.

Note: This material is from the Canadian National website: www.pch.gc.ca/ceremonial-symb/english/emb_anthem.html. There are many variations of both the French and English versions. The original French poem was by Sir Adolphe-Basile Routhier. It was first sung in 1880, and the first widely known translation was written by R. Stanley Weir in 1908.

The
Metalinguistic
Aspect
and
Miscellaneous
Materials

Contents

1: Glossary of Grammatical Terms

Absolute construction

A word or phrase which modifies the sentence as a whole, not any single element in it.

*The **game over**, the players left the field.*
*The **cattle having been branded**, the cowboys saddled up and rode off.*

Active

See Voice

Adjective

A word which modifies a noun or a pronoun.

*The **old** man walked across the **narrow** street.*

Adjective clause

A dependent clause serving an adjective function. See **Relative clause.**

*The woman **who performed** lives next door to me.*

Adjective phrase

A word or group of words that functions as an adjective.

dull, exceedingly dull, so very dull

Adverb

A word which modifies a verb, an adjective, or another adverb.

*The car moved **slowly** in very heavy traffic.*

Adverbial

A word or group of words which functions as an adverb.

*He works **in a large university.***
*It rained **very hard.***
*He was happy **when his friend arrived.***

Adverbial clause

A dependent clause serving an adverbial function, Common adverbial clauses include:

Comparison (as...as, as...than)

*I can't run **as fast as I used to.***

Concession (though, although, even if)

***Although I had a good time**, I was happy to leave.*

Condition - See Conditional sentences.

Reason (because, as, since)

*They turned on the lights **because it was too dark.***

Result (so...that, such ...that)

*He spoke **so fast that no one understood a thing.***

Time (when, as, while, until, as soon as)

***As soon as he lit his cigar**, people began to leave the room.*

Agreement

Correspondence between grammatically related elements. Agreement in number and person between a subject and its verb.

*The **children play.** The **child plays.***

Agreement in gender, number, and person between a pronoun and its antecedent.

*The girl washed **her face.***

Antecedent

The word to which a pronoun refers.

***Aunt Mary** fainted when **she** heard the news.*

Appositive

A word, phrase, or clause used as a noun and placed next to another noun to modify it.

*George Washington, **the president,** slept here.*

Article

A and *an* are indefinite articles. *The* is the definite article.

Auxiliary

Function words which help other verbs indicate tense, mood, or voice (be, do, have). Modal auxiliaries *(can, may, might, must, should, etc.)* serve also as structural signals and have a meaning of their own *(ability, obligation, possibility).*

Case

English has the remnants of three cases: *subjective, possessive,* and *objective*. Nouns are inflected for case in the possessive *(John's).* Some pronouns and the relative pronoun *who* are inflected.

subjective: I, *he, she, we, they, who.*
possessive: *my (mine), your (yours), his, her (hers), its, our (ours), their (theirs), whose.*
objective: *me, him, her, us, them, whom.*

Clause

A group of words containing a subject and a predicate. See Independent clause and Dependent clause.

Collective noun

A noun singular in appearance which indicates a class or group of persons or things.

*a **committee** of citizens, an **army***

246

Comparative

The form of adjectives and adverbs which is used to indicate relative superiority.

tall	**taller**	**less tall**
important	**more important**	**less important**
slowly	**more slowly**	**less slowly**

Complement

A word or group of words that follow the verb and complete the sentence.

*She is **in the kitchen.***
*I know **where she is.***

Compound sentence

A sentence which combines two or more independent clauses.

He whistled, and she worked.

Complex sentence

A sentence which contains one or more dependent clauses.

He whistled while she worked.

Compound complex sentence

A sentence which contains two or more independent clauses and one or more dependent clauses.

He whistled and she worked until they both got tired.

Conditional sentences

Conditional sentences have two parts, the conditional clause and the main clause. There are three types:

1. Real condition:

   If you bother the cat, it will scratch you.

2. Unreal, contrary-to-fact condition (present):

   If I were you, I would keep the money.
   If you took a trip, where would you go?

3. Unreal, contrary-to-fact condition (past):

   If I had known you were coming, I would have baked you a cake.
   If I had been Lincoln, I wouldn't have gone to the theater that night.

Conjunction

A word used to connect sentences or sentence parts. See also **Coordinating conjunctions, Subordinating conjunctions.**

Connective

See **Conjunction.**

Conjunctive adverbs

Adverbs used to relate two independent clauses separated by a semicolon:

then, consequently, however, moreover, therefore, etc.

Coordinating Conjunctions

The simple conjunction that connect sentences and sentence parts of equal rank:

and, but, or, nor, for, yet, so.

Correlative conjunctions

Pairs of conjunctions which join sentence parts:

either. . .or, neither. . . nor,
not only...but also, but...and.

Count noun

A noun that can be made plural, usually by adding -s.

Demonstrative adjectives and pronouns

Words used to point out someone or something:

this, that, these, those.
Also called demonstrative determiners.

Dependent (subordinate clause)

A group of words which contains both a subject and a predicate but which does not stand alone as a sentence. A dependent clause always serves a noun, adverb, or adjective function. See **Noun clause, Adjective clause, Adverbial clause, Relative clause.**

Determiners

A class of modifiers which includes articles *(a, an, the)*, possessives *(my, John's, his)*, demonstratives *(this, that)*, quantifiers *(some, any, two, each)*.

Diphthong

Two vowel sounds joined in one syllable to form one speech sound:

out, oil, I.

Direct object

A noun, pronoun, or other substantive which receives the action of the verb.

*Jack climbed the **bean stalk** into the sky.*

Direct speech

Repeats the speaker's exact words, enclosing them in quotation marks.

*He said, **"I've lost my umbrella."***

Elliptical clause

A clause in which one or more words necessary for the full subject-predicate structure are omitted but "understood."

*The manager admired no one else as much as **(he admired**—"understood") her.*

Expletive

The *it* or *there* which serves to fill the subject slot in *it is, there is,* and *there are* sentences.

***It** is easy to understand.*
***There is** a fly in my soup.*

247

Finite verb

A verb in the present or past form, e.g., the finite forms of the verb *be* are *is, am, are, was,* and *were.* The non-finite forms are *be, being,* and *been.*

Function words

Words which establish grammatical relationships within a sentence: articles, auxiliaries, conjunctions, prepositions, pronouns, determiners, intensifiers, and interjections.

Future

I will work, I shall work, I am going to work, I work tomorrow, etc.

Gender

The quality of nouns and pronouns that determines the choice between masculine, female, or neuter *(he, she, it.)*

Gerund

See **Verbal**.

Idiom

An expression that does not conform to general grammatical patterns but is established through usage as the way of conveying a given meaning.
hold up, hold down, be beside oneself, kick the bucket.

Indefinite pronouns

Pronouns not pointing out a particular person, thing, or definite quantity. *Some, any, each, every, everyone, everybody, nobody, anyone, anybody, one, neither* are among the most common.

Independent clause

A group of words which contains a subject and a predicate and which can stand alone as a sentence.

Indirect object

A word which indirectly receives the action of the verb.
*The witch gave **the pretty girl** a poisoned apple.*

Indirect speech

Paraphrases of the speaker's words.
He said he had lost his umbrella.

Infinitive

See **Verbal.**

Inflection

Changes in the form of words to reflect changes in grammatical relationships:
the cabins; he walks; she's talking; quickest.

Intensifier

Words that modify adjectives or adverbs and express degree: ***very** beautiful, **quite** young, **rather** old.*

Intensive pronoun

A reflexive pronoun ending in *-self -selves,* and used for emphasis.
*I'd rather do it **myself***

Interjection

A word used to exclaim or to express emotion: *ah, oh, ouch.*

Interrogative pronouns

Who, whose, whom, what, which, when used in questions.

Intonation

The rising and falling of the pitch of the voice in speech.

Intransitive verb

A verb which has no direct object
*The tide **turned** at noon.*

Linking verb

A verb which does not express action but links the subject to another word which names or describes it. *Be, become, seem, appear,* and *look* are common linking verbs.

Mass noun (Non-count noun)

A noun that refers to a quantity and cannot be preceded by a cardinal number, such as *three: sugar, milk, hunger.*

Modal verb

An auxiliary verb that adds meaning to the main verb: *can, may, might.*

Modifier

A word, phrase, or clause which limits or describes other sentence elements or the sentence as a whole.

Mood

The classification of verb forms as
indicative (plain or factual):
I am ready;
imperative (request or command):
Be ready at six; and
subjunctive (hypothetical or contrary-to-fact):
I wish you were ready.

Nominal

Any structure that functions as a noun.

Nominative case

See Case.

Non-restrictive relative clause

A clause which provides further information not essential to identification of the subject or complement and is set off usually with commas.
*John Jones, **who spends a lot of money**, has many friends.*

Noun

A word which names and classifies people, animals, things, ideas.
Thomas Jefferson, lemon, religion, alligator, Paris, worm, justice, school, committee.

Noun clause

A dependent clause serving a nominal function.
*Everyone agrees **that the play was a success.***

Noun phrase

The element in the sentence which functions as subject, object, or complement.
***The pretty girl** is **Julia**.*
***She** is **my younger sister**.*

Number

Forms that indicate singular or plural.

Object of a preposition

Completes the idea of time, position, direction, etc., begun by a preposition.
at his desk, towards the door

Objective complement

A complement after the direct object that provides another name for the object or otherwise amplifies it.
They elected him president.
The war made many women widows.
Everyone believed him crazy.

Participle

See **Verbal.**

Parts of speech

Noun, pronoun, adjective, adverb, conjunction, interjection, preposition, article.

Past

I worked, etc.

Perfect

I have worked, I had worked, I will have worked.

Person

Forms that express the person speaking, spoken to, or spoken about.
first person: I, *we*
second person: *you*
third person: *he, she, it, they*

Phoneme

A basic unit of sound in a language. (/i/, /p/, /iy/)

Phrasal verbs

A combination of a verb and a preposition or an adverb which forms a new vocabulary item. Phrasal verbs are classified as *intransitive, separable,* and *non-separable.*
intransitive: *John **got up** early this morning.*
separable: *John **calls up** his wife from the office.*
*John **calls** his wife **up** from the office.*
*John **calls** her **up** from the office.*
non-separable:
*Everybody **picks on** fat people.*

Possessive adjectives

My, your, his, her, its, our, their.

Predicate adjective

An adjective following a linking verb and describing the subject.
The flowers look artificial.

Predicate nominative

A word or group of words which follows a linking verb and identifies the subject.
The book is a bestselling science-fiction novel.

Preposition

A connective which joins a noun or a pronoun to the rest of the sentence. A prepositional phrase may serve either an adverb or an adjective function.
adverb: *The guide led us into the forest.*
adjective: *Jack is a master of many trades.*

Present

I work, she/he works, etc.

Progressive (Continuous)

I am working, I was working, I have been working.

Pronouns

Words which stand for nouns, classified as:
personal: (I, you, *he*)
possessive: *(mine, yours, his, hers)*
reflexive/intensive: *(myself, himself, ourselves)*
demonstrative: *(this, that, those)*
relative: *(who, which, what, that, whose)*
interrogative: *(who, which, what)*
indefinite: *(one, anyone, everyone)*

Quantifiers

Words denoting how much *(some, any, most, few, one, two, three)*

Reciprocal pronouns

Each other, one another.

Relative clause

A dependent clause that is related to the main clause by a relative pronoun.

*The book **that he recommended** is on sale.*

Restrictive relative clause: A clause that contributes to the identification of the noun it modifies, not separated by a comma from the noun. See Non-restrictive relative clause.

The man who called me up was a complete stranger.

Sentence

A grammatically complete unit of thought or expression, containing at least a subject and a predicate.

Simple sentence

A sentence consisting of only one independent clause.

Stress

Pronouncing a syllable or a word in such a way that it makes it more prominent in a word or sentence respectivley.

conductor, Let's go.

Substantive

See **Nominal.**

Subject

A word or group of words about which the sentence or clause makes a statement.

The dog jumped into the car.

Subject complement

See **Predicate nominative; Predicate adjective**

Subjunctive

See **Mood.**

Subordinating conjunctions

Conjunctions which join sentence parts of unequal rank. Usually they begin dependent clauses. Some of the most common ones are:

because, since, though, although,
if, when, while, before, after, as,
until, so that, as long as, whereas,
in order that.

Superlative

The form of adjectives and adverbs used to express absolute superiority.

the tallest	***the least tall***
the most important	*the least important*
the most slowly	*the least slowly*

Syntax

The rules of sentence formation.

Tag questions

Short *yes / no* questions added to statements.

*It's a beautiful day, **isn't it?***
*You haven't seen the film, **have you?***

Tense

The system of verb forms expressing primarily different relationships in time.

Transitive verb

A verb which normally requires an object.

*Monkeys **love** bananas.*

Verb

A word or group of words expressing action, being, or state of being.

*I **swallowed** a fly.*
*What **is** man?*
*She **seems** happy.*

Verbal

A word or phrase derived from a verb and used as a noun, an adjective, or an adverb. Verbals consist of infinitives, gerunds, or participles.

   infinitive: begins with to (sometimes understood) and is used as a noun, an adverb,or an adjective.

   noun: ***To do such a thing*** *would be disastrous.*

   adverb: *Many people jog **to keep physically fit.***

   adjective: *I'm ready **to testify,** your Honor.*

   gerund: ends in -ing and is used as a noun.

   Playing with matches *is a favorite passtime among children.*

   participle: ends in *-ing, -ed,* and is used as an adjective.

   *I can't live without **running** water.*

   Accompanied *by his faithful dog, Daniel roamed the woods.*

Verb phrase

Consists of the main verb and one or more auxiliaries.

*It **is beginning** to rain.*
*It **has been raining** for a long time.*

Modern grammarians use the term **verb phrase** to indicate the verb and all that goes with it (predicate) or the verb and its modifiers.

*The old man and the boy **had quietly taken the book from the library.***

Voice

A distinction in verb forms between *active* (the subject is acting) and passive (the subject is acted upon).

   active: *Elmer **fed** the chickens.*

   passive: *The chickens **were fed** by Elmer.*

2: A Comparison of Three Phonetic Alphabets
Consonants

Sounds   Representations

	I.P.A.*	T-S.**	Dict.***
may	/m/	/m/	m
bay	/b/	/b/	b
pay	/p/	/p/	p
way	/w/	/w/	w
whey	/hw/	/hw/	hw
vee	/v/	/v/	v
fee	/f/	/f/	f
thee	/ð/	/ð/	th
thigh	/θ/	/θ/	*th*
new	/n/	/n/	n
dew	/d/	/d/	d
too	/t/	/t/	t
Lou	/l/	/l/	l
zoo	/z/	/z/	z
Sue	/s/	/s/	s
you	/j/	/y/	y
rue	/r/	/r/	r
mea**s**ure	/ʒ/	/ž/	zh
show	/ʃ/	/š/	sh
joke	/dʒ/	/ǰ/	j
choo	/tʃ/	/č/	ch
ba**ng**	/ŋ/	/ŋ/	ng
ba**g**	/g/	/g/	g
ba**ck**	/k/	/k/	k
hi	/h/	/h/	h

*International Phonetic Alphabet
**Trager-Smith System
***American Heritage dictionary

Vowels

Sounds   **Representations**

	I.P.A.*	T-S.**	Dict.***
beat	/i/	/iy/	ē
bit	/ɪ/	/i/	ĭ
bait	/e/	/ey/	ā
bet	/ɛ/	/e/	ĕ
bat	/æ/	/æ/	ă
but	/ʌ/	/ə/	ŭ
alone	/ə/	/ə/	ə
boot	/u/	/uw/	o͞o
put	/ʊ/	/u/	o͝o
boat	/o/	/ow/	ō
bought	/ɔ/	/ɔ/	ô
pot	/ɑ/	/a/	ŏ
how	/aʊ/	/aw/ /æw/	ou
I	/aɪ/	/ay/	ī
boy	/ɔɪ/	/oy/	oi
ear		/ir/	îr
air		/er/	âr
marry		/ær/	ăr
father		/ər/	ər
fur		/ər/	ûr
poor		/ur/	o͞or
or		/or/	ôr
are		/ar/	är

3: A Brief Guide to Punctuation

Punctuation		Used for	Example(s)
Apostrophe	'	to indicate omissions in contractions	doesn't, won't
		to indicate possession	Mary's, the Joneses'
		to indicate plurals of letters and numerals	1870's, p's and q's
Brackets	[ ]	to indicate comment or question in quoted material	"He [Lincoln] was assassinated by a mad actor."
		to indicate comment or question within material in parentheses	(Kuwait was liberated [was turned into a desolate battleground] by the U.N. forces in March,1991).
Colon	:	in writing clock time	9:15, 2:47,17:09
		to introduce a list	We need the following items: soap, toothpaste, and hand lotion.
		after the names of speakers in a dialogue	Joe: Will you come, Honey? Sue: Are you nuts? No way!
		before a formal quotation	The tall speaker began: "Four score and seven years ago,....
		after salutations in formal or business letters	Dear Sir: Dear Ms. Landsdowne:
Comma	,	after *yes* or *no* in a response	Yes, we have no bananas.
		before the conjunction in a compound sentence except when the clauses are short	The oldest boy is going to school, and the youngest is going to work. He walked and she rode.
		to separate the elements in an address	New Orleans, Louisana, U. S. A. They live at 418 Cedar Street, Winnetka, Illinois
		to separate the elements in a date	He was born on Tuesday, January 25, 1944, in Chicago.
		to separate equivalent elements in a series	Watch the stocks of Target, Ames, and Walmart.
		to separate a speaker's words from the introductory statement	John asked, "May I leave?"
		to group large numbers into thousands	9,121; 1,268,421,135
		to set off the name of a person spoken to in direct speech	Mary, take this ring.
		to separate an introductory clause from the sentence	When the party was over, I walked home.

Punctuation	Used for	Example(s)
Comma, cont.	after a mild exclamation	Well, I don't care.
	before and after an appositive	George, a famous poet, spoke next.
	to separate a tag question from the rest of the sentence	It's cold, isn't it?
	before and after a non-restrictive adjective clause	Punctuation, which is essential for writing, seems complicated at first.
Dash —	to indicate an interruption or an afterthought	We'll be there—at last—in an hour! I'll do it—at least, I'll try.
	to indicate special emphasis in place of a comma	Give people what they want—money, fame, and power.
Exclamation Point !	to indicate strong feeling or emotion or for emphasis	Help! Watch out! She said she'd jump and she did!
Hyphen -	in certain fixed expressions	person-to-person, matter-of-fact, station-to-station
	in writing out compound numbers	twenty-one, ninety-nine, twenty-first, ninety-ninth
	in expressions of clock time	It's seven-thirty. It's one-fifteen.
	in joining a prefix to a proper name	pre-Columbian, post-Roosevelt, un-Christian
	in joining a prefix to a noun whose first letter is the same as the last letter of the prefix	anti-intellectual, pre-existing, post-temperance
Parenthesis ( )	to enclose remarks, comments, explanations that interrupt the main thought	She invited the two men (they are cousins) to the party. If it rains (it usually doesn't this time of year), we'll postpone the picnic.
Period .	at the end of a statement	I want to be alone.
	after initials and abbreviations	Mr. P. T. Barnum. It's 7 p.m.
	to indicate cents/decimals	$5.39; 257.0932; .00906
Question Mark ?	at the end of a direct question	Where does it all end?
	after a tag question	You like to talk, don't you?

Punctuation	Used for	Example(s)

Quotation " " to enclose direct quotations — "Come here," Jim said.

Marks

around titles of chapters — "The Return to Witchwood"

articles in magazines or newspapers — "Wood Stove Madness," *Country Journal*

songs, poems, radio and TV programs — "Michelle, Ma Belle" "Hurt Hawks" "Music from the Hearts of Space" "I Love Lucy"

with other punctuation, as follows: — "Come, " he said. "I'm going." I said, "I will;" I followed. "Can you see?" he asked. Did I answer, "No?"

Semicolon ; in a compound sentence without a connective — The singular form is "mouse;" the plural form is "mice."

in a sentence with two main clauses joined by a conjunctive adverb. — The teacher was sick; therefore, the class was called off. Roseanne ran a good race; however, she failed to qualify for the finals.

Underlining and *Italics* — Use underlining in handwritten or typed material and Italics in printed material:

for titles of periodicals and books — <u>Newsweek</u>, <u>A Farewell to Arms</u>

foreign phrases and words used in an English context — And then, *alors,* there she was. "<u>Cuidado,</u>" I warned myself, "You're a fool, but <u>que, sera, sera.</u>

words emphasized — I wanted *three* tickets, not four!

the names of ships, trains and airplanes — *Titanic,* <u>Orient Express,</u> *Constellation, Spirit of St. Louis*

4: Useful Spelling Rules

A. If a word ends in **y** preceded by a consonant, change the **y** to an **i** before every suffix except **-ing.**

salary	salaries	copy	copying
marry	married	try	trying
lonely	loneliness	fly	flying
worry	worried	worry	worrying

B. Write **i** before **e**, except after **c** or when sounded like **a**, as in *neighbor* and *weigh.*

i before **e:**   *brief, piece, chief, yield*
e before **i:**   *receive, deceive, ceiling, freight, sleigh*

Exceptions: *either, neither, seize, leisure, weird, species, financier*

C. If a word has only one syllable and ends with a single consonant preceded by a single vowel *(hop, bat)* and you add a suffix beginning with a vowel **(-er, -ed, -ing),** double the final consonant.

stop	stopped	trip	tripped
bat	batter	drop	dropping
rub	rubbing	spin	spinning

If the word has more than one syllable and the final syllable is stressed, double the final consonant.

occur	occurring	confer	conferred
admit	admitted	omit	omitted

D. If a word ends with a silent **e** and you add a suffix,

drop the **e** if the suffix begins with a vowel:

love	lovable	move	moving
desire	desirable	use	usable

but keep the e if the **e** is preceded by **c** or **g** and the suffix begins with **a, o,** or **u:**

notice	noticeable	manage	manageable
courage	courageous		

Exceptions: words ending in **ee** never drop the final **ee:**

agree	agreeing	flee	fleeing	see	seeing

keep the **e** if the suffix begins with a consonant:

use	useful	engage	engagement
love	lovely	move	movement

Exceptions: words that end in **-ple, -ble and -tle,** drop the -le before -**ly:**

simple	simply	probable	probably

256

5: Differences between British/Canadian* and American (U. S.) Spelling

American		British	
e	*anesthesia* *encyclopedia*	**ae**	*anaesthesia* *encyclopaedia*
-ection	*connection* *reflection*	**-exion***	*connexion* *reflexion*
-ed	*burned* *learned* *spelled*	**-t***	*burnt* *learnt* *spelt*
-ense	*license* *defense*	**-ence**	*licence* *defence**
-er	*center* *meter* *theater*	**-re**	*centre* *metre* *theatre*
-ization	*civilization* *naturalization*	**-isation***	*civilisation* *naturalisation*
-ize	*criticize* *memorize*	**-ise***	*criticise* *memorise*
-ll	*fulfill* *skillful*	**-l**	*fulfil* *skilful*
-ment	*judgment* *argument*	**-ement**	*judgement* *arguement**
-or	*color* *neighbor*	**-our**	*colour* *neighbour*

Note: **In British usage,** words ending in an l preceded by a single vowel usually double the l.

quarrel	quarrelling	model	modelling
travel	travelling	signal	signalling

In American usage, the consonant is doubled only if the last syllable is accented.

signal	signaling	excel	excellent
travel	traveling	propel	propeller

British spelling is often seen in the United States, and in some cases it is quite common; *encyclopaedia, centre, judgement, traveller, theatre,* for example, are frequently encountered. However, these spellings are not the normal, preferred spelling.

* In Canada, British spelling is generally preferred. However, newspapers often use U.S. spelling because it "saves space." In other words, although British spelling is generally considered the norm in Canada, Canadians often use U.S. spellings, particularly in the cases marked with an asterisk (*) above.

257

6: Some American - British Vocabulary Differences

American*	British
aisle (theater)	gangway (theatre)
apartment	flat
baby carriage	perambulator, pram
bar	pub
bartender	barman
bathtub	bath
battery (automobile)	accumulator
bill (money)	banknote
broiled (meat)	grilled
can	tin
candy	sweets
candy store	sweet shop
checkers (game)	draughts
cookie	biscuit
corn	maize
derby (hat)	bowler
detour	diversion
druggist	chemist
elevator	lift
eraser	rubber
faucet	tap
flashlight	torch
French fries	chips
garbage collector	dustman
gasoline	petrol
generator	dynamo
groceries	stores
hood (automobile)	bonnet
incorporated (Inc.)	limited (Ltd.)

* Canadians generally use U.S. American rather than British vocabulary.

American	British
installment plan	hire-purchase system
internal revenue	inland revenue
janitor	caretaker, porter
john (toilet)	loo
kerosene	paraffin
kindergarten	infant's school
lawyer	barrister
line	queue
living-room	sitting-room
liquor	spirits
long distance(telephone)	trunk
mailman	postman
molasses	treacle
oatmeal	porridge
pants	trousers
paste	gum
period (punctuation)	full stop
phonograph	gramophone
potato chips	crisps
private school	public school
raincoat	waterproof, mackintosh
rooster	cock
second floor	first floor
sedan	saloon car
sidewalk	pavement
soccer	football
subway	tube
suspenders (men's)	braces
taxes	rates
thermos bottle	flask
truck	lorry
underpants	pants
vacation	holiday
vest	waistcoat
windshield	windscreen
wrench	spanner

7: 600 High-Frequency Words:*
(1-300-word level – roman; *301-600-word level* – bold)

A A A A A A A A A A A

a/an

about

  (*approximately*)

adjective

adverb

after

afternoon

again

age

agree(ment)

ago

all

almost

also

always

and

another/the other

answer

any

April

arm

arrive/arrival

article (*grammar*)

as

ask

at

August

aunt

auto(mobile)

B B B B B B B B B B

back - n, adj

(in) back of

bad/worse/worst

bank

bathroom

be/am/are/is/was/

were

  /been

beautiful

because

become/became

bed

before

begin/began/begun

behind

believe

beside

between

big

black

blue

-body

    anybody

    everybody

    nobody

    somebody

book

born

both

boy

break/broke

  /broken

break (*take a*)

breakfast

bring/brought

brother

brown

building

bus

but

buy/bought

by (*near, beside*)

C C C C C C C C C C

call (*what do

  you x this*)

can - m

car

careful/careless

carry

cassette

cent

center - n

chair

change - v, n

change (*money*) -n

cheap

check in/out

child/children

choose/choice

city

class(room)

clean - v, adj

clear - adj

clock/o' clock

close - v/closed- adj

close(ly) - adj, adv

clothes

coat

coffee

cold

color - n

come/came

consonant

continue

cool - adj

copy - n,v

corner

(in)correct - adj,

  v/correction

cost - v, n

could - m

count -v

country

cup

D D D D D D D D D D

date (*today's*)

daughter

day

December

desk

dictionary

difficult

different/difference

dime

dinner

direction

discuss(ion)

do/did/done - v, av

doctor

dollar

door

down

drink/drank/drunk

drive/drove/driven

drop

drug/drugstore

E E E E E E E E E E

each

early

east(ern)

easy

eat/ate/eaten

eight

either

eleven

else

end - n, v

enjoy/enjoyable

enough

enter/entrance

evening

ever

every

example

excuse - v

exercise (*textbook*)

  - n

exit - n

expensive

explain

  /explanation

F F F F F F F F F F

face

fall (*season*)

fall/fell/fallen

family

far

fast

father

favorite

February

feel/felt

few/ a few

fill

fill out

find/found

fine - adj

finish - v

first

five

foot/feet (*12 inches*)

foot/feet (*body

  part*)

for

forget/forgot

  /forgotten

fork

four

Friday

friend

from

(in) front (of)

G G G G G G G G G G

gallon

game

get/got/gotten

  (*obtain, reach*)

get in/out of (*a car*)

get on/off (*a bus*)

get up (*arise*)

girl

give/gave/given

glass (*of water*)

go/went/gone

go away

(be) going to

good/better/best

goodbye/bye/bye-bye

gray

great (*wonderful*)

  - adj, excl

green

guess

H H H H H H H H H
half
hand
hand in/out
happen
happy
hard (*difficult*)
hat
have/has/had
have got to - m
have to/had to - m
he
head
hear/heard
heavy
hello
help - v, n
her(s)
here
high/height
him
his
holiday
home
hope - v
hospital
hot
hotel
hour
house
how
hundred
hungry
husband

I I I I I I I I I I I
I
idea
if
(un)important
in
inch
interesting
into
introduce/intro-
duction
it(s)

J J J J J J J J J J
January
job
July
June
just

K K K K K K K K K
keep/kept
key
kiss - n, v
kitchen
kind - adj
kind of
knife
know/knew/known

L L L L L L L L L
language
large
last - adj
late
laugh - n, v
learn
leave/left
left (*direction*)
leg
less
let
let's
letter (*alphabetic*)
letter (*correspon-
dence*)
light - n
light (*not heavy*)
like - v
like - prep
listen
little/a little
little (*small*)
live - v
look (at)
look (*appear*)
look up (*a word*)
lose/lost
lots of/a lot of
love - v, n
lunch

M M M M M M M
make/made
man/men
many
March
marry/married/
marriage
matter - v, n
may - m
May
maybe
me
mean/meant - v/
meaning - n
meet/met
meter/metric
    centi-
    milli-
    kilo-
middle
might - m
mile
million
mind - v
mine - pro
minute
miss - v
Miss
mistake
Monday
money
month
more/most
morning
mother
mouth
move
Mr.
Mrs.
Ms.
much
must - m
my

N N N N N N N
name - n
near
(un)necessary

need
neighbor
neither .. nor
nervous
never
new
news/newspaper
next
nice
nickel
night
nine
no
noon
north(ern)
nose
not
note
notice - v, n
noun
November
now
number

O O O O O O O
October
of
off
office
often
OK/okay
old
on
once
one
-one
    anyone
    everyone
    no one
    someone
only
open - adj, v
opposite
or
orange
ought to - m
ounce
our(s)

out
outside
over

P P P P P P P P P
package
page
pair/pair up/off
paper
paragraph
parents
part(ly)
past (*half past one*)
pay
pen
pencil
penny
pepper
period
    (*punctuation*)
person/people
phone/telephone
photo/photograph
pick up
picture
piece
pint
place - n
plane/airplane
play - v
please
police
(im)possible
pound (*lb.*)
practice
preposition
pretty - adj
pretty - int
price
probably
problem
pronoun
pronounce
    /pronunciation
pull
push
put

Q Q Q Q Q Q Q Q Q

quart

quarter

  (*coin, fraction*)

question

quick(ly)

quiet(ly)

R R R R R R R R

rain(y) - n, v, adj

read/read

ready

red

remember

restaurant

return

review - v, n

right

  (*correct, direction*)

road

room (*place*)

run/ran

S S S S S S S S S

sale

salt

same

say/said

Saturday

school

season

seat

second

  (*ordinal number*)

see/saw/seen

seem

-self/-selves

send/sent/sender

sentence

September

seven

several

share - v

she

shop - n, v

short

should - m

show - v, n

sick

sign - v/signature

since

sing/sang/sung

single (*unmarried*)

sir

sister

sit/sat

six

size

sleep/slept

slow(ly)

small

so - conj

soap

some

sometimes

son

soon

sorry

sort (of)

south(ern)

speak/spoke/spoken

spell

spoon

spring (*season*)

stairs

station

stamp (*postage*)

start - v

stay

still (*continuing*)

stop

store

story

straight

street

study/student

such

summer

Sunday

sure

T T T T T T T T T

table

take/took/taken

talk

tall

taxi

tea

teach/taught/teacher

television/TV

tell/told

ten

than

thank

the

then

there

there is/are

they/them/their(s)

thing

-thing

  anything

  everything

  nothing

  something

think/thought/

thought - n

thirsty

this/that/these/those

thousand

three/thirteen/thirty

  /third

through

throw

throw away

Thursday

ticket

time

tired

to

today

toilet

tomorrow

tonight

too - int

too (*also*)

top

toward(s)

towel

town

train

try

Tuesday

turn - v

turn on/off

turn up/down

  (*volume*)

twelve

twenty

two

U U U U U U U U

uncle

under

understand

  /understood

until

up

use - v

usual(ly)

V V V V V V V

verb

very

vocabulary

vowel

W W W W W W

wait

wake (up)/woke

  /woken

walk

want

warm

wash

watch - v

watch - n (*clock*)

water

way

we

weather

Wednesday

week

weekend

welcome - excl

well - excl

well - adv

west(ern)

wet

what

when

where

-where

  anywhere

  everywhere

  nowhere

  somewhere

which

while

white

who/whom/whose

why

wife

will/won't - m

winter

wish - v, n

with

woman/women

wonderful

word

work(er)

world

worry

would

would like to - m

would rather - m

write/wrote/written

wrong

X X X X X X X

Y Y Y Y Y Y Y

yard (*3 feet*)

year

yellow

yes/yeah

yesterday

yet

young

you(r)(s)

Z Z Z Z Z Z Z Z

zero

* **This word list is from** *The Learners Lexicon,* **published by Pro Lingua Associates.** The complete list contains 2,400 words.

8: Measurement Terms and Equivalents

Non-Metric

Linear measure

12 inches	= 1 foot
3 feet	= 1 yard
5 1/2 yards	= 1 rod
40 rods	= 1 furlong
8 furlongs	= 1 mile

Mariner's measure

6 feet	= 1 fathom
1,000 fathoms	= 1 nautical mile
3 nautical miles	= 1 league

Square measure

160 square rods	= 1 acre
640 acres	= 1 square mile

Avoirdupois weight

16 drams	= 1 ounce
16 ounces	= 1 pound
2,000 pounds	= 1 ton

Liquid measure

2 pints	= 1 quart
4 quarts	= 1 gallon

Dry measure

2 pints	= 1 quart
8 quarts	= 1 peck
4 pecks	= 1 bushel

Metric/English Measure Equivalents

Linear and square measure

1 centimeter (cm.)	= .3937 inch (in.)
1 meter (m.)	= 39.37 in.
	or 3.28 feet (ft.)
1 kilometer (km.)	= .62137 mile (mi.)
1,000 m²	= 1 hectare (ha.)
	or 2.471 acres

Liquid measure

1 centiliter (cl.)	= .338 fluid ounces (fl. oz.)
1 liter (l.)	= .9081 dry quart (qt.)
	or 1.0567 liquid quarts

Avoirdupois weight

1 gram (g.)	= .03527 ounces (oz.)
1 kilogram (kg.)	= 2.2046 pounds (lb.)

English/Metric Measure Equivalents

Linear and square measure

1 inch		= 2.54 centimeters	
12 in.	= 1 foot	= .3048 meters .	
3 ft.	= 1 yard	= .9144 meters	
16.5 ft.	= 1 rod	= 5.029 meters	
5,280 ft.	= 1 mile	=1.6093 kilometers	
4,840 yd	= 1 acre	= .4 hectatres	

Avoirdupois weight

1 ounce	= 28 grams	
16 oz.	= 1 pound	= .45 kilo (kg.)

Liquid Measure

1 teaspoon (tsp.)		=	5 milliliters
3 tsp.	= 1 tbs.	=	15 ml.
8 oz.	= 1 cup (c.)	=	.24 liters (l.)
2 cups	= 1 pint (pt.)		= .47 l.
2 pints	= 1 quart (qt.)		= .95 l.
4 quarts	= 1 gallon (gal.)		= 3.81 l.

Fahrenheit/Centigrade

$$(°F-32)x5÷9=°C$$
$$°Cx9÷5+32=°F$$

Degrees

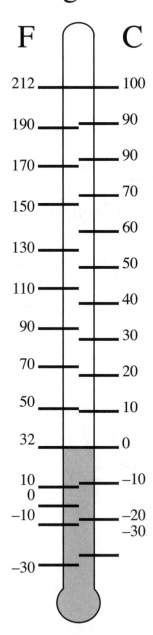

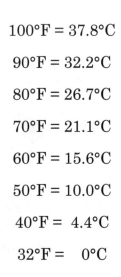

100°F = 37.8°C

90°F = 32.2°C

80°F = 26.7°C

70°F = 21.1°C

60°F = 15.6°C

50°F = 10.0°C

40°F = 4.4°C

32°F =   0°C

100°C = 212°F

40°C = 104°F

30°C = 86°F

20°C = 68°F

10°C = 50°F

0°C = 32°F

264

9: Common Elements*

Atomic number	Symbol	Element Name	Atomic Number	Symbol	Element Name
1	H	hydrogen	24	Cr	chromium
2	He	helium	25	Mn	manganese
3	Li	lithium	26	Fe	iron
4	Be	beryllium	27	Co	cobalt
5	B	boron	28	Ni	nickel
6	C	carbon	29	Cu	copper
7	N	nitrogen	30	Zn	zinc
8	O	oxygen	33	As	arsenic
9	F	fluoride	47	Ag	silver
10	Ne	neon	50	Sn	tin
11	Na	sodium	51	Sb	antimony
12	Mg	magnesium	53	I	iodine
13	Al	aluminum	56	Ba	barium
14	Si	silicon	78	Pt	platinum
15	P	phosphorous	79	Au	gold
16	S	sulfur	80	Hg	mercury
17	Cl	chlorine	82	Pb	lead
18	Ar	argon	83	Bi	bismuth
19	K	potassium	88	Ra	radium
20	Ca	calcium	92	U	uranium
			94	Pu	plutonium

* This list contains only the commonly known elements.

10: Common Symbols

♂ male

♀ female

\+ plus

− minus

× times

÷ divided by

= equals

> greater than

< less than

≠ not equal to

√ square root

π pi

∞ infinity

° degree (60°)

' minute (60° 30')

'' second (60° 30' 15")

@ at (@ 80¢ per quart)

≈ approximately

o/a on or about

% percent

number (#10 nail)

pounds (80#)

' foot (6')

'' inch (6'2")

× by (2" x 4")

$ dollar

¢ cent

£ pound (£ 3))

p penny, pence (6p)

€ Euro (€5 or 5 EUR

~ tilde (cañon)

^ circumflex (fetê)

ç cedilla (Français)

´ acute accent (passé)

` grave accent (à la carte)

•• dieresis (zoölogy)

© copyright

TM trademark

& ampersand (and)

* a hypothetical or wrong form (he *drinked)

* asterisk for note

† dagger for note

‡ double dagger for note

11: Proofreading and Correction Marks

∧ insert here *a word*

∧ insert comma

⊙ insert period⊙

⸲ delete ~~this~~

⌒ close up (foot ball)

¶ paragraph

No ¶ no paragraph

∿ transpose (a, b, d, c, e)

insert # space

.... let it stand

STET let it stand STET

≡ capitalize (washington) CAP

/ lower case (Capital) l.c.

Awk awkward construction

Frag sentence fragment

Sp spelling error hear *here*

12: Roman Numerals

I, i	1	VI, vi	6	XX	20	CD	400
II, ii	2	VII, vii	7	XL	40	D	500
III, iii	3	VIII, viii	8	L	50	CM	900
IV, iv	4	IX, ix	9	XC	90	M	1000
V, v	5	X, x	10	C	100	MM	2000

MCDXCII	1492
MDCXLVIII	1648
MCMXCIX	1999
MMI	2001

13: Abbreviations (abbr., abbrev.)
A. General (Gen.)

A.A.	Associate of Arts (degree)	K	thousand
A.D.	*anno Domini,* in the year of Our Lord	lang.	language
a.m.	*ante meridiem,* before noon	L., Lat.	Latin
Amer.	America, American	L.C., LC	Library of Congress
anon.	anonymous	Ltd.	Limited
assn.	association		
assoc.	associate(s)	m	thousand ($55m = $55,000)
		M.A.	Master of Arts
b.	born	M.A.T.	Master of Arts in Teaching
B.A.,A.B.	Bachelor of Arts	M.B.A.	Master of Business Administration
B.C.	before Christ	M.D.	Doctor of Medicine
B.S.	Bachelor of Science	misc.	miscellaneous
bibliog.	bibliography	mph, m.p.h.	miles per hour
biog.	biography	Mr.	Mister
		Mrs.	married woman (Mistress)
c.	hundred (4c = 400)	Ms.	Miss, Mrs., Woman
c., ca.	*circa,* about	ms.	manuscript
C.E.	common era = A.D.	M.S.	Master of Science
cf.	*confer,* compare		
ch., chap.	chapter	N.	north
Co.	Company	N.B.	*nota bene,* take note, note well
Coll.	College	no.	number
d.	died	p., pp.	page(s)
D.D.S.	Doctor of Dental Science (Surgery)	par.	paragraph
dept.	department	p.c.	politically correct
		Ph.D.	Doctor of Philosophy
E.	east	philos.	philosophy
E., Eng.,	English	p.m.	*post meridiem,* afternoon
ed.	edition, editor, edited by	pub.	published by
e.g.	*exempligratia,* for example		
esp.	especially	q.v.	*quod vide,* which see
et al	*et alii,* and others	rpm, r.p.m.	revolutions per minute
etc.	*et cetera,* and so forth		
ex.	example	S.	south
		Sr.	senior
f.,.ff.	and the following page(s)	sic.	thus
Fr.	French	Sp.	Spanish
		sp.	spelling
Gr.	German	St.	Saint
Gk.	Greek	St.	Street
hist.	history	T.M.	trademark
ibid.	*ibidem,* in the same place	U., Univ.	university
i.e.	*id est.* that is	vol.	volume
Inc.	Incorporated	W.	west
intro.	introduction		
It.	Italian		
Jr.	junior		

B. Days and Months (Mos.)

Jan.	January	Nov.	November
Feb.	February	Dec.	December
Mar.	March		
Apr.	April	Mon.	Monday
May	May	Tues.	Tuesday
June	June	Wed.	Wednesday
July	July	Thurs.	Thursday
Aug.	August	Fri.	Friday
Sept.	September	Sat.	Saturday
Oct.	October	Sun.	Sunday

Measures

in.	inch	mm.	millimeter
ft.	foot	cm.	centimeter
yd.	yard	m.	meter
mi.	mile	km.	kilometer
oz.	ounce	g., gr.	gram
fl. oz.	fluid ounce	c.	centigram
lb.	pound	kg.	kilo., kilogram
		t.	tonnes
tsp.	teaspoon		
tbs.,tbsp.	tablespoon	ml.	milliliter
		l.	liter
c.	cup		
pt.	pint		
qt.	quart		
gal.	gallon		

Many abbreviations are commonly used like words. There are two kinds: Acronyms are pronounceable words. Alphabetisms are pronounced by saying each letter, but they are usually written in capital letters without periods. Some familiar examples:

Acronyms

ACTFL
AIDS
Laser
NASA
NATO
OPEC
PIN
Radar
Scuba
TESOL
UNESCO
UNICEF

Alphabetisms

AA	IRS, INS
AAA	MIA
ATM	PC
ATV, SUV	RSVP
CBS, NBC, ABC,	TV
PBS, NPR, CNN	USA
CBC, BBC	UN
EFL, ESL, ESP	UPC
GED, GRE	UPS
GPS	USA
HIV	WMD

Postal Abbrs.

State	Traditional	New	State	Traditional	New	State	Traditional	New
Alabama	Ala.	AL	Maine	Me.	ME	Oklahoma	Okla.	OK
Alaska	Alas.	AK	Maryland	Md.	MD	Oregon	Ore.	OR
Arizona	Ariz.	AZ	Massachusetts	Mass.	MA	Pennsylvania	Penn.	PA
Arkansas	Ark.	AR	Michigan	Mich.	MI	Rhode Island	R.I.	RI
California	Cal.	CA	Minnesota	Minn.	MN	South Carolina	S.C.	SC
Colorado	Colo.	CO	Mississippi	Miss.	MS	South Dakota	S.D.	SD
Connecticut	Conn.	CT	Missouri	Mo.	MO	Tennessee	Tenn.	TN
Delaware	Del.	DE	Montana	Mont.	MT	Texas	Tex.	TX
Florida	Fla.	FL	Nebraska	Neb.	NE	Utah	Utah	UT
Georgia	Ga.	GA	Nevada	Nev.	NV	Vermont	Vt.	VT
Hawaii	Ha.	HI	New Hampshire	N.H.	NH	Virginia	Va.	VA
Idaho	Ida.	ID	New Jersey	N.J.	NJ	Washington	Wash.	WA
Illinois	Ill.	IL	New Mexico	N.M.	NM	West Virginia	W.V.	WV
Indiana	Ind.	IN	New York	N.Y.	NY	Wisconsin	Wisc.	WI
Iowa	Ia.	IA	North Carolina	N.C.	NC	Wyoming	Wyo.	WY
Kansas	Kan.	KS	North Dakota	N.D.	ND	Puerto Rico	P.R.	PR
Kentucky	Ky.	KY	Ohio	Ohio	OH	Guam	Guam	GU
Louisiana	La.	LA				Virgin Island	V.I.	VI

North America

United States of America	U.S. U.S.A.	Canada	Can.	Central America	C.A.
		Mexico	Mex.		

Cities

District of Columbia	D.C., DC	Miami	MIA	San Francisco	S.F., SF
Los Angeles	L.A., LA	New York City	N.Y.C., NYC	Seattle	SEA

Other Postal Abbrs.

APO	Army and Air Force Post Office	Cir.	Circle	Jct.	Junction
FPO	Naval Post Office	Ct.	Court	Ln.	Lane
RFD	Rural Free Delivery	Cres.	Crescent	Pl.	Place
PO Box	Post Office Box	Dr.	Drive	Pt.	Point
		Expy.	Expressway	Rd.	Road
		Ext.	Extension	Rte.	Route
Ave.	Avenue	Fwy.	Freeway	Sq.	Square
Blvd.	Boulevard	Gdns.	Gardens	St.	Street
Byp.	Bypass	Hts.	Heights	Ter.	Terrace
Cswy.	Causeway	Hwy.	Highway	Tpke.	Turnpike
Ctr.	Center				

14: Computer Acronyms

http	hyper text transfer protocol
html	hyper text markup language (how you build web pages)
ftp	file transfer protocol
ping	packet internet groper
ack	acknowledgment
url	uniform resource locator (aka a web page address)
ror	Ruby on Rails - a new programming language
ajax	Asynchronous JavaScript and XML - a newer approach to building rich, interactive web pages (such as Gmail)
dns	domain name server
ip	internet protocol
www	world wide web
ansi	American National Standards Institute
w3c	world wide web consortium (www.w3c.org)
ASCII	American Standard Code for Information Interchange
xml	eXtensible Markup Language
xsl	eXtensible Stylesheet Language
css	Cascading Style Sheets
wysiwyg	what you see is what you get (the technology whereby the word processor screen looks just like what is ultimately printed, pronounced wiz ee wig)
vm	virtual machine
usb	universal serial bus
tcp/ip	transmission control protocol/internet protocol
ssi	server side include
smtp	simple mail transfer protocol
sql	structured query language
ssl	secure sockets layer
ram	random access memory
dram	dynamic random access memory
eprom	eraseable programmable read only memory
rom	read only memory
p2p	peer to peer
pc	personal computer

pgp	pretty good privacy
PnP	Plug and Play
pots	plain old telephone service (as contrasted with digital phone systems)
ppp	Point to Point Protocol
ppoe	Point to Point Protocol over Ethernet
os	operating system
mapi	messaging application programming interface
pop	post office protocol
mpeg	motion picture experts group
mp3	mpeg third layer
jpeg	joint photographic experts group
gif	graphics interchange format
lan	local area network
lcd	liquid crystal display
jvm	java virtual machine
faq	frequently asked questions

Common Internet Slang Acronyms

k	OK	**bfn**	bye for now	**moo?**	**what?**
q	question	**btw**	by the way	**omg**	oh my gosh
r	are/our	**byo**	bring your own	**O RLY?**	oh really
u	you	**cuz**	because	**YA RLY!**	yeah really!
y	why	**fyi**	for your information	**NO WAI!!!**	no way!
am	above mentioned	**g2g**	got to go	**otp**	on the phone
cu	see you	**iaal**	I am actually laughing	**ppl**	people
nm	nothing much			**ROFl**	rolling on the floor laughing
np	no problem	**idc**	I don't care		
rl	real life	**idk**	I don't know	**RTFM**	read the fine manual
ty	thank you	**iirc**	if I remember correctly	**SAL**	smiling a little
wb	welcome back			**tbh**	to be honest
yw	you're welcome	**imho**	in my humble opinion	**thx**	thanks
afaik	as far as I know			**TIA**	thanks in advance
atm	at the moment	**l8r**	later	**ttyl**	talk to you later
brb	be right back	**LDR**	long-distance relationship	**tyt**	take your time
bbiab	be back in a bit			**kewl**	cool, awesome
bbl	be back later	**lol**	laughing out loud	**ke**	OK

14: Road Signs

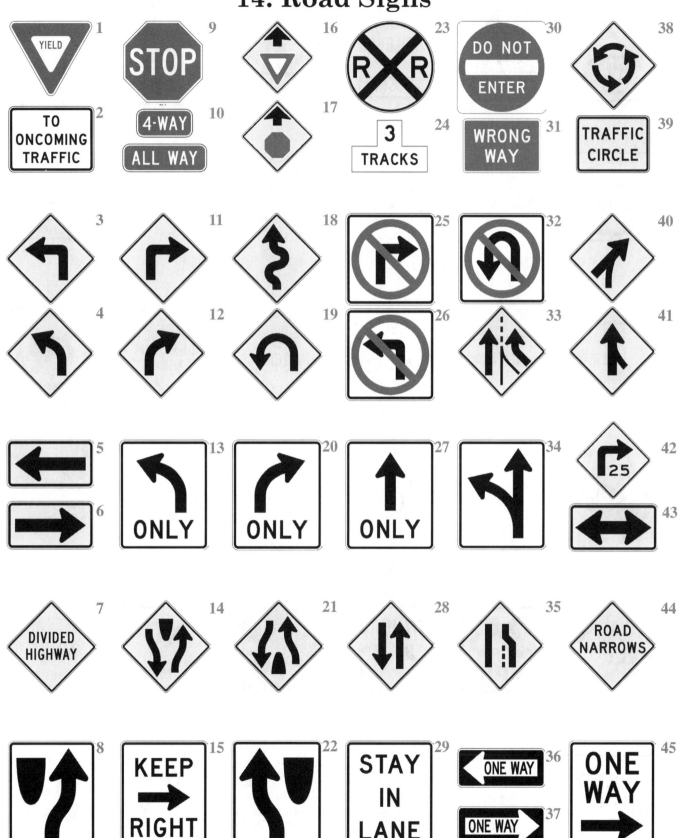

Explanations of the signs on page 276

 46

 52

 58
STOP
WHEN
CHILDREN
IN
CROSSWALK

 64

 70
PUSH
BUTTON
FOR

 76
CROSS
ONLY
ON
SIGNAL

 47

 53

 59

 65

 71

 77

 48

 54
SIGNAL
AHEAD

 60
BE
PREPARED
TO STOP

 66
STOP
AHEAD

 72
SCHOOL
BUS STOP
AHEAD

 78

 49

 55
HILL

 61
BUMP

 67
DIP

 73
BRIDGE
ICES BEFORE
ROAD

 79

 50
SPEED
LIMIT
55

 56
35
MPH

 62
TRUCKS
40

 68
NIGHT
45

 74
NO
TURNS

 80
LEFT LANE
MUST
TURN LEFT

 51
SPEED
LIMIT
50

 57
MINIMUM
SPEED
40

 63
EXIT
25
MPH

 69
CURVE
25
MPH

 75
DO
NOT
PASS

 81
PASS
WITH
CARE

 82

 89

 96

 103

 110

 117

 83

 90

 97

 104

 111

 118

 84

 91

 98

 105

 112

 119

 85

 92

 99

 106

 113

120

86

93

100

107

114

121

87

94

101

108

115

122

88

95

102

109

116

123

275

124 NO STANDING ANY TIME

126 NO PARKING ANY TIME

128  8:30 AM TO 5:30 PM

131 NO PARKING ANY TIME | ONE HOUR PARKING 9AM-7PM

133 EMERGENCY PARKING ONLY

134

125 NO PARKING LOADING ZONE

127 EMERGENCY SNOW ROUTE — NO PARKING IF OVER 2 INCHES

129 RESERVED PARKING

130 TOW-AWAY ZONE

132 NO PARKING BUS STOP

Key to Road Signs

1. Yield – *This shape is only used on yield signs.*
2. Yield to oncoming traffic – *Horizontal rectangles are used to give warnings, regulations or to supplement other signs.*
3. Warning left turn – *The diamond shape is only used for warning.*
4. Warning curve left
5. One way to left
6. One way to right
7. Divided highway
8. Keep right of divider – *This vertical rectangle shape is generally used to give regulations.*
9. Stop – *This shape is only used on stop signs.*
10. All cars must stop, used with stop signs.
11. Right turn
12. Curve right
13. Left turn only
14. Divided highway
15. Keep right
16. Yield sign ahead
17. Stop sign ahead
18. Winding road
19. Hair pin curve
20. Right turn only
21. Divided highway ends
22. Keep left of divider
23. Warning railroad crossing

24. Number of railroad tracks to be crossed.
25. No right turn – *This shape and symbol (a circle in a square barred from upper left to lower right) is used to say "no," to prohibit some activity.*
26. No left turn
27. Straight through only
28. Two way traffic
29. Stay in lane.
30. Do not enter
31. Wrong way
32. No U turn
33. Lane added
34. Left curve with optional lane going straight
35. Right lane ends; road narrows
36. One way going left
37. One way going right
38. Round-about or traffic circle ahead
39. Traffic circle
40. Entering roadway merge
41. Merge
42. Turn with speed advisory
43. Two way traffic
44. Road narrows
45. One way
46. Seat belts are mandatory
47. No bicycles
48. Signal light ahead
49. Hill
50. New speed limit ahead
51. Speed limit
52. School
53. Bicycles
54. Signal ahead
55. Hill

56. Speed limit, miles per hour
57. Minimum speed limit
58. Stop: children crossing
59. Playground
60. Be prepared to stop
61. Bump
62. Truck speed limit
63. Speed limit on exit
64. No pedestrians
65. Wheelchair warning
66. Stop ahead
67. Dip
68. Night speed limit
69. Speed limit on curve
70. Push button for pedestrian crossing signal
71. Pedestrian crossing
72. School bus stop ahead
73. Bridge ices before road
74. No turns
75. Do not pass
76. Cross only on signal
77. No hitch hiking
78. No trucks
79. Slippery when wet
80. Left land must turn left
81. Pass with care
82. Interstate route number
83. No commercial vehicles
84. Slower traffic keep right
85. Library – *Square signs are used for information.*
86. Emergency signal ahead
87. Emergency vehicles
88. Road work
89. Route number
90. Trucks use right lane
91. Walk on left
92. Hiking trail
93. By-pass
94. Horses in road

95. Flagman; work zone
96. Divided highway ends
97. HOV (high-occupancy vehicles) lane
98. Push button for green light
99. Hospital
100. Alternate route
101. Snowmobile crossing
102. No outlet
103. Soft shoulder
104. Bike lane; bike lane ahead
105. Cross only at cross walks
106. Airport
107. Temporary route
108. Deer crossing
109. Dead end
110. Left land ends
111. Left on green arrow only
112. Do not block intersection
113. Bus station
114. Truck route
115. Farm machinery
116. Detour
117. Pavement ends
118. No turn on red light
119. Spot here on red light
120. Train station
121. Business route
122. Clearance under bridge
123. End detour
124. No standing
125. No parking loading zone
126. No parking any time
127. No parking in snow
128. No parking time specified
129. Parking for handicapped
130. Tow-away zone
131. Two parking signs
132. No parking: bus stop
133. Emergency parking only
134. No parking: bus stop

The design of these signs are set by the U.S. government. These images are available in color for educational use from the *Manual of Traffic Signs*, by

Pedagogical Atlas of the World 2007

with keyed outline maps

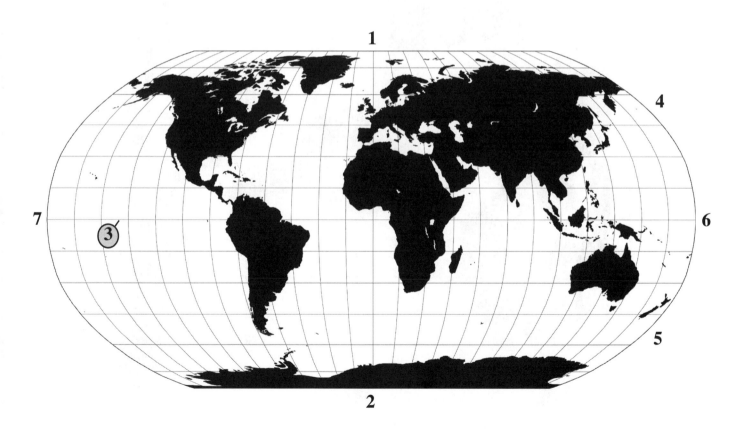

Map 1 World

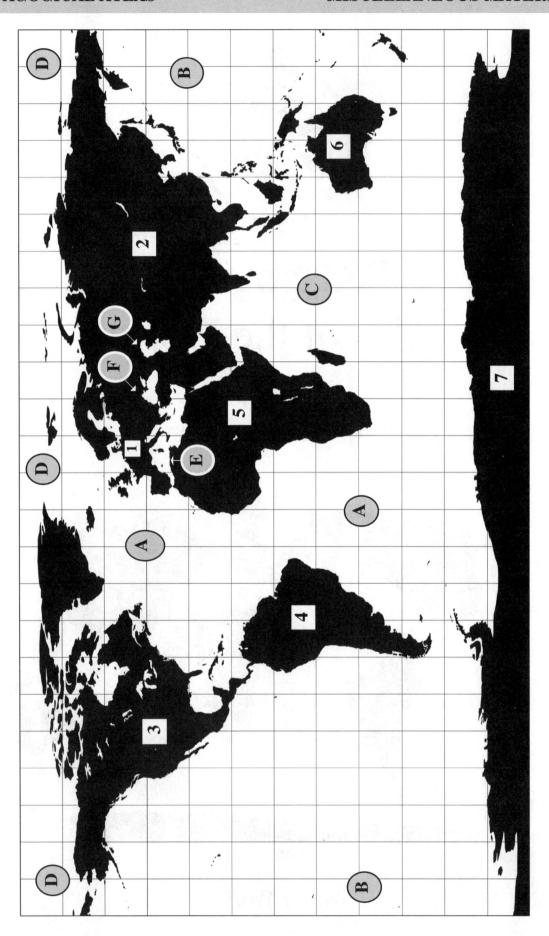

Map 2 Continents and Seas

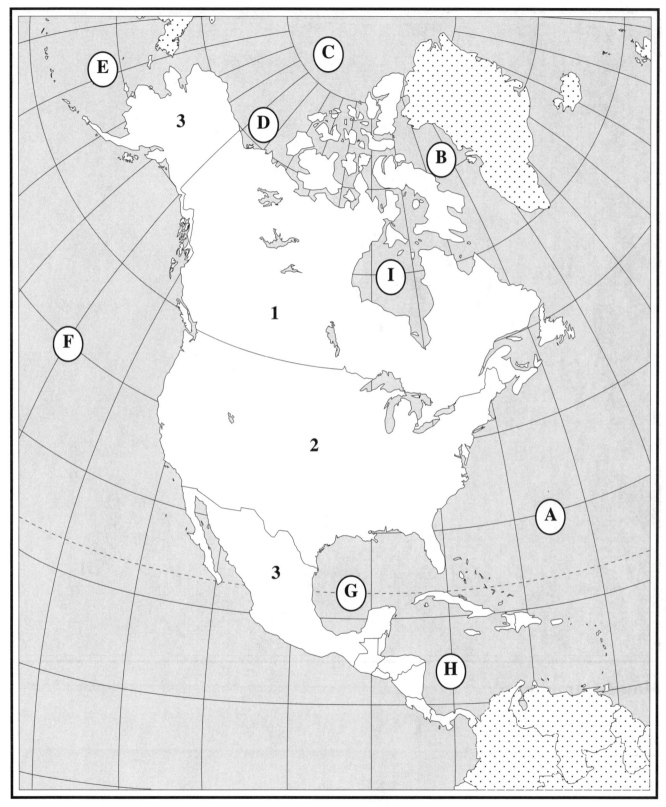

Map 3 North America

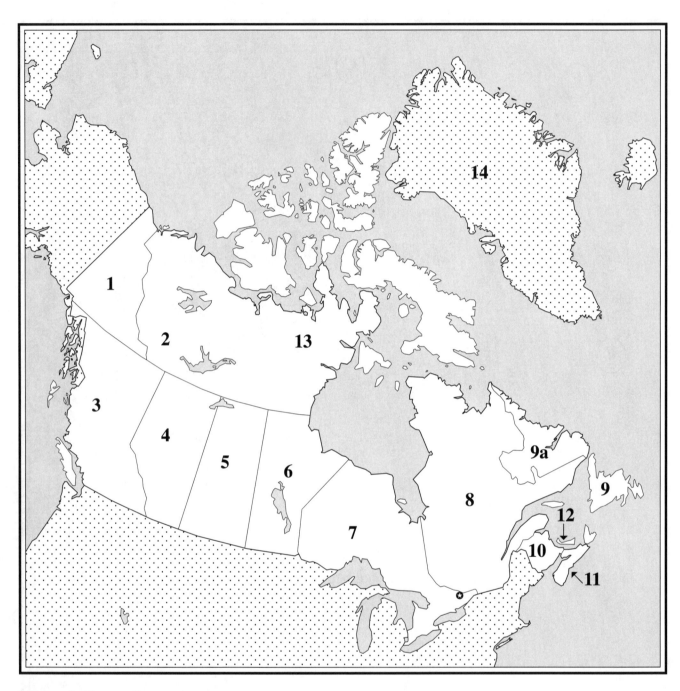

Map 4 Canada

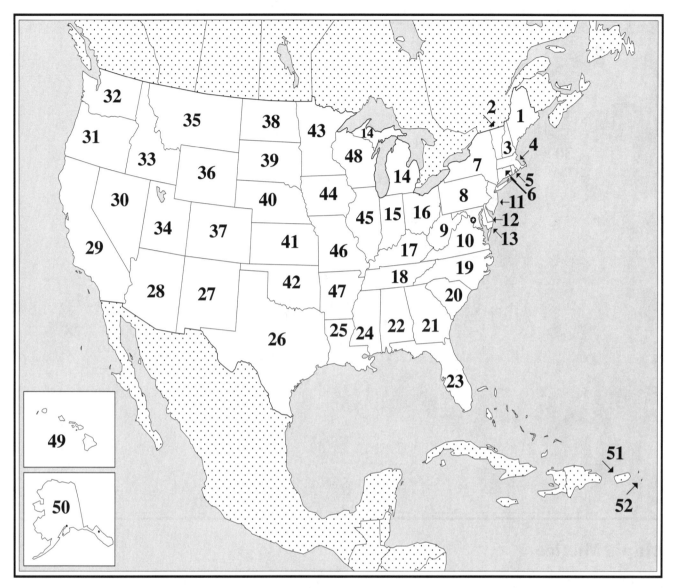

Map 5 United States of America

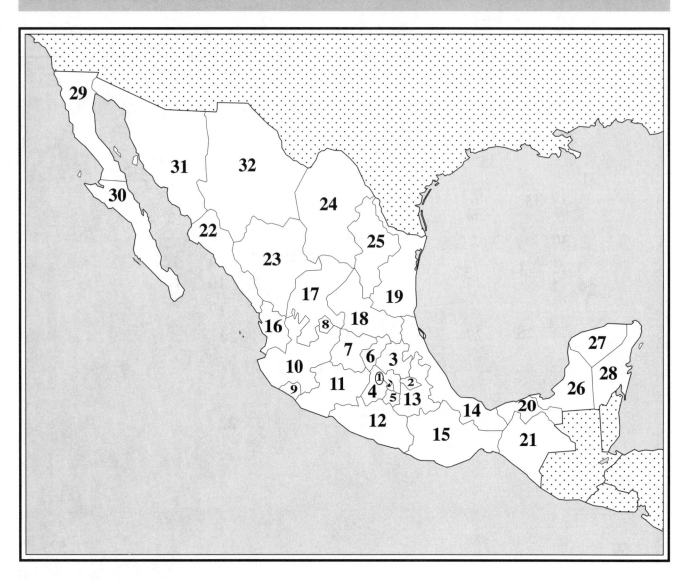

Map 6 Mexico

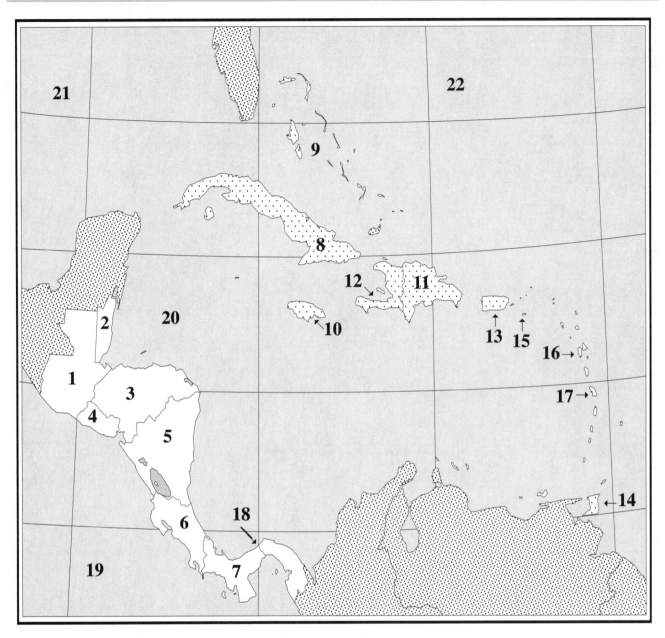

Map 7 Central America and the Caribbean

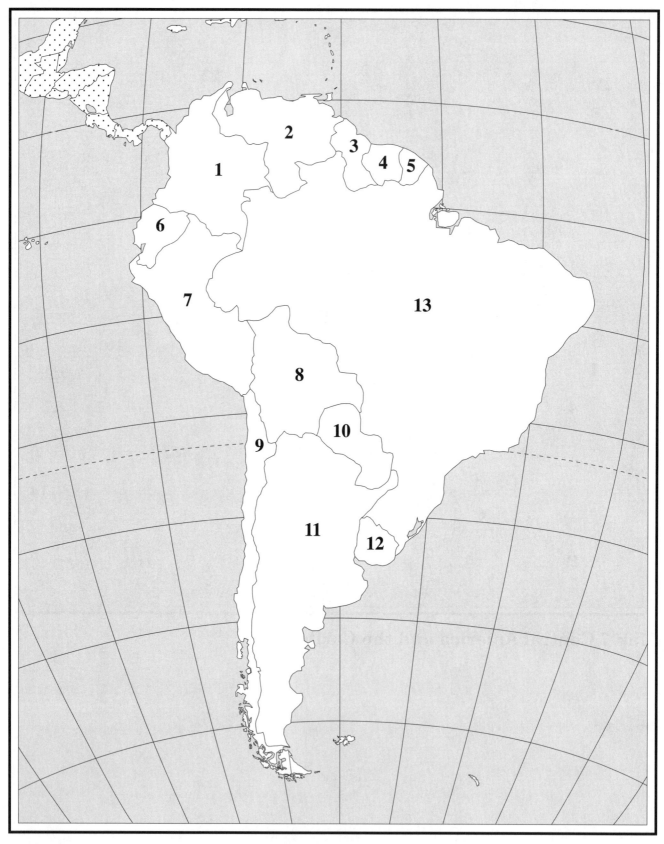

Map 8 South America

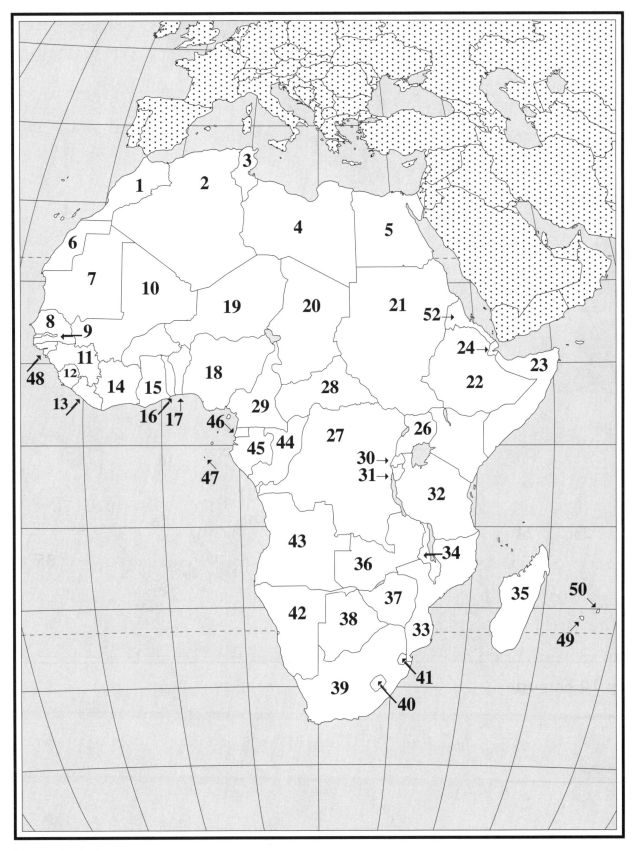

Map 9 Africa

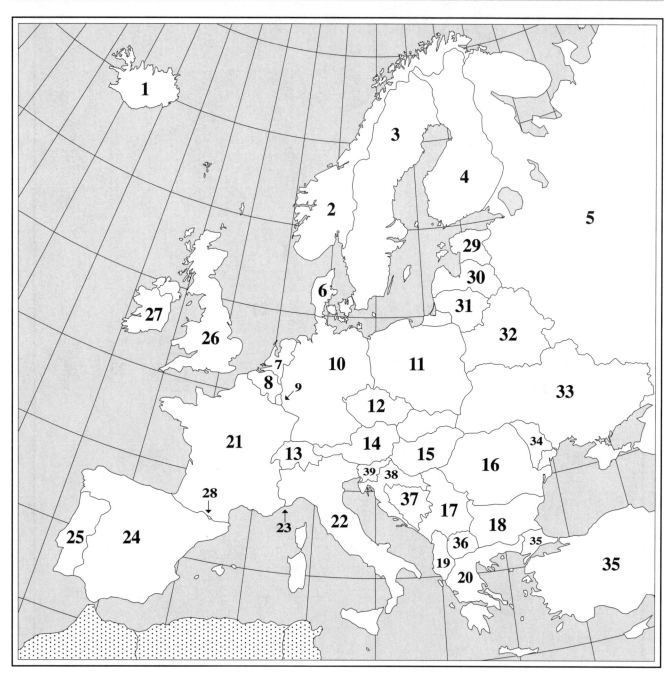

Map 10 Europe

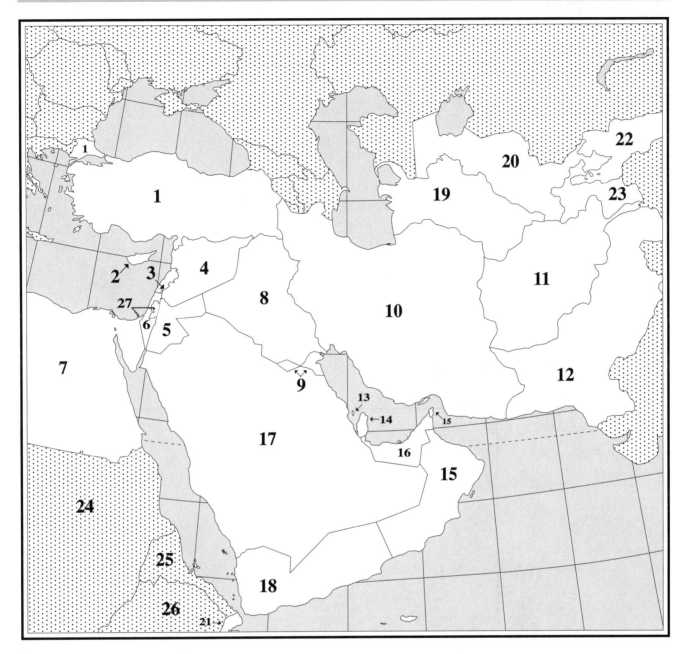

Map 11 Middle East

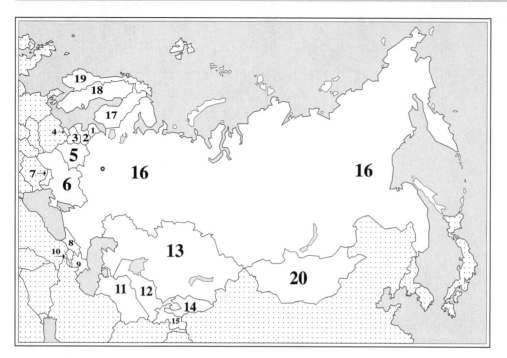

Map 12 Northern Eurasia

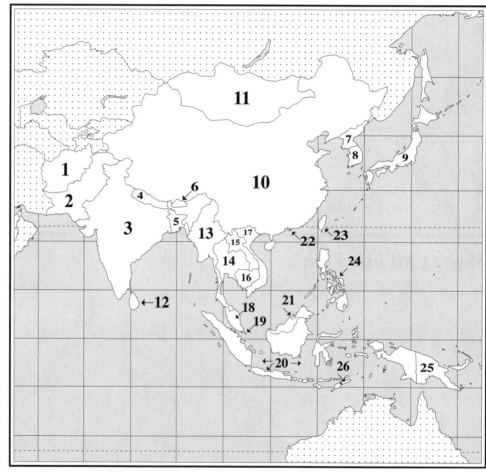

Map 13 East and Southeast Asia

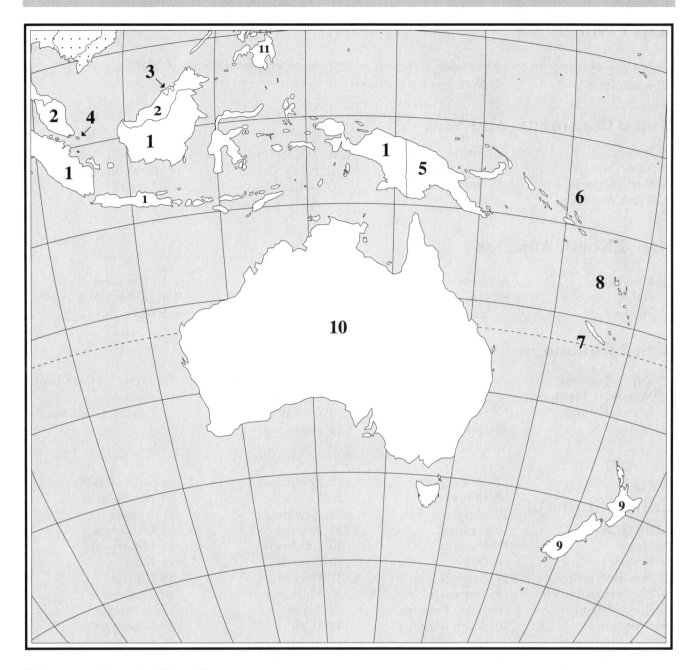

Map 14 South Pacific

Map 1 World

1 North Pole
2 South Pole
3 Equator
4 Northern Hemisphere
5 Southern Hemisphere
6 East
7 West

Map 2 Continents and Seas

1 Europe
2 Asia
3 North America
4 South America
5 Africa
6 Australia
7 Antarctica

A Atlantic Ocean
B Pacific Ocean
C Indian Ocean
D Arctic Ocean

E Mediterranean Sea
F Black Sea
G Caspian Sea

Map 3 North America

1 Canada
2 U.S.A.
3 Mexico

A North Atlantic
B Baffin Bay
C Arctic

D Beaufort Sea
E Bering Sea
F Pacific

G Gulf of Mexico
H Caribbean Sea
I Hudson Bay

Map 4 Canada

1 Yukon Territory
2 Northwest Territories
3 British Columbia
4 Alberta
5 Saskatchewan
6 Manitoba
7 Ontario
8 Quebec
9 Newfoundland
9a (including Labrador)
10 New Brunswick
11 Nova Scotia
12 Prince Edward Island
13 Nunavut
14 Greenland (Denmark)

Map 5 United States of Amenca

1 Maine
2 Vermont
3 New Hampshire
4 Massachusetts
5 Rhode Island
6 Connecticut
7 New York
8 Pennsylvania
9 West Virginia
10 Virginia
11 New Jersey
12 Delaware
13 Maryland
14 Michigan
15 Indiana
16 Ohio
17 Kentucky
18 Tennessee
19 North Carolina
20 South Carolina
21 Georgia
22 Alabama
23 Florida
24 Mississippi
25 Louisiana
26 Texas
27 NewMexico
28 Arizona
29 California
30 Nevada
31 Oregon
32 Washington
33 Idaho
34 Utah
35 Montana
36 Wyoming
37 Colorado
38 North Dakota
39 South Dakota
40 Nebraska
41 Kansas
42 Oklahoma
43 Minnesota
44 Iowa
45 Illinois
46 Missouri
47 Arkansas
48 Wisconsin
49 Hawaii
50 Alaska
51 Puerto Rico
52 Virgin Islands

Map 6 Mexico

1 Distrito Federal
2 Tlaxcala
3 Hidalgo
4 Mexico
5 Morelos
6 Queretaro
7 Guanajuato
8 Aguascalientes
9 Colima
10 Jalisco
11 Michoacan
12 Guerrero
13 Puebla
14 Veracruz
15 Oaxaca
16 Nayarit
17 Zacatecas
18 San Luis Potosi
19 Tamaulipas
20 Villahermosa
21 Chiapas
22 Sinaloa
23 Durango
24 Coahuila
25 Nuevo Leon
26 Campeche
27 Yucatan
28 Quintana Roo
29 Baja California Norte
30 Baja California Sur
31 Sonora
32 Chihuaha

Map 7 Central America and the Caribbean

1 Guatemala	7 Panama	12 Haiti	18 Panama Canal
2 Belize	8 Cuba	13 Puerto Rico	19 Pacific Ocean
3 Honduras	9 The Bahamas	14 Trinidad/Tobago	20 Caribbean Sea
4 El Salvador	10 Jamaica	15 US Virgin Islands	21 Gulf of Mexico
5 Nicaragua	11 Dominican	16 Martinique	22 Atlantic Ocean
6 Costa Rica	Republic	17 Guadeloupe	

Map 8 South America

1 Colombia	5 French Guiana	8 Bolivia	11 Argentina
2 Venezuela	6 Ecuador	9 Chile	12 Uruguay
3 Guyana	7 Peru	10 Paraguay	13 Brazil
4 Suriname			

Map 9 Africa

1 Morocco	14 Ivory Coast	27 Dem. Republic of Congo	40 Lesotho
2 Algeria	15 Ghana	28 Central African Republic	41 Swaziland
3 Tunisia	16 Togo	29 Cameroun	42 Namibia
4 Libya	17 Benin	30 Rwanda	43 Angola
5 Egypt	18 Nigeria	31 Burundi	44 Republic of Congo
6 Western Sahara	19 Niger	32 Tanzania	45 Gabon
7 Mauritania	20 Chad	33 Mozambique	46 Equatorial Guinea
8 Senegal	21 Sudan	34 Malawi	47 Sao Tome/Principe
9 Gambia	22 Ethiopia	35 Madagascar	48 Guinea Bissau
10 Mali	23 Somalia	36 Zambia	49 Reunion
11 Guinea	24 Djibouti	37 Zimbabwe	50 Mauritius
12 Sierra Leone	25 Kenya	38 Botswana	51 Burkina Faso
13 Liberia	26 Uganda	39 South Africa	52 Eritrea

Map 10 Europe

1 Iceland	11 Poland	21 France	31 Lithuania
2 Norway	12 Czech Republic	22 Italy	32 Belarus
3 Sweden	13 Switzerland	23 Monaco	33 Ukraine
4 Finland	14 Austria	24 Spain	34 Moldova
5 Russia	15 Hungary	25 Portugal	35 Turkiye
6 Denmark	16 Romania	26 The United Kingdom	36 Macedonia
7 Netherlands	17 Yugoslavia	27 Ireland	37 Bosnia
8 Belgium	18 Bulgaria	28 Andorra	38 Croatia
9 Luxembourg	19 Albania	29 Estonia	39 Slovenia
10 Germany	20 Greece	30 Latvia	40 Slovakia

Map 11 Middle East

1 Turkey	8 Iraq	15 Oman	22 Kyrgyzstan
2 Cyprus	9 Kuwait	16 United Arab Emirates	23 Tajikistan
3 Lebanon	10 Iran	17 Saudi Arabia	24 Sudan
4 Syria	11 Afghanistan	18 Yemen	25 Eritrea
5 Jordan	12 Pakistan	19 Turkmenistan	26 Ethiopia
6 Israel	13 Bahrain	20 Uzbekistan	27 Occupied Territories:
7 Egypt	14 Qatar	21 Djibouti	West Bank and Gaza

Map 12 Northern Eurasia

1 Estonia	6 Ukraine	11 Turkmenistan	16 Russia
2 Latvia	7 Moldova	12 Uzbekistan	17 Finland
3 Lithuania	8 Georgia	13 Kazakhstan	18 Sweden
4 Kaliningrad	9 Azerbaijan	14 Kyrgyztan	19 Norway
5 Belarus	10 Armenia	15 Tajikistan	20 Mongolia

Map 13 East snd Southeast Asia

1 Afghanistan	8 South Korea	15 Laos	22 Hong Kong
2 Pakistan	9 Japan	16 Kampuchea	23 Taiwan
3 India	10 China	17 Vietnam	24 The Philippines
4 Nepal	11 Mongolia	18 Malaysia	25 Papua New Guinea
5 Bangladesh	12 Sri Lanka	19 Singapore	26 East Timor
6 Bhutan	13 Burma/Myanmar	20 Indonesia	
7 North Korea	14 Thailand	21 Brunei	

Map 14 South Pacific

1 Indonesia	4 Singapore	7 New Caledonia	10 Australia
2 Malaysia	5 Papua New Guinea	8 Vanuatu	11 The Philippines
3 Brunei	6 Solomon Islands	9 New Zealand	

The Paralinguistic Aspect

We are using the term paralinguistic to include a variety of acts that accompany language or are used in place of language to communicate a message. Sometimes sound itself is used, e.g. a "wolf whistle;" sometimes the body is used, e.g. a smile. In short, this Aspect is about non-verbal communication. But let us hasten to say, it is not about all kinds of non-verbal communication. Painting and sculpture, for example, could be considered non-verbal forms of communication, but because they are only very distant cousins of language, they are not of primary interest to the language learner and teacher.

We have not dealt with the entire spectrum of non-verbal communication partly because to do so would make the book overly long and partly because paralinguistic communication does not lend itself to exploration in a book such as this one. Such paralinguistic events as a whistle and a smile are not easily classified or captured and catalogued in print, as are nouns, verbs, and topical vocabulary. Paralinguistic communication is very important, however, and we want to give students and teachers a handle on the subject. To do this we have outlined the field of paralinguistics and non-verbal communication. This outline, in checklist form, as usual, is included as a reminder that at some point in the language program it would be useful to discuss and explore the various sounds and actions suggested by the list. Also, as usual, the outline is far from exhaustive; it is suggestive and is intended only as a start.

Because they do fit into the format of this book, we have chosen to present three forms of paralinguistic communication in some detail: the International Sign Alphabet, Classroom Gestures, and a selection or sampling of common American Gestures. The alphabet of the International Sign Language has been included because we feel it is of potential value to language teachers and learners. For example, it can be used in the classroom in instances where a teacher might want to avoid oral spelling. The signs for the vowels might be especially useful because of the discrepancy between the sounds and the names of English vowels (*A, E,* and *I* give students a lot of trouble). And in general, a sign alphabet might be a useful tool for teachers who try to keep their own verbalizations at a minimum.

The Classroom Gestures are included here only to suggest that there can be a pedagogical use for paralinguistic gestures. To a certain extent, such gestures are idiosyncratic, but our brief page of sketches is, we hope, illustrative of some rather widely used classroom gestures. We would like to suggest that teachers and students might be well advised to establish their own system of classroom gestures at the outset of the language program. Our illustration can be used as a starting point.

The sampling of common American Gestures speaks for itself. These gestures were originally collected, photographed, labeled, and categorized by Peg Clement in 1981. The images and some of the gestures became somewhat dated over the next twenty-five years, and so we have recreated her collection using new models and some new gestures. However, with a few minor changes, we have used her classification system in presenting the photos. We have also included additional information about the meanings and the sounds that might accompany the gestures.

The two children who demonstrated the American gestures are Veronica McKay and Cole Madden. The adults are Liza Aldana and Adrienne Antrim Major. All the photos were taken by Mike Jerald.

Contents

1: An Outline of Paralinguistic Communication

A. Sounds

❏ 1. Individual sounds
  a. Fricatives—Shh!
  b. Nasals— Mmmm.
  c. Trills—Brrr.
  d. Clicks and stops—Tsk, tsk; Pst.

❏ 2. Emotional Intonation
  a. Surprise
  b. Fear
  c. Anger
  d. Irony
  e. Sarcasm
  f. Teasing
  g. Mockery
  h. Complaint
  i. Persuasion
  j. Pleading
  k. Flirtation
  l. Intimacy
  m. Pleasure

❏ 3. Exclamations and Interjections

❏ 4. Voice qualities and styles
  a. Whisper
  b. Baby talk
  c. Falsetto
  d. Command, stern and calm
  e. Command, gruff

❏ 5. Whistling

❏ 6. Humming

❏ 7. Yelling

❏ 8. Laughing

❏ 9. Crying

❏ 10. Coughing and throat clearing

B. Body Language (Kinesics)

❏ 1. Facial expressions

❏ 2. Eye contact

❏ 3. Gestures

❏ 4. Touching (Haptics)

C. Other Areas of Paralinguistic Communication

❏ 1. Silence

❏ 2. Time

❏ 3. Space and distance (Proxemics)

2: International Sign Alphabet

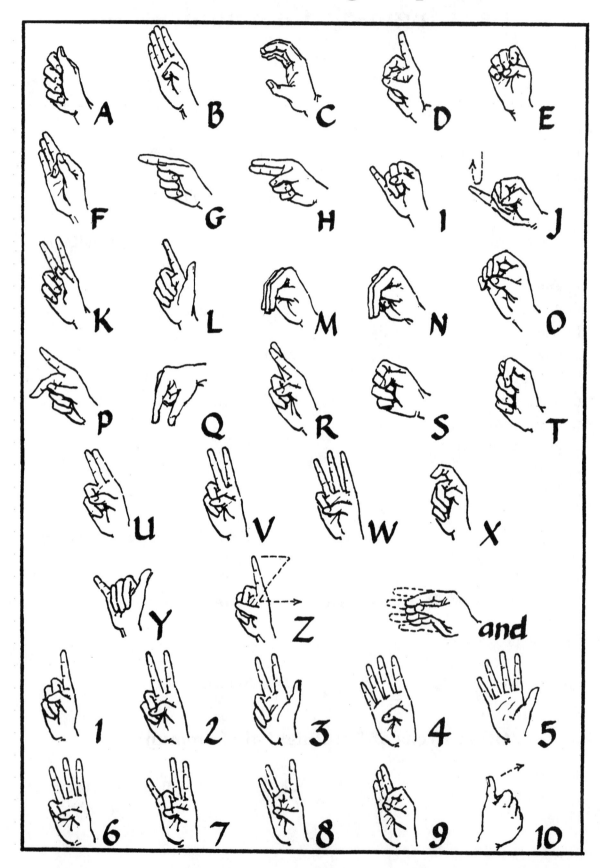

3: Classroom Gestures

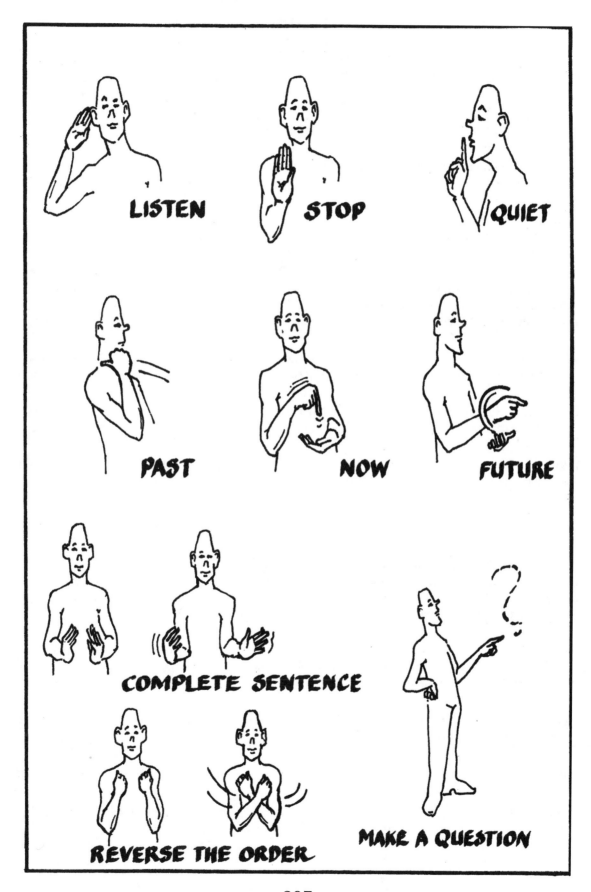

4: Selected American Gestures

Checklist

Classification: Children's Gestures			page 305
Number	What it means	What it's called, if anything	What sounds or words are used with it
❑ 1.	An act of defiance, often teasing, to someone giving orders.	Sticking out your tongue	Nnn, nnnn
❑ 2.	Teasing ridicule meaning: "Ha ha! you got caught (and I didn't). It serves you right. You made a mistake. I'm right and you're wrong."	* * *	"Naa naa!" "Yaa yaa!"
❑ 3.	Teasing ridicule meaning, literally, something or someone smells bad. It implies, "I don't like that. It is awful!"	Holding your nose.	"PU!" "Yuck!" "That stinks!"
❑ 4.	Secretly giving a person who is having their picture taken "devil's horns" as a teasing joke or trick. This is very common childish behavior before a camera.	* * *	No noise, because the joke is secret; giggling is typical.
❑ 5.	Crossing your fingers behind your back means that you really don't mean to do what you are promising to do.	Fingers crossed	No noise, because the joke is secret
❑ 6.	Making the "L" sign referring to someone means that the person indicated is a "Loser." It is a secret signal.	* * *	No noise, because the message is secret
❑ 7.	Making the "W" sign referring to someone means that the person indicated is a "Winner." It is a secret signal.	* * *	No noise, because the message is secret

Parental Gestures			page 306
❑ 8.	Beckoning by wiggling the index finger means: "Come here. I want you here, now!" It is not always imperative and not always done to a child, although the person beckoned is usually of inferior status.	* * *	"Come here." "Come on." – said encouragingly.
❑ 9.	A reprimand or scolding gesture, often teasing, usually done to a child or inferior. The index/forefinger is pointed up and wagged back and forth.	Shaking your finger at someone.	"Naughty, Naughty!" "Bad girl! (or boy) "Tsk, tsk!" "No!"
❑ 10.	Scraping your index fingers together at someone usually a child or inferior, often teasingly.	Reprimand	"Shame, shame." "No, no."
❑ 11.	A signal to be quiet.	Shushing someone.	Sometimes done silently to avoid noise or with whispered "Shh" "Be quiet!"
❑ 12.	A reprimand or scolding gesture, often teasing, usually done to a child or inferior. The index/forefinger is pointed at the child.	Scolding, pointing your finger at someone	12. Same as 9

298

Societal Gestures   page 307

☐ 13. A civilian style salute most commonly used when pledging allegiance to the national flag or singing the national anthem. *See National Documents at the end of the* Topics *section.*

    Holding your hand over your heart.

    * * *

☐ 14. The formal stance assumed while taking an oath. The right hand is raised, the left is placed on a Bible or other sacred book. Those who prefer not to swear to the truth using a book (which is forbidden in some religions) can affirm the truth putting a hand over their heart.

    Taking an oath. Putting your hand on the Bible.

    "I swear (on the Bible/on my honor) that I will...."

☐ 15. A military salute, a gesture of respect given to a superior commissioned officer and often returned. It is also used by others in uniform (such as police) as a formal greeting, and by most people in uniform during the pledge of allegiance or the national anthem, or to honor the raising or passing of the national flag, usually while standing stiffly at formal attention.

    Saluting_____. (the flag, an officer, etc.)

    * * *

Gestures of Greeting and Leave Taking   pages 307-308

There are many forms of greeting and leave taking used in North America. These vary regionally and between age groups and ethnic groups. A very informal "salute" or wave is most common. More formally people shake right hands. In some groups, an "air kiss" on one or two cheeks is typical among friends as is a quick hug, even among men. People say different things, such as "Hi." "Hey there." "Good to see you." How're you doing?" For somewhat formal introductions: "Hello." "How do you do." "It's nice to meet you."

☐ 16. Between two members of some cultural, ethnic, and age groups, elaborate special hand shakes are popular. "High five," clapping raised right hands is used, particularly by athletes, both as a greeting and as a celebratory gesture.

    High five

    "Slap me five, Brother!"

☐ 17. Elaborate "handshake" greetings go in and out of fashion. One purpose is to indicate that the people involved are initiates, "brothers." Groups which have typically invented and used such rituals include children, athletes, members of secret societies, and people who identify themselves with a specific ethnic group and/or a specific social or political philosophy. Knowing and using the ritual gesture is a way of identifying oneself and celebrating one's beliefs or success. The one pictured is very common. A "high five" is followed by a "low five," tapping palms or finger tips.

    Low five

☐ 18. A wave of the hand with fingers extended is the most common gesture of greeting or goodbye used either informally or from a distance. It is also used to get someone's attention. Emotions or strength of feeling are indicated by the vigor of the gesture and the person's expression.

    A wave.

    "Hi." "Hello." "Bye." "Yoo hoo." "Here I am."

❑ 19. To say goodbye to a loved one. Men or women kiss their finger tips and then either toss or blow the "kiss" to the departing person.	Blowing a kiss.	"I love you."
❑ 20. The "Vulcan salute" (now often comical) is a leave taking and blessing. It originated with the character Mr. Spock, a Vulcan officer on space ship Enterprise, in the TV series *Star Trek*. It became popular with young people of the 1960's and remains so with fans today, perhaps because it is similar to a "Peace" gesture.	Vulcan farewell salute	"Live long and prosper."

Gestures of Complicity and Fraternity   page 309

❑ 21. Tapping your temple with your forefinger or making a circular motion around your ear, usually while rolling your eyes towards someone and then pointing at them, means that you disapprove (good naturedly) of that person's behavior or opinions as being abnormal.	Crazy sign	"He's crazy." "...nuts." "...wacko." "...batty." "...loco." "...got a screw loose." "... out of his mind." and other such comic overstatements.
❑ 22. Pointing with one's thumb, often while extending the lower lip and rolling one's eyes upwards, is a gesture generally of mockery, disapproval, or approval shared with someone who will agree with the opinion expressed. It is a common comic gesture.	* * *	"Get a load of this!" This expession is generally thought, not said out loud.
❑ 23. This comic gesture suggests that you have a good and clever idea for some action. It is sometimes done simply to show anticipation, but when it is exaggerated (often with a grin of evil delight and a low chuckling sound), it suggests that you are being crafty.	Rubbing your hands (in glee).	"Oh, boy!" "Hee, hee, hee!" "Oh, just wait 'til I ..."
❑ 24. A wink is a friendly facial gesture. It may mean many different things depending on the context and the people communicating. It may mean that you are taking someone into your confidence and that you agree with them: Don't let on, but I agree with you. Don't really believe me; I was only kidding. A wink may also be a gesture on quiet congratulations: I won't make a fuss, but, between us, you did a great job! Or it may be a gesture of greeting or invitation. A politician may wink to say: I see you are with me and I like you! Others may wink to say: You're attractive to me, Handsome (or Beautiful). Come over and get to know me! People are generally careful who they wink at.	Winking.	Nothing is usually said. Winks are often combined with a slight nod of agreement or encouragement. There is an old saying: "A wink's as good as a nod."
❑ 25. A gesture of resignation or non-involvement meaning: So, don't ask me, it's not my problem, how should I know? I know nothing about it. What can I do? Who cares?	A shrug	"Damned if I know." "Who knows?" "So what?"
❑ 26. A dramatic gesture showing shock or disappointment, particularly with oneself. Variations are clutching your forehead, covering your eyes, or slapping yourself on the forehead. It is often used when you have made a costly or stupid mistake.	***	"No!" " Daaah!" "Stupid me!" "How could I?"

Gestures of Identification   page 310

❑ 27. Pointing to yourself.   ***   "Me?"

❑ 28. Pointing to, recognizing or acknowledging someone else.   ***   "You!" "It's you!"

Gestures of Hope or Good Luck   page 310

The following gestures were originally magic rituals addressed to the powers of Fate or the goddess Fortune. To some strongly religious people these are gestures of pagan superstition and evil, while some true believers in magic take such rituals very seriously. However, most people practice these gestures, or at least refer to them, as good-natured jokes. Such rituals and other superstitions may amuse people, but they often make them slightly nervous as well. For this reason, some hotels do not have thirteenth floors, and many people will not walk under ladders, and they avoid black cats.

❑ 29. This gesture, knocking on wood, is done to avoid tempting fate, to avoid bad luck, when someone says something very positive about you or when you or someone else has just predicted some good luck or fortune. A common joke is to knock on your head, making gentle fun of the ritual and ridiculing yourself as having a wooden head – a block head – stupid enough to go through with the ritual, which, of course, you always do, religiously.   Knocking on wood.   "I hope so — it is going to work – knock on wood."

❑ 30. Traditionally, the believer looks for something made of wood to knock on.

❑ 31. A gesture expressing the hope that some specific good thing will happen. This gesture is also sometimes used with arms crossed over the chest (heart), particularly by children, as a pledge of truthfulness: "It's true! Cross my fingers, hope to die, if it's not!"   Crossing your fingers.   "I think we're in luck, but I'm keeping my fingers crossed – just in case."

❑ 32. The crossed fingers gesture may also express concern that something will go wrong. A worried look suggests that the person would prevent bad luck it they could.   "Oh, I'm so afraid it won't work, but I've got my fingers crossed!"

Gestures of Jubilation   page 311

❑ 33. Shaking your hands enthusiastically above your head, like pumping a person's hand enthusiastically, is a gesture of enthusiastic approval.   Cheering.   Hooray

❑ 34. Putting your hands on your cheeks, showing surprise.   Surprize   Wow

❑ 35. Raising your arm, making a fist, jerking your fist down fast to waist level is an expression of exultation.   Cheering   Yes!!!.

Gestures of Congratulation and Self-Congratulation   page 312

❏ 36. Shaking your hand with the palm out, thumb and index finger touching, and the rest of the fingers extended is a quiet, happy sign of approval and encouragement. *However, it should be noted that Americans from some non-U.S. cultural backgrounds may mistake the meaning of this gesture; elsewhere it is a vulgar gesture with strongly sexual implications.*   * * *   "All right!"
"That'a way!"
"That's A OK!"
"Right on!" said with a smile.

❏ 37. A comic gesture of self-congratulation. Dampening your nails with your breath and then rubbing them on your chest is interpreted variously as polishing a prize, medal. or apple.   * * *   The gesture speaks for itself.

❏ 38. A gesture meaning that you or someone else has scored a point, either literally, in a game, or figuratively, in a discussion, argument, or some other competitive situation. You wet you finger and then make a motion as if you were making a wet mark on the air.   Chalking one up.   "OK, that's one for me" (you, him, her, them, etc.)

Gestures of Nervousness, Impatience, Worry, and Boredom   page 313

❏ 39. Americans from many ethnic groups chew their fingernails when they are anxious or nervous. This gesture refers to the habit meaning that you are, or should be, nervous. It is often done dramatically for comic effect.   Biting your nails.   * * *

❏ 40. Hands on hips, foot tapping, head tilted. This full-body gesture shows that you are impatient and most probably angry.   Tapping your foot.   * * *

❏ 41. All humans and even monkeys yawn when they are tired, bored, or impatient. Usually Americans politely stifle or hide their yawns, but they may gesture, pretending to yawn, to show their feelings.   A fake yawn   A loud intake of breath, like a yawn

❏ 42. Drumming with your fingers, tapping a surface with one finger after another, is another gesture showing boredom, impatience, and probably anger.   Finger drumming   * * *

❏ 43. Baring your teeth, wrinkling your forehead with your eyes to one side is a gesture showing worry or concern. It is often done with your arms folded, suggesting a hug.   Grimace   * * *

❏ 44. Putting your hands together with the fingers linked while rolling ("twiddling") your thumbs is a common gesture of impatience. When it is done openly while someone is talking, it is rude. It is often done covertly to tell someone that you are bored with what someone else is saying or with the situation you are in. Although it can show real annoyance, it is generally a comic or mocking expression.   Twiddling your thumbs.   A sigh. "Ho hum!"
"Really!"
"I'm just bored to death!"

Miscellaneous Gestures Showing Other Emotions   pages 314-315

❑ 45. A gesture meaning "stop" or "slow down." It can be a command or an expression of concern, depending on your facial expression and the authority of your movement.   * * *   "Whoa!" "Slow down!" "Just a minute!" "Hold it right there!"

❑ 46. Making and sometimes shaking a fist while frowning shows anger and threatens retaliation.   * * *   "I'll get you!" "You just wait!"

❑ 47. Frowning is a facial gesture of anger or concern   Frowning   Generally silent

❑ 48. Standing with your weight on your back foot, your hands on your hips, and aa expression shock suggests outrage.   * * *   "No way!" "You're wrong!" "That's terrible!"

❑ 49. Turning away from someone while holding up you hand as if to block them is a gesture meaning "stop" or "wait."   * * *   "Just wait a minute!" "Stop it, now!"

❑ 50. The gesture of snapping your fingers along with an expression of delight and surprise means that you have just thought of or remembered something you have been trying to think of. Snapping your fingers with a stern, impatient, or angry expression generally means that you want someone to do something immediately. Snapping your fingers to get someone's attention (a waiter in a crowded restaurant, for example) is often effective but is considered to be very offensive; it will often get the waiter's attention but bad service as well.   Snapping your fingers.   "I've got it!" "That's it!" "Ah, ha!" "Eureka!"

"Now, this minute!"

"You, over here! Come here! I want you now!"

❑ 51. Scratching your head is an expression of puzzlement or bewilderment.   Scratching your head.   "What?" "I don't get it!" "Huh?" "What's that supposed to mean?"

❑ 52. Brushing your forehead with your fingers while blowing air through your pursed lips is a gesture of relief after avoiding a serious misfortune. The same gesture is also used to complain about the heat.   Wiping your forehead. Wiping your brow.   "Phew!" "That was a close call!" "Oh, that was too close for comfort."

❑ 53. Covering your ears, gasping, and staring is a gesture of horror or fright, suggesting that you don't want to hear.   * * *   "No! It can't be! I don't want to hear it! I don't want to look!"

❑ 54. Covering your mouth, gasping, and staring is a gesture of of horror, suggesting that you don't want to speak or scream.   * * *   Aaah! I want to scream! What should I do?"

Miscellaneous Gestures With Specific Meanings   page 316

❏ 55. Measurement gestures are common to most languages and cultures. The one shown means the object or person was about as high or tall as the woman's hand. Length is shown by holding the thumb and forefinger apart the right distance or by holding the two hands apart with the fingers extended and the palms held inward.

* * *

"Oh, it (he or she) was about this high (tall, deep)."

❏ 56. The gesture of holding your hand up when you are in a group of people is the accepted way of indicating that you want to be called on or recognized to speak next. It is polite when it is silent. Children may raise their hands high and even wave. Adults generally make the least gesture necessary to get attention.

Putting your hand up

Silent, except when done comically to get attention and show enthusiasm with expressions like "I'm ready!" "Call on me!"

❏ 57. Gesturing to get the attention of a waiter is extremely difficult in American English, unless the waiter is attentive. You may wave discreetly or lift your index finger as shown here. You may even say "Excuse me," very softly and politely, as he or she passes close by. However, these gestures often go unseen in a busy restaurant, and snapping your fingers, clapping your hands, whistling, and shouting out for service are all considered to be very objectionable. They are outdoor behavior, suitable for hailing taxicabs in heavy traffic, an art which may also look like the gesture pictured when practiced by a master.

Catching a waiter's eye.

Done either silently or with very quiet, polite noises like a gentle cough, "um," or "oh." "Excuse me, please." "Ah. Could we please...."

"Taxi!" or a loud whistle

❏ 58. Gestures of approval and disapproval, dating back to ancient Rome, when "thumbs up" meant 'let the gladiator up; let him live." Gesture made with a smile.

Thumbs up

"I'm for it." "Great!" "That's good!"

❏ 59. "Thumbs down" meant "let them die without mercy." In America, the signal means "my reaction is negative. I don't like it, him, or her. No, I vote against it. The gesture is often made while sticking out your lower lip or frowning.

Thumbs down

"No, I'm against it!" "Bad!" "That's no good!" "That's awful!"

❏ 60. This gesture with your thumb stretched back next to your ear and your little finger stretched forward in front of your mouth means "call me on the telephone: A similar gesture, putting your thumb to your lips and then tipping your hand up like a bottle with your little finger raised, means you want a drink.

Call me

A silent signal, though sometimes the person mouths, "Call me."

❏ 61. This signal is a request for a break in the action. Originally it was used in team sports asking the officials for "time out." It is now used to ask for or suggest that a class or meeting should be stopped for a few minutes so that the participants can "take a break." The hands are raised to form a T for "Time."

Time out

Generally silent, but in sports particularly the person may reinforce the gesture by yelling, "Time out."

1

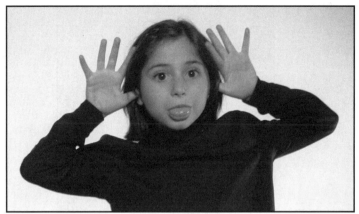

2

3

4

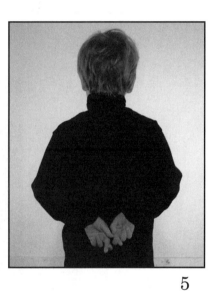

5

6

7

Meanings: page 298

8

9

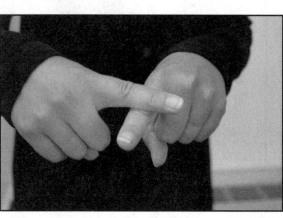

10

11

12

Meanings: page 298

13

14

15

GESTURES OF GREETING

16

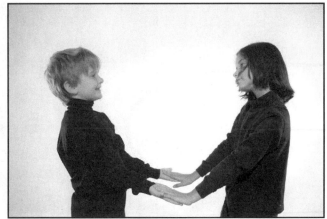

17

Meanings: page 299

18

19

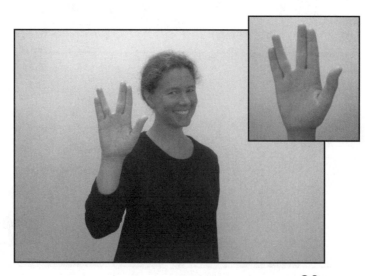

20

Meanings: pages 299 - 300

21

22

23

24

25

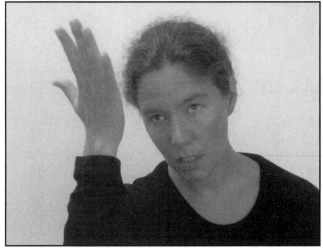

26

Meanings: page 309

27

28

29

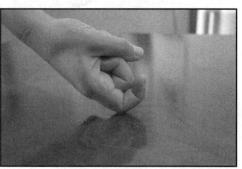

30

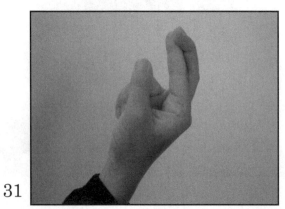

31

32

Meanings: page 310

33

34

35

Meanings: page 301

36

37

38

Meanings: page 302

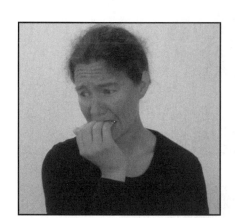

39

40

41

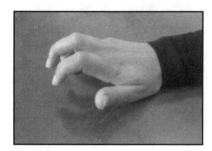

42

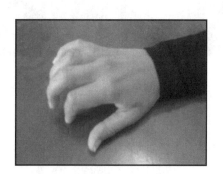

43

44

Meanings: page 302

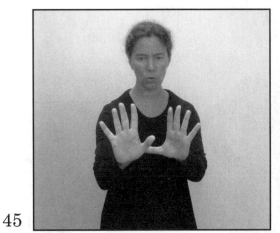

45

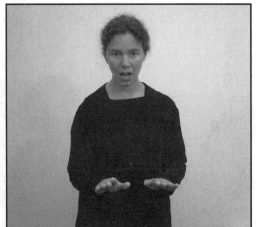

46

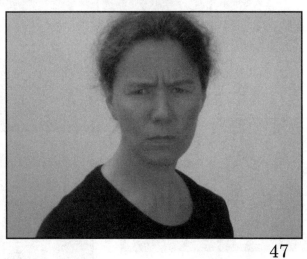

47

48

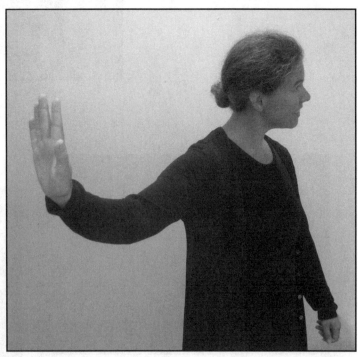

49

Meanings: page 303

50

51

52

53

54

Meanings: page 303

315

55

56

57

58

59

60

61

Meanings: page 304

SOURCES

Allison, Alexander W., Herbert Barrows, et al. *The Norton Anthology of Poetry,* Third Edition. New York, N.Y.: W. W. Norton & Co., 1986

Boone, Eleanor; Rick Gildea, and Pat Moran. *Resources for TESOL Teaching* (Program and Training Journal 26). Washington, D.C.: ACTION/ Peace Corps, 1978

Beilenson, Evelyn, and Ann Tenenbaum, eds. *Wit and Wisdom of Famous American Women.* White Plains, N.Y.: Peter Pauper Press, Inc., 1986

Carruth, Gordon, and Eugene Ehrlich, eds. *The Harper Book of American Quotations.* New York, N.Y.: Harper & Row, 1988

Celce-Murcia and Diane Larsen-Freeman. *The Grammar Book, 2nd edition.* Boston: Heinle and Heinle, 1999

Chase, William D., and Helen M. Chase. *Chase's Annual Events: Special Days, Weeks, and Months.* Chicago, Ill.: Contemporary Books, Inc.

Clement, Margaret A. *A Handful of English.* Unpublished MAT Thesis, School for International Training, 1978

The Concise Columbia Encyclopedia., New York, N.Y.: Avon Books (Columbia University Press), Hearst Corp., 1983

Crystal, David. *The Cambridge Encyclopedia of Language.* Cambridge: Cambridge University Press, 1987

Dobler, Lavinia. *Customs and Holidays Around the World.* New York, N.Y.: Fleet Publishing Co., 1962

The Encyclopaedia Britannica. Chicago, Ill., 1990

Encyclopedia of Knowledge. Danbury, CT.: Grolier, 1991

Evans, Bergen. *Dictionary of Quotations.* New York, N.Y.: Delacorte Press, 1968

Frank, Marcella. *Modern English: A Practical Reference Guide.* Englewood Cliffs, N.J.: Prentice-Hall, 1972

Gunterman, Gail. "Purposeful Communication Practice: Developing Functional Proficiency in a Foreign Language." *FLAnnals (NI* No.3), 1979

Hacker, Andrew. *U.S.:A Statistical Portrait of the American People.* New York, N.Y.: Viking Press,1983

The Hammond Almanac. Maplewood, N.J.: Hammond Almanac, Inc.,1981

Indian and Northern Affairs Canada website: www.ina.gc.ca 1999

Jacquet, Constant H., ed. *Yearbook of American and Canadian Churches, 1987,* Nashville, Tenn.: Abington Press,1989

Kehoe, Alice B. *North American Indians: A Comprehensive Account.* Englewood Cliffs, N.J.: Prentice-Hall,1981

Keller, Charles. *Tongue Twisters.* New York, N.Y.: Simon and Schuster,1989

Key, Mary Ritchie. *Paralanguage and Kinesics.* Metuchen, N.J.: The Scarecrow Press, 1975

Kin, David. ed. *Dictionary of American Proverbs.* New York, N.Y.: Philosophical Library

Moeur, Richard C. *Manual of Traffic Signs.* www,trafficsign.us

Murdock, George P. "The Common Denominators of Culture" in *The Science of Man in the World Crisis,* Ralph Linton, ed. New York, N.Y.: Columbia University Press,1945

Munro, David. *Oxford Dictionary of the World.* New York: Oxford University Press, 1995

The New American Desk Encyclopedia. New York, N.Y.: New American Library (A Signet Book), 1989

1996 Census/ Statistics Canada website: www.statcan.ca 1999

The New York Times Almanac. New York, N.Y. Penguin Books, 2002

Parnwell, E. C. *Oxford Picture Dictionary of American English.* New York: Oxford University Press, 1978

Praninskas, Jean. *Rapid Review of English Grammar* (Second Edition). Englewood Cliffs, N.J.: Prentice-Hall, 1975

Quirk, Randolph. *A Concise Grammar of Contemporary English*. New York: Harcourt, Brace, 1973

Radford, E. and M.A. *Encyclopaedia of Superstitions*. New York: Philosophical Library, 1949

Reader's Digest Almanac, 1987. Pleasantville, N.Y.: The Reader's Digest Association, Inc., 1986

Richards, Jack C., John Platt, and Heidi Platt. *Longman Dictionary of Teaching and Applied Linguistics*. London: Longman 1992

Silber, Irwin and Fred. *The Folksinger's Word Book*. New York: Oak Publications, 1973

Time Almanac 2007 with Information Please. Boston: Time, Inc. Pearson Education, 2006

U. S. Department of State. *Background Notes*

Untermeyer, Louis, ed. *Golden Treasury of Poetry*. New York, N.Y.: Golden Press, 1989

Wallechinsky, David, and Irving Wallace. *The People's Almanac*. Garden City, N.J.: Doubleday & Company, Inc., 1975

Whitford, Harold C. and Robert J. Dixon. *Handbook of American Idioms and Idiomatic Usage*. New York: Regents, 1953

The World Almanac and Book of Facts, 2006. New York: World Almanac Books 2006

INDEX

Other teacher resources from Pro Lingua Associates:

• **The Great Big BINGO Book.** 44 varied, creative, and *photcopyable* BINGO games make it fun for students to learn about grammar, vocabulary, writing, pronunciation, and cultural topics.

• **The Great Big Book of Crosswords.** Working independently, in pairs, or in triads, students solve these 66 fun **photocopyable** puzzles rich with vocabulary and culture.

• **Go Fish.** 7 speaking and listening games for learning languages. 126 everyday objects from around the home are pictured in color on large playing/flash cards. Students practice conversation and learn vocabulary in any language. English word lists are in the book. Many other languages are free at Pro Lingua's web site.

• **Match It!** 83 *photocopyable* sets of cards for playing the index card game, Matched Pairs (Concentration), a grammar/vocabulary game for beginning to high intermediate students.

• **Shenanigames:** Grammar Focused ESL/EFL Activities and Games. A *photocopyable* teacher resource with 49 easy-to-understand-and-play game exercises that practice specific, clearly indicated grammar points appropriate for low to high intermediate students at the middle school, high school, university, and adult levels.

• **Index Card Games for ESL.** A new edition of one of Pro Lingua's all-time best sellers. The 7 card game techniques explained are easy to prepare and play using 3x5 index cards. These are student-centered, group activities which provide practice with vocabulary, structure, spelling, questioning, and conversation. Sample games for beginning to advanced students are all *photocopyable.* •*Also available,* **More Index Card Games**, with 9 techniques.

• **Conversation Inspirations.** Over 2,400 conversation topics and 9 distinctive conversation activities. The topics range from lighthearted fun to serious subjects for discussion, from the universal – human nature and interpersonal relationships – to the culturally vital – cutting edge issues in North American society and how people from other cultures feel about them and deal with them. All *photocopyable*.

• **Writing Inspirations:** A Fundex of Individualized Writing Activities for English Language Practice. The book includes 176 *photocopyable* masters for topic cards. Each topic has several variations, so that student have over 600 writing tasks to choose from. This student-centered material is appropriate for students of all ages, interests, and skill levels since students work at their own level. The Fundex is ideal for tutorials and for use in learning centers and libraries. •*Also available and* ***photocopyable***, **Write for You**, creative writing activities for intermediate students, and **Breaking the Writing Barrier**, fun activities for adolescents developing writing skills.

• **From Sound to Sentence.** Learning to read and write English, basic literacy and spelling, phonics and sight words. A simple to use and often entertaining beginning text. And to provide important practice in a game context, **Superphonic Bingo: Breaking the Sounds Barrier,** 15 photocopyable games, each with 8 different Bingo cards, plus 2 incomplete, student-fill-in cards. An easy, fun way to practice English phonics.

• **Stress Rulz: Pronunciation Through Rap.** The irresistible rap CD, supplemented with *photocopyable* handouts from the teacher's book, teach and demonstrate the rules of stress in American English.

• **The Interactive Tutorial:** An Activity Parade. 57 *photocopyable* activities for beginning Adult ESL/ EFL. The student and tutor work/play together, developing communicative skills. Everything needed – game forms, boards, cards, and picture cubes – is provided. Easily adaptable for use with younger students and in classes.

• **Pronunciation Card Games.** 16 pronunciation games are explained in simple terms. They use ***photocopyable*** sets of illustrated game cards. The games work with the production and discrimination of difficult consonant and vowel sounds and stress and intonation.

Recent texts to explore at www.ProLinguaAssociates.com: The Grammar Review Book, Writing Strategies I & II, Conversation Strategies, Discussion Strategies, The Modal Book, A Phrasal Verb Affair/CD, Lexicarry, Surveys for Conversation, Dictations for Discussion/CD, How and Why Folktales from Around the World, and Pearls of Wisdom: African and Caribbean Folktales - a reader and integrated skills workbook with *3 CD's.*

American Culture from Pro Lingua Associates:

Living in the United States: How to feel at home, make friends, and enjoy everyday life. This is a brief introduction to the culture of the United States for visitors, students, and business travelers. It is used in cultural orientation programs in high schools, colleges and exchange programs across the country and around the world. •*In the same series* are "Living in" books on Mexico, Italy, Greece, France, Japan, South Korea, and China.

• **All Around America: The Time Traveler's Talk Show.** American history and geography are made vivid as students listen to and participate in 18 talk shows visiting sites from the ancient pueblos of the Anasazi to the skyscrapers of Chicago and meeting historical figures from Lincoln and Lee at Gettysburg to Vitus Bering in Alaska and Queen Liliuokalani of Hawaii. Using the scripts, workbook, and two CD's, students work on all their language skills: reading, speaking, writing, and vocabulary development with an emphasis on idioms and adjectives.

• **Legends: 52 People Who Made a Difference.** *Graded readings from American History.* Brief bio-sketches for reading, retelling, listening, writing, and research. There are 13 groups of legendary Americans (folk heroes, anti-slavery heroes, Native Americans, inventors, reformers, human rights leaders, Presidents, military heroes, writers, entertainers, sports heroes, etc.) each represented by 4 biographies; these range in length and difficulty - 100 words long to 250. Pages can be removed and used as story cards, each with a timeline on the back for retelling and discussion and a web site reference for research.

• **Celebrating American Heroes.** *13 brief plays* about significant historical figures. Written to be read aloud dramatically, each play has a few main characters and a chorus. The heroes are Betsy Ross and Washington; Dolley Madison; Sacagawea; Stowe; Lincoln; Edison; Muir; Jackie Robinson; Salk; Frost; Cesar Chavez; Astronauts Armstrong, Aldrin, and Collins; and Jaime Escalante – all people who contributed to making this a better nation. The stories are upbeat and inspiring. The plays are excellent ways to introduce or reinforce specific social studies or history topics. They fit well in citizenship classes and multilevel classes – the more proficient students enjoy the lead roles; the less confident are part of the chorus. Everybody shines. There is a teacher's guide with *photocopyable* masters for exercises and activities.

• **Heroes from American History,** an ESL/Civics text. This companion to Celebrating American Heroes can be used independently. An integrated-skills reader, it covers the same great Americans plus Eleanor Roosevelt, Maya Lin, and the average American citizen.

• **Plays for the Holidays:** Historical and Cultural Celebrations. In each play a few characters (stars) are supported by a chorus (the rest of the class) which comments, advises, warns, and cajoles the stars while at the same time giving the big picture behind the drama. Most of the plays have historical subjects relating to the traditions and origins of the holidays; the author adapts *Scrooge* for Christmas and *The Headless Horseman* for Halloween.

• **American Holidays**: Exploring Traditions, Customs, and Backgrounds – 2nd Edition. July 4th, Election Day, Christmas, and New Year's Eve: reading about our American national holidays is not only fun, it is a way of exploring our diverse culture and values. How do we celebrate Memorial Day and Kwanzaa? What is the history of Cinco de Mayo and Thanksgiving? What does "Be my valentine" mean? How are Ramadan, Chinese New Year, Easter, and Rosh Hashana celebrated? *Special features:* 4 appendices of traditional holiday songs, readings for the holidays, typical holiday gifts, and a listing of state holidays. A *CD* of the readings is available.

• **North American Indian Tales** – *Story Cards*. 48 animal stories collected from American Indian tribes across North America, from Canada, Mexico, and the United States. The tales explain how the world came to be as it is—*How Chipmunk Got Her Stripes; Why Dogs Don't Talk; Wind; Bluebird and Coyote; How Fire Came to the Sierras; Butterflies.* The illustrations, by a popular Native American artist and story teller, draw on symbols and motifs from the many cultures represented to impart the wisdom and mystery of the great oral tradition of the "animal people" tales. • Other collections of *Story Cards*: **Aesop's Fables** and **Tales of Nasreddin Hodja.**